I0755858

Wisdom of Andrew Murray Volume II

Waiting on God
The Two Covenants
School of Obedience

Wisdom of Andrew Murray Volume II

by Andrew Murray

Start Publishing PD LLC

Manufactured in the United States of America

Cover art: Shutterstock/Taisiya Kozorez

Cover design: Jennifer Do

10 9 8 7 6 5 4 3 2 1

ISBN 979-8-8809-2487-5

Waiting on God

Table of Contents

Day 1. The God of Our Salvation

"*My soul waiteth only upon God [marg: is silent unto God]; from Him cometh my salvation.*" *Ps. 62:1*

If salvation indeed comes from God, and is entirely His work, just as creation was, it follows, as a matter of course, that our first and highest duty is to wait on Him to do the work that pleases Him. Waiting becomes then the only way to the experience of a full salvation, the only way, truly, to know God as the God of our salvation. All the difficulties that are brought forward as keeping us back from full salvation, have their cause in this one thing: the defective knowledge and practice of waiting upon God. All that the Church and its members need for the manifestation of the mighty power of God in the world, is the return to our true place, the place that belongs to us, both in creation and redemption, the place of absolute and unceasing dependence upon God. Let us strive to see what the elements are that make up this most blessed and needful waiting upon God: it may help us to discover the reasons why this grace is so little cultivated, and to feel how infinitely desirable it is that the Church, that we ourselves, should at any price learn its blessed secret.

The deep need for this waiting on God lies equally in the nature of man and the nature of God. God, as Creator, formed man, to be a vessel in which He could show forth His power and goodness. Man was not to have in himself a fountain of life, or strength, or happiness: the ever-living and only living One was each moment to be the

Communicator to him of all that he needed. Man's glory and blessedness was not to be independent, or dependent upon himself, but dependent on a God of such infinite riches and love. Man was to have the joy of receiving every moment out of the fulness of God. This was his blessedness as an unfallen creature.

When he fell from God, he was still more absolutely dependent on Him. There was not the slightest hope of his recovery out of his state of death, but in God, His power and mercy. It is God alone who began the work of redemption; it is God alone who continues and carries it on each moment in each individual believer. Even in the regenerate man there is no power of goodness in himself: he has and can have nothing that he does not each moment receive; and waiting on God is just as indispensable, and must be just as continuous and unbroken, as the breathing that maintains his natural life.

It is, then, because Christians do not know their relation to God of absolute poverty and helplessness, that they have no sense of the need of absolute and unceasing dependence, or the unspeakable blessedness of continual waiting on God. But when once a believer begins to see it, and consent to it, that he by the Holy Spirit must each moment receive what God each moment works, waiting on God becomes his brightest hope and joy. As he apprehends how God, as God, as Infinite Love, delights to impart His own nature to His child as fully as He can, how God is not weary of each moment keeping charge of his life and strength, he wonders that he ever thought otherwise of God than as a God to be waited on all the day. God unceasingly giving and working; His child unceasingly waiting and receiving: this is the blessed life.

"Truly my soul waiteth upon God; from Him cometh my salvation." First we wait on God for salvation. Then we learn that salvation is only to bring us to God, and teach us to wait on Him. Then we find what is better still, that waiting on God is itself the highest salvation. It is the ascribing to Him the glory of being All; it is the experiencing that He is All to us.

May God teach us the blessedness of waiting on Him.

"My soul, wait thou only upon God!"

Day 2. The Keynote of Life

I have waited for Thy salvation, O Lord! Gen 49:18.

It is not easy to say exactly in what sense Jacob used these words, in the midst of his prophecies in regard to the future of his sons. But they do certainly dictate that both for himself and for them his expectation was from God alone. It was God's salvation he waited for; a salvation which God had promised and which God Himself alone could work out. He knew himself and his sons to be under God's charge. Jehovah the Everlasting God would show in them what His saving power is and does. The words point forward to that wonderful history of redemption which is not yet finished, and to the glorious future in eternity whither it is leading. They suggest to us how there is no salvation but God's salvation, and how waiting on God for that, whether for our personal experience, or in wider circles, is our first duty, our true blessedness.

Let us think of ourselves, and the inconceivably glorious salvation God has wrought for us in Christ, and is now purposing to work out and to perfect in us by His Spirit. Let us meditate until we somewhat realize that every participation of this great salvation, from moment to moment, must be the work of God Himself. God cannot part with His grace, or goodness, or strength, as an external thing that He gives us, as He gives the raindrops from heaven. No; He can only give it, and we can only enjoy it, as He works it Himself directly and unceasingly. And the only reason that He does not work it more effectually and continuously is, that we do not let Him. We hinder Him either by our indifference or by our self-effort, so that He cannot do what He would.

What He asks of us, in the way of surrender, and obedience, and desire, and trust, is all comprised in this one word: waiting on Him, waiting for His salvation. It combines the deep sense of our entire helplessness of ourselves to work what is divinely good, and our perfect confidence that our God will work it all in His divine power.

Again, I say, let us meditate on the divine glory of the salvation God purposes working out in us, until we know the truths it implies. Our heart is the scene of a divine operation more wonderful than Creation. We can do as little towards the work as towards creating the world, except as God works in us to will and to do. God only asks of us to yield, to consent, to wait upon Him, and He will do it all. Let us meditate and be still, until we see how meet and right and blessed it is that God alone do all, and our soul will of itself sink down in deep humility to say: "I have waited for Thy salvation, O Lord." And the deep blessed background of all our praying and working will be: "Truly my soul waiteth upon God."

The application of the truth to wider circles, to those we labor among or intercede for, to the Church of Christ around us, or throughout the world, is not difficult. There can be no good but what God works; to wait upon God, and have the heart filled with faith in His working, and in that faith to pray for His mighty power to come down, is our only wisdom. Oh for the eyes of our heart to be opened to see God working in ourselves and in others, and to see how blessed it is to worship and just to wait for His salvation!

Our private and public prayer are our chief expression of our relation to God: it is in them chiefly that our waiting upon God must be exercised. If our waiting begin by quieting the activities of nature, and being still before God; if it bows and seeks to see God in His universal and almighty operation, alone able and always ready to work all good; if it yields itself to Him in the assurance that He is working and will work in us; if it maintains the place of humility and stillness, and surrenders until God's Spirit has quickened the faith that He will perfect His work: it will indeed become the strength and the joy of the soul. Life will become one deep blessed cry: "I have waited for Thy salvation, O Lord."

"My soul, wait thou only upon God"

Day 3. The True Place of the Creature

"These wait all upon Thee; That Thou mayest give them their meat in due season. That Thou givest unto them, they gather: Thou openest Thine hand, they are satisfied with good." Ps.104:27-28

This Psalm, in praise of the Creator, has been speaking of the birds and the beasts of the forest; of the young lions, and man going forth to his work; of the great sea, wherein are things creeping innumerable, both small and great beasts. And it sums up the whole relation of all creation to its Creator, and its continuous and universal dependence upon Him in the one word: "These all wait upon Thee." Just as much as it was God's work to create, it is His work to maintain. As little as the creature could create itself, it is it left to provide for itself. The whole creation is ruled by the one unalterable law of — waiting upon God!

The word is the simple expression of that for the sake of which alone the creature was brought into existence, the very groundwork of its constitution. The one object for which God gave life to creatures was that in them He might prove and show forth His wisdom, power, and goodness, in His being each moment their life and happiness, and pouring forth unto them, according to their capacity, the riches of His goodness and power. And just as this is the very place and nature of God, to be unceasingly the supplier of every want in the creature, so the very place and nature of the creature is nothing hut this — to wait upon God and receive from Him what He alone can give, what He delights to give.

If we are in this little book at all to apprehend what waiting on God is to be to the believer, to practice it and to experience its blessedness, it is of consequence that we begin at the very beginning, and see the deep reasonableness of the call that comes to us. We shall understand how the duty is no arbitrary command. We shall see how it is not only rendered necessary by our sin and helplessness. It is simply and truly our restoration to our original destiny and our highest nobility, to our true place and glory as creatures blessedly dependent on the All-Glorious God.

If once our eyes are opened to this precious truth, all Nature will become a preacher, reminding us of the, relationship which, founded in creation, is now taken in grace. As we read this Psalm, and learn to look upon all life in Nature as continually maintained by God Himself, waiting on God will be seen to be the very necessity of our being. As we think of the young lions and the ravens crying to Him, of the birds and the fishes and every insect waiting on Him, till He give them their meat in due season, we shall see that it is the very nature and glory of God that He is a God who is to be waited on. Every thought of what Nature is, and what God is, will give new force to the call: "Wait thou only upon God."

"These all wait upon Thee, that thou mayest give." It is God who giveth all: let this faith enter deeply into our hearts. Ere yet we fully understand all that is implied in our waiting upon God, and ere we have even been able to cultivate the habit, let the truth enter our souls: waiting on God, unceasing and entire dependence upon Him, is, in heaven and earth, the one only true religion, the one unalterable and all-comprehensive expression for the true relationship to the ever-blessed one in whom we live.

Let us resolve at once that it shall be the one characteristic of our life and worship, a continual, humble, truthful waiting upon God. We may rest assured that He who made us for Himself, that He might give Himself to us and in us, that He will never disappoint us. In waiting on Him we shall find rest and joy and strength, and the supply of every need.

"My soul, wait thou only upon God."

Day 4. For Supplies

"The Lord upholdeth all that fall, And raiseth up all those that be bowed down. The eyes of all wait upon Thee; And Thou givest them their meat in due season." Ps 145:14-15

PSALM 104 is a Psalm of Creation, and the words, "These all wait upon Thee," were used with reference to the animal creation. Here we have a Psalm of the Kingdom, and "The eyes of all wait upon Thee" appears specially to point to the needs of God's saints, of all that fall and them that be bowed down. What the universe and the animal creation do unconsciously, God's people are to do intelligently and voluntarily. Man is to be the interpreter of Nature. He is to prove that there is nothing more noble or more blessed in the exercise of our free will than to use it in waiting upon God.

If an army has been sent out to march into an enemy's country, and tidings are received that it is not advancing, the question is at once asked, what may be the cause of delay. The answer will very often be: "Waiting for supplies." All the stores of provisions or clothing or ammunition have not arrived; without these it dare not proceed. It is no otherwise in the Christian life: day by day, at every step, we need our supplies from above. And there is nothing so needful as to cultivate that spirit of dependence on God and of confidence in Him, which refuses to go on without the needed supply of grace and strength.

If the question be asked, whether this be anything different from what we do when we pray, the answer is, that there may be much praying with but very little waiting on God. In praying we are often occupied with ourselves, with our own needs, and our own efforts in the presentation of them. In waiting upon God, the first thought is of the God upon whom we wait. We enter His presence, and feel we need just to be quiet, so that He, as God, can overshadow us with Himself. God longs to reveal Himself, to fill us with Himself. Waiting on God gives Him time in His own way and divine power to come to us.

It is specially at the time of prayer that we ought to set ourselves to cultivate this spirit.

Before you pray, bow quietly before God, just t remember and realize who He is, how near He is, how certainly He can and will help. Just be still before Him, and allow His Holy Spirit to waken and stir up in your soul the child-like disposition of absolute dependence and confident expectation. Wait upon God as a Living Being, as the Living God, who notices you, and is just longing to fill you with His salvation. Wait on God till you know you have met Him; prayer will then be come so different.

And when you are praying, let there be intervals of silence, reverent stillness of soul, in which you yield yourself to God, in case He may have aught He wishes to teach you or to work in you. Waiting on Him will become the most blessed part of prayer, and the blessing thus obtained will be doubly precious as the fruit or such fellowship with the Holy One, God has so ordained it, in harmony with His holy nature, and with ours, that waiting on Him should be the honor we give Him. Let us bring Him the service gladly and truthfully; He will reward it abundantly.

"The eyes of all wait upon Thee, and Thou givest them their meat in due season." Dear soul, God provides in Nature for the creatures He has made: how much more will He provide in Grace for those He has redeemed. Learn to say of every want, and every failure, and every lack of needful grace: I have waited too little upon God, or He would have given me in due season all I needed. And say then too,

"My soul, wait thou only upon God!"

Day 5. For Instruction

"Shew me thy ways, O Lord; Teach me Thy paths. Lead me in Thy truth, and teach me; For Thou art the God of my salvation; On Thee do I wait all the day." Ps. 25:4-5

I spoke of an army on the point of entering an enemy's territories. Answering the question as to the cause of delay: "Waiting for supplies." The answer might also have been: "Waiting for instructions," or "Waiting for orders." If the last despatch had not been received, with the final orders of the commander-in-chief, the army dared not move. Even so in the Christian life: as deep as the need of waiting for supplies, is that of waiting for instructions.

See how beautiful this comes out in Ps. 25. The writer knew and loved God's law exceedingly, and meditated in that law day and night. But he knew that this was not enough. He knew that for the right spiritual apprehension of the truth, and for the right personal application of it to his own peculiar circumstances, he needed a direct divine teaching.

The psalm has at all times been a very peculiar one, because of its reiterated expression of the felt need of the Divine teaching, and of the childlike confidence that that teaching would be given. Study the psalm until your heart is filled with the two thoughts — the absolute need, the absolute certainty of divine guidance. And with these how entirely it is in this connection that he speaks, "On Thee do I wait all the day." Waiting for guidance, waiting for instruction, all the day, is a very blessed part of waiting upon God.

The Father in heaven is so interested in His child, and so longs to have his life at every step in His will and His love, that He is willing to keep his guidance entirely in His own hand. He knows so well that we are unable to do what is really holy and heavenly, except as He works it in us, that He means His very demands to become promises of what He will do, in watching over and leading us all the day. Not only in special difficulties and times of perplexity, but in the common course of everyday life, we may count upon Him to teach us His war, and show us His path.

And what is needed in us to receive this guidance? One thing: waiting for instructions, waiting on God. "On Thee do I wait all the day." We want in our times of prayer to give clear expression to our sense of need, and our faith in His help. We want definitely to become conscious of our ignorance as to what God's war may be, and the need of the Divine light shining within us, if our way is to be as of the sun, shining more and more unto the perfect day. And we want to wait quietly before God in prayer, until the deep, restful assurance fills us: It will be given — "the meek will He guide in the way."

"On Thee do I wait all the day." The special surrender to the Divine guidance in our seasons of prayer must cultivate, and be followed up by, the habitual looking upwards "all the day." As simple as it is, to one who has eyes, to walk all the day in the light of the sun, so simple and delightful can it become to a soul practiced in waiting on God, to walk all the day in the enjoyment of God's light and leading. What is needed to help us to such a life is just one thing: the real knowledge and faith of God as the one only source of wisdom and goodness, as ever ready, and longing much to be to us all that we can possibly require — yes! this is the one thing we need. If we but saw our God in His love, if we but believed that He waits to be gracious, that He waits to be our life and to work all in us, — how this waiting on God would become our highest joy, the natural and spontaneous response of our hearts to His great love and glory!

"My soul, wait thou only upon God!"

Day 6. For All Saints

"Let none that wait on Thee be ashamed." Ps. 25:3

Let us now, in our meditation of today, each one forget himself, to think of the great company of God, saints throughout the world, who are all with us waiting on Him. And let us all join in the fervent prayer for each other, "Let none that wait on Thee be ashamed."

Just think for a moment of the multitude of waiting ones who need that prayer; how many there are, sick and weary and solitary, to whom it is as if their prayers are not answered, and who sometimes begin to fear that their hope will be put to shame. And then, how many servants of God, ministers or missionaries, teachers or workers, of various name, whose hopes in their work have been disappointed, and whose longing for power and blessing remains unsatisfied. And then, too, how many, who have heard of a life of rest and perfect peace, of abiding light and fellowship, of strength and victory, and who cannot find the path. With all these, it is nothing but that they have not yet learned the secret of full waiting upon God. They just need, what we all need, the living assurance that waiting on God can never be in vain. Let us remember all who are in danger of fainting or being weary, and all unite in the cry, "Let none that wait on Thee be ashamed!"

If this intercession for all who wait on God becomes part of our waiting on Him for ourselves, we shall help to bear each other's burdens, and so fulfil the law of Christ.

There will be introduced into our waiting on God that element of unselfishness and love, which is the path to the highest blessing, and the fullest communion with God. Love to the brethren and love to God are inseparably linked. In God, the love to His Son and to us are one: "That the love wherewith Thou hast loved Me, may be in them." In

Christ, the love of the Father to Him, and His love to us, are one: "As the Father loved me, so have I loved you." In us, He asks that His love to us shall be ours to the brethren: "As I have loved you, that ye love one another." All the love of God, and of Christ, are inseparably linked with love to the brethren. And how can we, day by day, prove and cultivate this love otherwise than by daily praying for each other? Christ did not seek to enjoy the Father's love for Himself; He passed it all on to us. All true seeking of God and His love for ourselves, will be inseparably linked with the thought and the love of our brethren in prayer for them.

"Let none that wait on Thee be ashamed." Twice in the psalm David speaks of his waiting on God for himself; here he thinks of all who wait on Him. Let this page take the message to all God's tried and weary ones, that there are more praying for them than they know. Let it stir them and us in our waiting to make a point of at times forgetting ourselves, and to enlarge our hearts, and say to the Father, "These all wait upon Thee, and Thou givest them their meat in due season." Let it inspire us all with new courage-for who is there who is not at times ready to faint and be weary? "Let none that wait on Thee be ashamed" is a promise in a prayer, "They that wait on Thee shall not be ashamed!" From many and many a witness the cry comes to every one who needs the help, brother, sister, tried one, "Wait on the Lord; be of good courage, and He shall strengthen your heart; wait, I say, on the Lord. Be of good courage, and He shall strengthen your heart, all ye that wait on the Lord."

Blessed Father! We humbly beseech Thee, Let none that wait on Thee be ashamed; no, not one. Some are weary, and the time of waiting appears long. And some are feeble, and scarcely know how to wait. And some are so entangled in the effort of their prayers and their work, they think that they can find no time to wait continually. Father, teach us all how to wait. Teach us to think of each other, and pray for each other. Teach us to think of Thee, the God of all waiting ones. Father! Let none that wait on Thee be ashamed. For Jesus' sake. Amen.

"My soul, wait thou only upon God!"

Day 7. A Plea in Prayer

"Let integrity and uprightness preserve me; for I wait on Thee." Ps 25:21

For the third time in this psalm we have the word wait. As before in verse 5, "On Thee do I wait all the day," so here, too, the believing supplicant appeals to God to remember that he is waiting on Him, looking for an answer. It is a great thing for a soul not only to wait upon God, but to be filled with such a consciousness that its whole spirit and position is that of a waiting one, that it can, in childlike confidence, say, Lord! Thou knowest, I wait on Thee. It will prove a mighty plea in prayer, giving ever-increasing boldness of expectation to claim the promise, "They that wait on Me shall not be ashamed!"

The prayer in connection with which the plea is put forth here is one of great importance in the spiritual life. If we draw nigh to God, it must be with a true heart. There must be perfect integrity, whole-heartedness, in our dealing with God. As we read in the next Psalm (26:1, 11). "Judge me, O Lord, for I have walked in mine integrity," "As for me, I walk in my integrity," there must be perfect uprightness or single-heartedness before God, as it is written, "His righteousness is for the upright in heart." The soul must know that it allows nothing sinful, nothing doubtful; if it is indeed to meet the Holy One, and receive His full blessing, it must be with a heart wholly and singly given up to His will. The whole spirit that animates us in the waiting must be, "Let integrity and uprightness" — Thou seest that I desire to come so to Thee, Thou knowest I am looking to Thee to work them perfectly in me; — let them "preserve me, for I wait on Thee."

And if at our first attempt truly to live the life of fully and always waiting on God, we begin to discover how much that perfect integrity is wanting, this will just be one of the blessings which the waiting was meant to work. A soul cannot seek close fellowship with God, or attain the abiding consciousness of waiting on Him all the day, without a very honest and entire surrender to all His will.

"For I wait on Thee": it is not only in connection with the prayer of our text but with every prayer that this plea may be used. To use it often will be a great blessing to ourselves. Let us therefore study the words well until we know all their bearings. It must be clear to us what we are waiting for. There may be very different things. It may be waiting for God in our times of prayer to take his place as God, and to work in us the sense of HIS holy presence and nearness. It may be a special petition, to which we are expecting an answer. It may be our whole inner life, in which we are on the lookout for God's putting forth of His power. It may be the whole state of His Church and saints, or some part of His work, for which our eyes are ever toward Him. It is good that we sometimes count up to ourselves exactly what the things are we are waiting for, and as we say definitely of each of them, "On Thee do I wait," we shall be emboldened to claim the answer, "For on Thee do I wait."

It must also be clear to us, on Whom we are waiting. Not an idol, a God of whom we have made an image by our conceptions of what He is. No, but the living God, such as He really is in His great glory, His infinite holiness, His power, wisdom, and goodness, in His love and nearness. It is the presence of a beloved or a dreaded master that wakens up the whole attention of the servant who waits on him. It is the presence of God, as He can in Christ by His Holy Spirit make Himself known, and keep the soul under its covering and shadow, that will waken and strengthen the true waiting spirit. Let us be still and wait and worship till we know how near He is, and then say, "On Thee do I wait."

And then, let it be very clear, too, that we are waiting. Let that become so much our consciousness that the utterance comes spontaneously, "On Thee I do wait all the day; I wait on Thee." This will indeed imply sacrifice and separation, a soul entirely given up to God as its all, its only joy. This waiting on God has hardly yet been acknowledged as the only true Christianity. And yet, if it be true that God alone is goodness and joy and love; if it be true that our highest blessedness is in having as much of God as we can; if it be true that Christ has redeemed us wholly for God, and made a life of continual abiding in His presence possible, nothing less ought to satisfy than to be ever breathing this blessed atmosphere, "I wait on Thee."

"My soul, wait thou only on God!"

Day 8. Strong and of Good Courage

"Wait on the Lord: be strong, And let your heart take courage Yea, wait thou on the Lord." Ps. 27:14

The psalmist had just said, "I had fainted, unless I had believed to see the goodness of the Lord in the land of the living." If it had not been for his faith in God, his heart had fainted. But in the confident assurance in God which faith gives, he urges himself and us to remember one thing above all, — to wait upon God. "Wait on the Lord: be strong, and let your heart take courage: yea, wait thou on the Lord." One of the chief needs in our waiting upon God, one of the deepest secrets of its blessedness and blessing, is a quiet, confident persuasion that it is not in vain; courage to believe that God will hear and help; we are waiting on a God who never could disappoint His people.

"Be strong and of good courage." These words are frequently found in connection with some great and difficult enterprise, in prospect of the combat with the power of strong enemies, and the utter insufficiency of all human strength. Is waiting on God a work so difficult, that, for that too, such words are needed, "Be strong, and let your heart take courage"? Yes, indeed. The deliverance for which we often have to wait is from enemies, in presence of whom we are impotent. The blessings for which we plead are spiritual and all unseen; things impossible with men; heavenly, supernatural, divine realities. Our heart may well faint and fail.

Our souls are so little accustomed to hold fellowship with God; the God on whom we wait so of ten appears to hide Himself. We who have to wait are often tempted to fear that we do not wait aright, that our faith is too feeble, that our desire is not as upright or as earnest as it should be, that our surrender is not complete. Amid all these causes of fear or doubt, how blessed to hear the voice of God, "Wait on the Lord! Be strong, and let thine heart take Courage! *Yea, Wait Thou on the Lord!*" Let nothing in heaven or earth or hell — let nothing keep thee from waiting on thy God in full assurance that it cannot be in vain.

The one lesson our text teaches us is this, that when we set ourselves to wait on God we ought beforehand to resolve that it shall be with the most confident expectation of God's meeting and blessing us. We ought to make up our minds to this, that nothing was ever so sure, as that waiting on God will bring us untold and unexpected blessing. We are so accustomed to judge of God and His work in us by what we feel, that the great probability is that when we begin more to cultivate the waiting on Him, we shall be discouraged, because we do not find any special blessing from it. The message comes to us, "Above everything, when you wait on God, do so in the spirit of abounding hopefulness. It is God in His glory, in His power, in His love longing to bless you that you are waiting on."

If you say that you are afraid of deceiving yourself with vain hope, because you do not see or feel any warrant in your present state for such special expectations, my answer is, it is God, who is the warrant for your expecting great things. Oh, do learn the lesson. You are not going to wait on yourself to see what you feel and what changes come to you. You are going to *Wait on God*, to know first, *What He is*, and then, after that, what He will do. The whole duty and blessedness of waiting on God has its root in this, that He is such a blessed Being, full, to overflowing, of goodness and power and life and joy, that we, however wretched, cannot for any time come into contact with Him, without that life and power secretly, silently beginning to enter into him and blessing him. God is Love! That is the one only and all-sufficient warrant of your expectation. Love seeketh out its own: God's love is just His delight to impart Himself and His blessedness to His children.

Come, and however feeble you feel, just wait in His presence. As a feeble, sickly invalid is brought out into the sunshine to let its warmth go through him, come with all that is dark and cold in you into the sunshine of God's holy, omnipotent love, and sit and wait there, with the one thought: Here I am, in the sunshine of His love. As the sun does its work in the weak one who seeks its rays, God will do His work in you. Oh, do trust Him fully. "Wait on the Lord! Be strong, and let your heart take courage! Yea, wait thou on the Lord!"

"My soul, wait thou only upon God!"

Day 9. With the Heart

"Be strong, and let your heart take courage, All ye that wait for the Lord." Ps. 31:24

The words are nearly the same as in our last meditation. But I gladly avail myself of them again to press home a much-needed lesson for all who desire to learn truly and fully what waiting on God is. The lesson is this: It is with the heart we must wait upon God. "Let your heart take courage"

All our waiting depends upon the state of the heart. As a man's heart is, so is he before God. We can advance no further or deeper into the holy place of God's presence to wait on Him there, than our heart is prepared for it by the Holy Spirit. The message is, "Let your heart take courage, all ye that wait on the Lord."

The truth appears so simple, that some may ask, Do not all admit this? Where is the need of insisting on it so specially? Because very many Christians have no sense of the great difference between the religion of the mind and the religion of the heart, and the former is far more diligently cultivated than the latter. They know not how infinitely greater the heart is than the mind. It is in this that one of the chief causes must be sought of the feebleness of our Christian life, and it is only as this is understood that waiting on God will bring its full blessing.

A text in Proverbs (3:5) may help to make my meaning plain. Speaking of a life in the fear and favor of God, it says, "Trust in the Lord with all thine heart, and lean not upon thine own understanding." In all religion we have to use these two powers. The mind as to gather knowledge from God's word, and prepare the food by which the heart with the inner life is to be nourished. But here comes in a terrible danger, of our leaning to our own understanding, and trusting in our apprehension of divine things.

People imagine that if they are occupied with the truth, the spiritual life will as a matter of course be strengthened. And this is by no means the case. The understanding deals with conceptions and images of divine things, but it cannot reach the real life of the soul. Hence the command, "Trust in the Lord with all thine heart, and lean not upon thine own understanding." It is with the heart man believeth, and comes into touch with God. It is in the heart God has given His Spirit, to be there to us the presence and the power of God working in us. In all our religion it is the heart that must trust and love and worship and obey. My mind is utterly impotent in creating or maintaining the spiritual life within me: the heart must wait on God for Him to work it in me.

It is in this even as in the physical life. My reason may tell me what to eat and drink, and how the food nourishes me. But in the eating and feeding my reason I can do nothing: the body has its organs for that special purpose. Just so, reason may tell me what God's word says, but it can do nothing to the feeding of the soul on the bread of life — this the heart alone can do by its faith and trust in God. A man may be studying the nature and effects of food or sleep; when he wants to eat or sleep he sets aside his thoughts and study, and uses the power of eating or sleeping. And so the Christian needs ever, when he has studied or heard God's word, to cease from his thoughts, to put no trust in them, and to waken up his heart to open itself before God, and seek the living fellowship with Him.

This is now the blessedness of waiting upon God, that I confess the impotence of all my thoughts and efforts, and set myself still to bow my heart before Him in holy silence, and to trust Him to renew and strengthen His own work in me. And this is just the lesson of our text, "Let your heart take courage, all ye that wait on the Lord." Remember the difference between knowing with the mind and believing with the heart. Beware of the temptation of leaning upon your understanding, with its clear strong thoughts. They only help you to know what the heart must get from God: in themselves they are only images and shadows.

"Let your heart take courage, all ye that wait on the Lord." Present it before Him as that wonderful part of your spiritual nature in which God reveals Himself, and by which you can know Him. Cultivate the greatest confidence that, though you cannot see into your heart, God is working there by His Holy Spirit. Let the heart wait at times in perfect silence and quiet; in its hidden depths God will work. Be sure of this, and just wait on Him. Give your whole heart, with its secret workings, into God's hands continually. He wants the heart, and takes it, and as God dwells in it. "Be strong, and let your heart take courage, all ye that wait on the Lord."

"My soul, wait thou only upon God!"

Day 10. Waiting on God: in Humble Fear and Hope

"Behold, the eye of the Lord is upon them that fear Him, upon them that hope in His mercy; To deliver their soul from death, And to keep them alive in famine. Our soul hath waited for the Lord; He is our help and our shield. For our heart shall rejoice in Him, Because we have trusted in His holy name. Let thy mercy, O Lord, be upon us, According as we wait for thee." Ps. 33:18-22

God's eye is upon His people: their eye is upon Him. In waiting upon God, our eye, looking up to Him, meets His looking down upon us. This is the blessedness of waiting upon God, that it takes our eyes and thoughts away from ourselves, even our needs and desires, and occupies us with our God. We worship Him in His glory and love, with His all-seeing eye watching over us, that He may supply our every need. Let us consider this wonderful meeting between God and His people, and mark well what we are taught here of them on whom God's eye rests, and of Him on whom our eye rests.

"The eye of the Lord is on them that fear Him, on them that hope in His mercy." Fear and hope are generally thought to be in conflict with each other, in the presence and worship of God they are found side by side in perfect and beautiful harmony. And this because in God Himself all apparent contradictions are reconciled. Righteousness and peace, judgment and mercy, holiness and love, infinite power and infinite gentleness, a majesty that is exalted above all heaven, and a condescension that bows very low, meet and kiss each other.

There is indeed a fear that hath torment, that is cast out entirely by perfect love. But there is a fear that is found in the very heavens. In the song of Moses and the Lamb they sing, "Who shall not fear Thee, O

Lord, and glorify Thy name?" And out of the very throne the voice came, "Praise our God, all ye His servants, and ye that fear Him." Let us in our waiting ever seek "to fear the glorious and fearful name, *the Lord Thy God.*" The deeper we w bow before His holiness in holy fear and adoring awe, in deep reverence and humble self-abasement, even as the angels veil their faces before the throne, the more will His holiness rest upon us, and the soul be filled to have God reveal Himself; the deeper we enter into the truth "that no flesh glory in His presence," will it be given us to see His glory. "The eye of the Lord is on them that fear Him."

"On them that hope in His mercy." So far will the true fear of God be from keeping us back from hope, it will stimulate and strengthen it. The lower we bow, the deeper we feel we have nothing to hope in but His mercy. The lower we bow, the nearer God will come, and make our hearts bold to trust Him. Let every exercise of waiting, let our whole habit of waiting on God, be pervaded by abounding hope — a hope as bright and boundless as God's mercy. The fatherly kindness of God is such that, in whatever state we come to Him, we may confidently hope in His mercy.

Such are God's waiting ones. And now, think of the God on whom we wait. "The eye of the Lord is on them that fear Him, on them that hope in His mercy; to deliver their soul from death, and to keep them alive in famine." Not to prevent the danger of death and famine — this is often needed to stir the waiting on Him — but to deliver and to keep alive. For the dangers are often very real and dark; the situation, whether in the temporal or spiritual life, may appear to be utterly hopeless. There is always one hope: God's eye is on them.

That eye sees the danger, and sees in tender love His trembling waiting child, and sees the moment when the heart is ripe for the blessing, and sees the way in which it is to come. This living, mighty God, oh, let us fear Him and hope in His mercy. And let us humbly but boldly say, "Our soul waiteth for the Lord; He is our help and our shield. Let Thy mercy be upon us, O Lord, according as we wait for Thee."

Oh, the blessedness of waiting on such a God! a very present help in every time of trouble; a shield and defense against every danger.

Children of God! will you not learn to sink down in entire helplessness and impotence and in stillness to wait and see the salvation of God?

In the utmost spiritual famine, and when death appears to prevail, oh, wait on God. He does deliver, He does keep alive. Say it not only in solitude, but say it to each other — the psalm speaks not of one but of God's people — "Our soul waiteth on the Lord: He is our help and our shield." Strengthen and encourage each other in the holy exercise of waiting, that each may not only say of it himself, but of his brethren, "We have waited for Him; we will be glad and rejoice in His salvation."

"My soul, wait thou only upon God!"

Day 11. Waiting on God: Patiently

"Rest in the Lord, and wait patiently for Him, Those that wait upon the Lord, they shall inherit the land." Ps. 37:7, 9

"In patience possess your souls." "Ye have need of patience." "Let patience have its perfect work, that ye may be perfect and entire." Such words of the Holy Spirit show us what an important element in the Christian life and character patience is. And nowhere is there a better place for cultivating or displaying it than in waiting on God. There we discover how impatient we are, and what our impatience means. We confess at times that we are impatient with men, and circumstances that hinder us, or with ourselves and our slow progress in the Christian life. If we truly set ourselves to wait upon God, we shall find that it is with Him we are impatient, because He does not at once, or as soon as we could wish, do our bidding. It is in waiting upon God that our eyes are opened to believe in His wise and sovereign will, and to see that the sooner and the more completely we yield absolutely to it, the more surely His blessing can come to us.

"It is not of him that willeth, nor of him that runneth, but of God that sheweth mercy." Rom 9:16. We have as little power to increase or strengthen our spiritual life, as we had to originate it. We "were born not of the will of the flesh, nor of the will of man, but of the will of God." Even so, our willing and running, our desire and effort, avail nought; all is "of God that sheweth mercy."

All the exercises of the spiritual life, our reading and praying, our willing and doing, have their very great value. But they can go no farther than this, that they point the way and prepare us in humility to look to and to depend alone upon God Himself, and in patience to wait His good time and mercy. The waiting is to teach us our absolute dependence upon God's mighty working, and to make us in perfect patience place ourselves at His disposal. They that wait on the Lord shall inherit the land; the promised land and its blessing. The heirs must wait; they can afford to wait.

"Rest in the Lord, and wait patiently for Him." The margin gives for "Rest in the Lord," "Be silent to the Lord," or R. V., "Be still before the Lord." It is resting in the Lord, in His will, His promise, His faithfulness, and His love, that makes patience easy. And the resting in Him is nothing but being silent unto Him, still before Him. Having our thoughts and wishes, our fears and hopes, hushed into calm and quiet in that great peace of God which passeth all understanding. That peace keeps the heart and mind when we are anxious for anything, because we have made our request known to Him. The rest, the silence, the stillness, and the patient waiting, all find their strength and joy in God Himself.

The need for patience, and the reasonableness, and the blessedness of patience will be opened up to the waiting soul. Our patience will be seen to be the counterpart of God's patience. He longs far more to bless us fully than we can desire it. But, as the husbandman has long patience till the fruit be ripe, so God bows Himself to our slowness and bears long with us. Let us remember this, and wait patiently: of each promise and every answer to prayer the word is true: "I the Lord will hasten it in its time." Isa 60:22.

"Rest in the Lord, and wait patiently for Him." Yes, for *Him*. Seek not only the help, the gift, thou needest seek: *Himself*; wait for *Him*. Give God His glory by resting in Him, by trusting him fully, by waiting patiently for Him. This patience honors Him greatly; it leaves Him, as God on the throne, to do His work; it yields self wholly into His hands. It lets God be God. If thy waiting be for some special request, wait patiently. If thy waiting be more the exercise of the spiritual life seeking to know and have more of God, wait patiently. Whether it be in the shorter specific periods of waiting, or as the continuous habit of the souls. Rest in the Lord, be still before the Lord, and wait patiently. "They that wait on the Lord shall inherit the land."

"My soul, wait thou only upon God!"

Day 12. Waiting on God: Keeping His Ways

"Wait on the Lord, and keep His way, And He shalt exalt thee to inherit the land." Ps. 37:34.

If we desire to find a man whom we long to meet, we inquire where the places and the ways are where he is to be found. When waiting on God, we need to be very careful that we keep His ways; out of these we never can expect to find Him. "Thou meetest him that rejoiceth and worketh righteousness; those that remember Thee in Thy ways." Isa 64:5. We may be sure that God is never and nowhere to be found but in His ways. And that there, by the soul who seeks and patiently waits, He is always most surely to be found. "Wait on the Lord, and keep His ways, and He shall exalt thee."

How close the connection between the two parts of the injunction, "Wait on the Lord," — that has to do with worship and disposition; "and keep His ways," — that deals with walk and work. The outer life must be in harmony with the inner; the inner must be the inspiration and the strength for the outer. It is our God who has made known His ways in His Word for our conduct, and invites our confidence for His grace and help in our heart. If we do not keep His ways, our waiting on Him can bring no blessing. The surrender to full obedience to all His will is the secret of full access to all the blessings of His fellowship.

Notice how strongly this comes out in the psalm. It speaks of the evildoer who prospereth in his way, and calls on the believer not to fret himself. When we see men around us prosperous and happy while they forsake God's ways, and ourselves left in difficulty or suffering, we are in danger of first fretting at what appears so strange, and then gradually yielding to seek our prosperity in their path. The psalm says, "Fret not thyself; trust in the Lord, and do good. Rest in the Lord, and wait patiently for Him; cease from anger, and forsake wrath. Depart from evil, and do good; the Lord forsaketh not His saints. The righteous shall inherit the land. The law of his God is in his heart; none of his steps shall slide." "And then follows — the word occurs for the third time in the psalm — "Wait on the Lord, and keep His way." Do what God asks you to do; God will do more than you can ask Him to do.

And let no one give way to the fear: I cannot keep His way; it is this robs one of every confidence. It is true you have not the strength yet to keep all His ways. But keep carefully those for which you have received strength already. Surrender yourself willingly and trustingly to keep all God's ways, in the strength which will come in waiting on Him. Give up your whole being to God without reserve and without doubt; He will prove Himself God to you, and work in you that which is pleasing in His sight through Jesus Christ.

Keep His ways, as you know them in the Word. Keep His ways, as nature teaches them, in always doing what appears right. Keep His ways, as Providence points them out. Keep His ways, as the Holy Spirit suggests. Do not think of waiting on God while you say you are not willing to work in His path. However weak you feel, only be willing, and He who has worked to will, will work to do by His power.

"Wait on the Lord, and keep His way." It may be that the consciousness of shortcoming and sin makes our text look more like a hindrance than a help in waiting on God. Let it not be so.

Have we not said more than once, the very starting-point and ground-work of this waiting is utter and absolute impotence? Why then not come with everything evil you feel in yourself, every memory of unwillingness, unwatchfulness, unfaithfulness, and all that causes such unceasing self-condemnation? Put your power in God's omni-potence, and find in waiting on God your deliverance.

Your failure has been owing to only one thing: you sought to conquer and obey in your own strength. Come and bow before God until you learn that He is the God who alone is good, and alone can work any good thing. Believe that in you, and all that nature can do, there is no true power. Be content to receive from God each moment the inworking of His mighty grace and life, and waiting on God will become the renewal of your strength to run in His ways and not be weary, to walk in His paths and never faint. "Wait on the Lord, and keep His way" will be command and promise in one.

"My soul, wait thou only upon God!"

Day 13. Waiting on God: for More than We Know

"And now, Lord, what wait I for? My hope is in Thee. Deliver me from all my transgressions." Ps. 39:7, 8.

There may be times when we feel as if we knew not what we are waiting for. There may be other times we think we do know, and when it would just be so good for us to realize that we do not know what to ask as we ought. God is able to do for us exceeding abundantly above what we ask or think, and we are in danger of limiting Him, when we confine our desires and prayers to our own thoughts of them. It is a great thing at times to say, as our psalm says: "And now, Lord, what wait I for?" I scarce know or can tell; this only I can say — "My hope is in Thee."

How we see this limiting of God in the case of Israel! When Moses promised them meat in the wilderness, they doubted, saying, "Can God furnish a table in the wilderness? He smote the rock that the water gushed out; can He give bread also? Can He provide flesh for His people?" If they had been asked whether God could provide streams in the desert, they would have answered, Yes. God had done it: He could do it again. But when the thought came of God doing something new, they limited Him; their expectation could not rise beyond their past experience, or their own thoughts of what was possible.

Even so we may be limiting God by our conceptions of what He has promised or is able to do. Do let us beware of limiting the Holy one of Israel in our very prayer. Let us believe that the very promises of God we plead have a divine meaning, infinitely beyond our thoughts of them. Let us believe that His fulfilment of them can be, in a power and an abundance of grace, beyond our largest grasp of thought. And let us therefore cultivate the habit of waiting on God, not only for what we think we need, but for all His grace and power are ready to do for us.

In every true prayer there are two hearts in exercise. The one is your heart, with its little, dark, human thoughts of what you need and God can do. The other is God's great heart, with its infinite, its divine purposes of blessing. What think you? To which of these two ought the larger place to be given in your approach to Him? Undoubtedly, to the heart of God: every thing depends upon knowing and being occupied with that. But how little this is done. This is what waiting on God is meant to teach you. Just think of God's wonderful love and redemption, in the meaning these words must have to Him. Confess how little you understand what God is willing to do for you, and say each time as you pray: "And now, what wait I for?" My heart cannot say, God's heart knows and waits to give. "My hope is in Thee." Wait on God to do for you more than you can ask or think.

Apply this to the prayer that follows: "Deliver me from all my transgressions." You have prayed to be delivered from temper, or pride, or self-will. It is as if it is in vain. May it not be that you have had your own thoughts about the way or the extent of God's doing it, and have never waited on the God of glory, according to the riches of His glory, to do for you what hath not entered the heart of man to conceive? Learn to worship God as the God who doeth wonders, who wishes to prove in you that He can do something supernatural and divine. Bow before Him, wait upon Him, until your soul realizes that you are in the hands of a divine and almighty worker. Consent but to know what and how He will work; expect it to be something altogether godlike, something to be waited for in deep humility, and received only by His divine power. Let, the, "And now, Lord, what wait I for? My hope is in Thee" become the spirit of every longing and every prayer. He will in His time do His work.

Dear soul, in waiting on God you may often be ready to be weary, because you hardly know what you have to expect. I pray you, be of good courage — this ignorance is often one of the best signs. He is teaching you to leave all in His hands, and to wait on Him alone. "Wait on the Lord! Be strong, and let your heart take courage. Yea, wait thou on the Lord"

"My soul, wait thou only upon God!"

Day 14. Waiting on God: the Way to the New Song

"I waited patiently for the Lord, and He inclined unto me, and heard my cry. . . and He hath put a new song in my mouth, even praise unto our God." Ps. 40:1-3.

Come and listen to the testimony of one who can speak from experience of the sure and blessed outcome of patient, waiting upon God. True patience is so foreign to our self-confident nature, it is so indispensable in our waiting upon God, it is such an essential element of true faith, that we may well once again meditate on what the word has to teach us.

The word patience is derived from the Latin word for suffering. It suggests the thought of being under the constraint of some power from which we fain would be free. At first we submit against our will; experience teaches us that when it is vain to resist, patient endurance is our wisest course. In waiting on God it is of infinite consequence that we not only submit, because we are compelled to, but because we lovingly and joyfully consent to be in the hands of our blessed Father. Patience then becomes our highest blessedness and our highest grace. It honors God, and gives Him time to have His way with us. It is the highest expression of our faith in His goodness and faithfulness. It brings the soul perfect rest in the assurance that God is carrying on His work. It is the token of our full consent that God should deal with us in such a way and time as He thinks best. True patience is the losing of our self-will in His perfect will.

Such patience is needed for the true and full waiting on God. Such patience is the growth and fruit of our first lessons in the school of waiting. To many a one it will appear strange how difficult it is truly to wait upon God. The great stillness of soul before God that sinks into its own helplessness and waits for Him to reveal Himself; the deep humility that is afraid to let own will or own strength work aught except as God works to will and to do; the meekness that is content to be and to know nothing except as God gives His light; the entire resignation of the will that only wants to be a vessel in which His holy will can move and mold: all these elements of perfect patience are not found at once. But they will come in measure as the soul maintains its position, and ever again says: "Truly my soul waiteth upon God; from *Him* cometh my salvation: He only is my rock and my salvation."

Have you ever noticed what proof we have that patience is a grace for which very special grace is given, in these words of Paul: "Strengthened with all might, according to His glorious power, unto all" — what? "patience and long-suffering with joyfulness." Yes, we need to be strengthened with all God's might, and that according to the measure of His glorious power, if we are to wait on God in all patience. It is God revealing Himself in us as our life and strength, that will enable us with perfect patience to leave all in His hands. If any are inclined to despond, because they have not such patience, let them be of good courage; it is in the course of our feeble and very imperfect waiting that God Himself by His hidden power strengthens us and works out in us the patience of the saints, the patience of Christ Himself.

Listen to the voice of one who was deeply tried: "I waited patiently for the Lord, and He inclined unto me, and heard my cry." Hear what he passed through: "He brought me up also out of an horrible pit, out of the miry clay, and set my feet upon a rock, and established my goings. And He hath put a new song in my mouth, even praise unto our God." Patient waiting upon God brings a rich reward; the deliverance is sure; God Himself will put a new song into your mouth. O soul! be not impatient, whether it be in the exercise of prayer and worship that you find it difficult to wait, or in the delay in respect of definite requests, or in the fulfilling of your heart's desire for the revelation of God Himself in a deeper spiritual life — fear not, but rest in the Lord, and wait patiently for Him.

And if you sometimes feel as if patience is not your gift, then remember it is God's gift, and take that prayer (2 Thess. 3:5): "The Lord direct your hearts into the patience of Christ." Into the patience with which you are to wait on God, He Himself will guide you.

"My soul, wait thou only upon God!"

Day 15. Waiting on God: for His Counsel

"They soon forgot His works: they waited not for His counsel." Ps. *106:13.*

This is said of the sin of God's people in the wilderness. He had wonderfully redeemed them, and was prepared as wonderfully to supply their every need. But, when the time of need came, "they waited not for His counsel." They thought not that the Almighty God was their Leader and Provider; they asked not what His plans might be. They simply thought the thoughts of their own heart, and tempted and provoked God by their unbelief. "They waited not for His counsel."

How this has been the sin of God's people in all ages! In the land of Canaan, in the days of Joshua, the only three failures of which we read were owing to this one sin. In going up against Ai, in making a covenant with the Gibeonites, in settling down without going up to possess the whole land, they waited not for His counsel. And so even the advanced believer is in danger from this most subtle of temptations — taking God's word and thinking his own thoughts of them, and not waiting for His counsel. Let us take the warning and see what Israel teaches us. And let us very specially regard it not only as a danger to which the individual is exposed, but as one against which God's people, in their collective capacity, need to be on their guard.

Our whole relation to God is ruled in this, that His will is to be done in us and by us as it is in heaven. He has promised to make known His will to us by His Spirit, the Guide into all truth. And our position is to be that of waiting for His counsel as the only guide of our thoughts and actions. In our church worship, in our prayer-meetings, in our conventions, in all our gatherings as managers, or directors, or committees, or helpers in any part of the work for God, our first object ought ever to be to ascertain the mind of God. God always works according to the counsel of His will; the more that counsel of His will is sought and found and honored, the more surely and mightily will God do His work for us and through us.

The great danger in all such assemblies is that in our consciousness of having our Bible, and our past experience of God' s leading, and our sound creed, and our honest wish to do God's will, we trust in these, and do not realize that with every step we need and may have a heavenly guidance. There may be elements of God's will, application of God's word, experience of the close presence and leading of God, manifestations of the power of His Spirit, of which we know nothing as yet. God may be willing, nay, God is willing to open up these to the souls who are intently set upon allowing Him to have his way entirely, and who are willing in patience to wait for His making it known.

When we come together praising God for all He has done and taught and given, we may at the same time be limiting Him by not expecting greater things. It was when God had given the water out of the rock that they did not trust Him for bread. It was when God had given Jericho into his hands that Joshua thought the victory over Ai was sure, and waited not for counsel from God. And so, while we think that we know and trust the power of God for what we may expect, we may be hindering Him by not giving time, and not definitely cultivating the habit of waiting for His counsel.

A minister has no more solemn duty than teaching people to wait upon God. Why was it that in the house of Cornelius, when "Peter spake these words, the Holy Ghost fell upon all that heard him"? They had said, "We are here before God to hear all things that are commanded thee of God." We may come together to give and to listen to the most earnest exposition of God's truth with little spiritual profit if there be not the waiting for God's counsel.

And so in all our gatherings we need to believe in the Holy Spirit as the Guide and Teacher of God's saints when they wait to be led by Him into the things which God hath prepared, and which the heart cannot conceive. More stillness of soul to realize God's presence; more consciousness of ignorance of what God's great plans may be; more faith in the certainty that God has greater things to show us; that He Himself will be revealed in new glory: these must be the marks of the assemblies of God's saints if they would avoid the reproach, "They waited not for His counsel."

"My soul, wait thou only upon God!"

Day 16. Waiting on God: and His Light in the Heart

"I wait for the Lord, my soul doth wait, And in His word do I hope. My soul waiteth for the Lord. More than they that watch for the morning: More than they that watch for the morning." Ps. 130:5-6.

With what intense longing the morning light is often waited for. By the mariners in a shipwrecked vessel; by a benighted traveler in a dangerous country; by an army that finds itself surrounded by an enemy. The morning light will show what hope of escape there may be. The morning may bring life and liberty. And so the saints of God in darkness have longed for the light of His countenance, more than watchmen for the morning. They have said, "More than watchmen for the morning, my soul waiteth for the Lord." Can we say that too? Our waiting on God can have no higher object than simply having His light shine on us, and in us, and through us, all the day.

God is Light. God is a Sun. Paul says: "God hath shined in our hearts to give the light," What light? "The light of the glory of God, in the face of Jesus Christ." Just as the sun shines its beautiful, life-giving light on and into our earth, so God shines into our hearts the light of His glory, of His love, in Christ His Son. Our heart is meant to have that light filling and gladdening it all the day. It can have it, because God is our sun, an it is written, "Thy sun shall no more go down for ever." God's love shines on us without ceasing.

But can we indeed enjoy it all the day? We can. And how can we? Let nature give us the answer. Those beautiful trees and flowers, with all this green grass, what do they do to keep the sun shining on them? They do nothing; they simply bask in the sunshine, when it comes. The sun is millions of miles away, but over all that distance it comes, its own light and joy; and the tiniest flower that lifts its little head up- wards is met by the same exuberance of light and blessing as flood the widest landscape. We have not to care for the light we need for our day's work; the sun cares, and provides and shines the light around us all the day. We simply count upon it, and receive it, and enjoy it.

The only difference between nature and grace is this, that what the trees and the flowers do unconsciously, as they drink in the blessing of the light, is to be with us a voluntary and a loving acceptance. Faith, simple faith in God's word and love, is to be the opening of the eyes, the opening of the heart, to receive and enjoy the unspeakable glory of His grace. And just as the trees, day by day, and month by month, stand and grow into beauty and fruitfulness, just welcoming whatever sunshine the sun may give, so it is the very highest exercise of our Christian life just to abide in the light of God, and let it, and let Him, fill us with the life and the brightness it brings.

And if you ask, But can it really be, that just as naturally and heartily as I recognize and rejoice in the beauty of a bright sunny morning, I can rejoice in God's light all the day? It can, indeed. From my breakfast-table I look out on a beautiful valley, with trees and vineyards and mountains. In our spring and autumn months the light in the morning is exquisite, and almost involuntarily we say, How beautiful! And the question comes, Is it only the light of the sun that is to bring such continual beauty and joy? And is there no provision for the light of God being just as much an unceasing source of joy and gladness? There is, indeed, if the soul will but be still and wait on Him, *Only Let God Shine*.

Dear soul! learn to wait on the Lord, more than watchers for the morning. All within you may be very dark; is that not the very best reason for waiting for the light of God? The first beginnings of light may be just enough to discover the darkness, and painfully to humble you on account of sin. Can you not trust the light to expel the darkness? Do believe it will. Just bow, even now, in stillness before God, and wait on Him to shine into you. Say, in humble faith, God is light, infinitely brighter and more beautiful than that of the sun. God is light: the Father. The eternal, inaccessible, and incomprehensible light: the Son. The light concentrated, and embodied, and manifested: the Spirit, the light entering and dwelling and shining in our hearts. God is light, and is here shining on my heart. I have been so occupied with the rushlights of my thoughts and efforts. I have never opened the shutters to let His light in. Unbelief has kept it out.

I bow in faith: God, light, is shining into my heart; the God of whom Paul wrote, "God hath shined into our heart," is my God. What would I think of a sun that could not shine? What shall I think of a God that does not shine? No, God shines! God is light! I will take time, and just be still, and rest in the light of God. My eyes are feeble, and the windows are not clean, but I will wait on the Lord. The light does shine, the light will shine in me, and make me full of light. And I shall learn to walk all the day in the light and joy of God. My soul waits on the light of the Lord, more than the watcher for the morning.

"My soul, wait thou only upon God"

Day 17. Waiting on God: in Times of Darkness

"I will wait upon the Lord, that hideth His face from the house of Jacob; and I will look for Him." Isa 8:17.

Here we have a servant of God, waiting upon Him, not on behalf of himself, but of his people, from whom God was hiding His face. It suggests to us how our waiting upon God, though it commences with our personal needs, with the desire for the revelation of Himself, or for the answer to personal petitions, need not, may not, stop there. We may be walking in the full light of God's countenance, and God yet be hiding His face from His people around us; far from being content to think that this is nothing but the just punishment of their sin, or the consequence of their indifference, we are called with tender hearts to think of their sad estate, and to wait on God on their behalf. The privilege of waiting upon God is one that brings great responsibility. Even as Christ, when He entered God's presence, at once used His place of privilege and honor as intercessor, so we, no less, if we know what it is really to enter in and wait upon God, must use our access for our less favored brethren. "I will wait upon the Lord, who hideth His face from the house of Jacob."

You worship with a certain congregation. Possibly there is not the spiritual life or joy either in the preaching or in the fellowship that you could desire. You belong to a Church, with its many congregations. There is so much of error or worldliness, of seeking after human wisdom and culture, or trust in ordinances and observances, that you do not wonder that God hides His face, in many cases, and that there is but little power for conversion or true edification.

Then there are branches of Christian work with which you are connected — a Sunday school, a gospel hall, a young men's association, a mission work abroad — in which the feebleness of the Spirit's working appears to indicate that God is hiding His face. You think, too, you know the reason, There is too much trust in men and money; there is too much formality and self-indulgence; there is too little faith and prayer; too little love and humility; too little of the spirit of the crucified Jesus. At times you feel as if things were hopeless; nothing will help.

Do believe that God can help and will help. Let the spirit of the prophet come into you, as you value his words, and set yourself to wait on God, on behalf of His erring children. Instead of the tone of judgment or condemnation, of despondency or despair, realize your calling to wait upon God. If others fail in doing it, give yourself doubly to it. The deeper the darkness, the greater the need of appealing to the one only Deliverer. The greater the self-confidence around you, that knows not that it is poor and wretched and blind, the more urgent the call on you who profess to see the evil and to have access to Him who alone can help, to be at your post waiting upon God. Say on each new occasion, when you are tempted to speak or to sigh: "I will wait on the Lord, who hideth His face from the house of Jacob."

There is a still larger circle — the Christian Church throughout the world. Think of Greek, Roman Catholic, and Protestant churches, and the state of the millions that belong to them. Or think only of the Protestant churches with their open Bible and orthodox creeds. How much nominal profession and formality, how much of the rule of the flesh and of man in the very temple of God! And what abundant proof that God does hide his face!

What are those who see and mourn this to do? The first thing to be done is this: "I will wait on the Lord, who hideth His face from the house of Jacob." Let us wait on God, in the humble confession of the sins of His people. Let us take time and wait on Him in this exercise. Let us wait on God in tender, loving intercession for all saints, our beloved brethren, however wrong their lives or their teaching may appear. Let us wait on God in faith and expectation, until He shows us that He will hear. Let us wait on God, with the simple offering of ourselves to Himself, and the earnest prayer that He would send us to our brethren. Let us wait on God, and give Him no rest till He makes Zion a joy in the earth.

Yes, let us rest in the Lord, and wait patiently for Him who now hides His face from so many of His children. And let us say of the lifting up of the light of His countenance we long for all His people, "I wait for the Lord, my soul doth wait, and my hope is in His word. My soul waiteth for the Lord, more than the watchers for the morning, the watchers for the morning."

"My soul, wait thou only upon God!"

Day 18. To Reveal Himself

And it shall be said in that day, Lo, this is our God; we have waited for him, and he will save us: this is the *Lord*; we have waited for Him, we will be glad and rejoice in his salvation.—Isaiah 25:9

In this passage, we have two precious thoughts. The one, that it is the language of God's people who have been unitedly waiting on Him. The other, that the fruit of their waiting has been that God has so revealed Himself, that they could joyfully say, "Lo, this is our God . . . this is the *Lord*." The power and the blessing of united waiting is what we need to learn.

Note that this phrase is repeated twice, "We have waited for him." In some time of trouble, the hearts of the people had been drawn together, and they had, ceasing from all human hope or help, with one heart set themselves to wait for their God. Is this not just what we need in our churches and conventions and prayer meetings? Is not the need of the church and the world great enough to demand it? Are there not in the church of Christ evils to which no human wisdom is equal? Have we not ritualism and rationalism, formalism and worldliness, robbing the church of its power? Have we not culture and money and pleasure threatening its spiritual life? Are not the powers of the church utterly inadequate to cope with the powers of infidelity and iniquity and wretchedness in Christian countries and in heathendom? And, is there not, in the promise of God and in the power of the Holy Spirit, a provision made that can meet the need and give the church the restful assurance that she is doing all her God expects of her? And would not united waiting upon God for the supply of His Spirit most certainly seem the needed blessing? We cannot doubt it.

The object of a more definite waiting upon God in our gatherings would be very much the same as in personal worship. It would mean a deeper conviction that God must and will do all. It would require a more humble and abiding entrance into our deep helplessness, and the need of entire and unceasing dependence upon Him. We need a more living consciousness that the essential thing is to give God His place of honor and of power. We must have a confident expectation that to those who wait on Him, God will, by His Spirit, give the secret of His acceptance and presence, and then, in due time, the revelation of His saving power. The great aim would be to bring everyone in a praying and worshiping company under a deep sense of God's presence, so that when they part there will be the consciousness of having met God Himself, of having left every request with Him, and of now waiting in stillness while He works out His salvation.

It is this experience that is indicated in our text. The fulfillment of the words may, at times, be in such striking interpositions of God's power that all can join in the cry, "Lo, this is our God . . . this is the *Lord*." They may equally become true in spiritual experience, when God's people, in their waiting times, become so conscious of His presence that, in holy awe, souls feel, "Lo, this is our God . . . this is the *Lord*." It is this, alas, that is too much missed in our meetings for worship. The godly minister has no more difficult, no more solemn, no more blessed task, than to lead his people out to meet God. And, before he preaches, he must bring each one into contact with Him. "We are now here in the presence of God"—these words of Cornelius show the way in which Peter's audience was prepared for the coming of the Holy Spirit. Waiting before God, waiting for God, and waiting on God are the conditions of God showing His presence.

A company of believers gathered with the one purpose, helping each other by little intervals of silence, to wait on God alone, opening the heart for whatever God may have of new discoveries of evil, of His will, of new openings in work or methods of work, would soon have reason to say, "Lo, this is our God; we have waited for him, and he will save us: this is the *Lord*; we have waited for him, we will be glad and rejoice in his salvation."

My soul, wait thou only upon God!

Day 19. As a God of Judgment

Yea, in the way of thy judgments, O Lord, have we waited for thee . . . For when thy judgments are in the earth, the inhabitants of the world will learn righteousness.—Isaiah 26:8–9

The Lord is a God of judgment: blessed are all they that wait upon him.—Isaiah 30:18

God is a God of mercy and a God of judgment. Mercy and judgment are forever together in His dealings. In the Flood, in the deliverance of Israel out of Egypt, in the overthrow of the Canaanites, we ever see mercy in the midst of judgment. I n these, the inner circle of His own people, we see it, too. The judgment punishes the sin, while mercy saves the sinner. Or, rather, mercy saves the sinner, not in spite of, but by means of, the very judgment that came upon his sin. In waiting on God, we must beware of forgetting this—as we wait we must expect Him as a God of judgment.

"In the way of thy judgments, O *Lord*, have we waited for thee." That will prove true in our inner experience. If we are honest in our longing for holiness—in our prayers to be wholly the Lord's—His holy presence will stir up and discover hidden sin. It, will bring us very low in the bitter conviction of the evil of our nature, its opposition to God's law, and its inability to fulfill that law. The words will come true: "Who may abide the day of his coming? . . . For he is like a refiner's fire" (Mal. 3:2). "Oh that thou wouldest . . . come down . . . As when the melting fire burneth" (Isa. 64:1). In great mercy, God executes, within the soul, His judgments upon sin, as He makes it feel its wickedness and guilt. Many try to flee from these judgments. The soul that longs for God, and for deliverance from sin, bows under them in humility and in hope.

In silence of soul, it says, "Rise up, *Lord*, and let thine enemies be scattered" (Num. 10:35). "In the way of thy judgments . . . have we waited for thee."

Let no one who seeks to learn the blessed art of waiting on God, wonder if at first the attempt to wait on Him only reveals more of sin and darkness. Let no one despair because unconquered sins, evil thoughts, or great darkness appear to hide God's face. Was not, in His own beloved Son, the gift and bearer of His mercy on Calvary, the mercy as hidden and lost in the judgment? Oh, submit and sink down deep under the judgment of your every sin. Judgment prepares the way and breaks out in wonderful mercy. It is written, "Zion shall be redeemed with judgment" (Isa. 1:27). Wait on God, in the faith that His tender mercy is working out His redemption in the midst of judgment. Wait for Him; He will be gracious to you.

There is another application still, one of unspeakable solemnity. We are expecting God, in the way of His judgments, to visit his earth; we are waiting for Him. What a thought! We know of these coming judgments. We know that there are tens of thousands of professing Christians who live on in carelessness, and who, if no change comes, must perish under God's hand. Oh, will we not do our utmost to warn them, to plead with and for them, if God may lave mercy on them! If we feel our lack of boldness, zeal, and cower, will we not begin to wait on God more definitely and persistently as a God of judgment? Will we not ask Him to so reveal Himself in the judgments that are coming on our very friends, that we may be inspired with a new fear of Him and them, and constrained to speak and pray as never yet before? Verily, waiting on God is not leant to be a spiritual self-indulgence. Its object is to let God and His holiness, Christ and the love that died on Calvary, the Spirit and fire that burns in heaven and came to earth, get possession of us to warn and arouse men with the message that we are waiting for God in the way of His judgments. Oh, Christian, prove that you really believe in the God of judgment!

My soul, wait thou only upon God!

Day 20. Who Waits on Us

And therefore will the Lord wait, that he may be gracious unto you, and therefore will He be exalted, that he may have mercy upon you: for the Lord is a God of judgment: blessed are all they that wait for him.—Isaiah 30:18

We must not only think of our waiting upon God, but also of what is more wonderful still, of God's waiting upon us. The vision of Him waiting on us will give new impulse and inspiration to our waiting upon Him. It will give us an unspeakable confidence that our waiting cannot be in vain. If He waits for us, then we may be sure that we are more than welcome—that He rejoices to find those He has been seeking for. Let us seek even now, at this moment, in the spirit of lowly waiting on God, to find out, something of what it means. "Therefore will the *Lord* wait, that he may be gracious unto you." We will accept and echo back the message, "Blessed are all they that wait for him."

Look up and see the great God upon His throne. He is love an unceasing and inexpressible desire to communicate His own goodness and blessedness to all His creatures. He longs and delights to bless. He has inconceivably glorious purposes concerning every one of His children, by the power of His Holy Spirit, to reveal in them His love and power. He waits with all the longings of a father's heart. He waits that He may be gracious unto you. And, each time you come to wait upon Him, or seek to maintain in daily life the holy habit of waiting, you may look up and see Him ready to meet you. He will be waiting so that He may be gracious unto you. Yes, connect every exercise, every breath of the life of waiting, with faith's vision of your God waiting for you.

And if you ask: How is it, if He waits to be gracious, that even after I come and wait upon Him, He does not give the help I seek, but waits on longer and longer? There is a double answer. The one is this. God is a wise husbandman, who "waiteth for the precious fruit of the earth, and hath long patience for it (James 5:7). He cannot gather the fruit until it is ripe. He knows when we are spiritually ready to receive the blessing to our profit and His glory. Waiting in the sunshine of His love is what will ripen the soul for His blessing. Waiting under the cloud of trial, that breaks in showers of blessing, is as necessary. Be assured that if God waits longer than you could wish, it is only to make the blessing doubly precious. God waited four thousand years, until the fullness of time, before He sent His Son. Our times are in His hands. He will avenge His elect speedily. He will make haste for our help and not delay one hour too long.

The other answer points to what has been said before. The giver is more than the gift; God is more than the blessing. And our being kept waiting on Him is the only way for our learning to find our life and joy in Himself. Oh, if God's children only knew what a glorious God they have, and what a privilege it is to be linked in fellowship with Him, then they would rejoice in Him! Even when He keeps them waiting, they will learn to understand better than ever. "Therefore will the *Lord* wait, that he may be gracious unto you." His waiting will be the highest proof of His graciousness.

"Blessed are all they that wait for him." A queen has her ladies-in-waiting. The position is one of subordination and service, and yet it is considered one of the highest dignity and privilege, because a wise and gracious sovereign makes them companions and friends. What a dignity and blessedness to be attendants-in-waiting on the everlasting God, ever on the watch for every indication of His will or favor, ever conscious of His nearness, His goodness, and His grace! "The *Lord* is good unto them that wait for him" (Lam. 3:25). "Blessed are all they that wait for him." Yes, it is blessed when a waiting soul and a waiting God meet each other. God cannot do His work without His and our waiting His time. Let waiting be our work, as it is His. And, if His waiting is nothing but goodness and graciousness, let ours be nothing but a rejoicing in that goodness, and a confident expectancy of that grace. And, let every thought of waiting become to us the simple expression of unmingled and unutterable blessedness, because it brings us to a God who waits that He may make Himself known to us perfectly as the gracious One.

My soul, wait thou only upon God!

Day 21. The Almighty One

They that wait upon the Lord shall renew their strength; they shall mount up with wings as eagles; they shall run, and not be weary; and they shall walk, and not faint.—Isaiah 40:31

Our waiting on God will depend greatly on our faith of what He is. In our text, we have the close of a passage in which God reveals Himself as the everlasting and almighty One. It is as that revelation enters into our soul that the waiting will become the spontaneous expression of what we know Him to be — a God altogether most worthy to be waited upon.

Listen to the words, "Why sayest thou, 0 Jacob . . . My way is hid from the *Lord* . . .? Hast thou not known? hast thou not heard, that the everlasting God, the *Lord*, the Creator of the ends of the earth, fainteth not, neither is weary?" (Isa. 40:27-28). So far from it: "He giveth power to the faint; and to them that have no might he increaseth strength. Even the youths shall faint . . . and the young men shall utterly fall" (vv. 29-30). And consider that "the glory of young men is their strength" (Prov. 20:29). All that is deemed strong with man shall come to nothing. "But they that wait upon the *Lord*," on the Everlasting One, who does not faint, and is not weary, they "shall renew their strength; they shall mount up with wings as eagles; they shall run, and"—listen now, they will be strong with the strength of God, and, even as He, they will "not be weary; and they shall walk, and" even as He, they will "not faint."

Yes, "they shall mount up with wings as eagles." You know what eagles' wings mean. The eagle is the king of birds; it soars the highest into the heavens. Believers are to live a heavenly life, in the very presence and love and joy of God. They are to live where God lives;

they need God's strength to rise there. It will be given to them that wait on Him.

You know how the eagles' wings are obtained. Only in one way—by the eagle birth. You are born of God. You have the eagles' wings. You may not have known it; you may not have used them; but God can and will teach you how to use them.

You know how the eagles are taught the use of their wings. See yonder cliff rising a thousand feet out of the sea. See high up a ledge on the rock, where there is an eagle's nest with its treasure of two young eaglets. See the mother bird come and stir up her nest, and with her beak push the timid birds over the precipice. See how they flutter and fall and sink toward the depth. See now how she "fluttereth over her young, spreadeth abroad her wings, taketh them, beareth them on her wings" (Deut. 32:11), and so, as they ride upon her wings, brings them to a place of safety. And so, she does this once and again, each time casting them out over the precipice, and then again taking and carrying them. "So the *Lord* alone did lead him" (v. 12). Yes, the instinct of that eagle mother was God's gift, a single ray of that love in which the Almighty trains His people to mount as on eagles' wings.

He stirs up your nest. He disappoints your hopes. He brings down your confidence. He makes you fear and tremble, as all your strength fails, and you feel utterly weary and helpless. And all the while He is spreading His strong wings for you to rest your weakness on and offering His everlasting Creator strength to work in you. And all He asks is that you sink down in your weariness and wait on Him. Allow Him in His Jehovah strength to carry you as you ride upon the wings of His omnipotence.

Dear child of God, I pray you, lift up your eyes, and behold your God! Listen to Him who says that He "fainteth not, neither is weary" (Isa. 40:28), who promises that you too will not faint or be weary, who asks nothing but this one thing, that you should wait on Him. And, let your answer be, With such a God, so mighty, so faithful, so tender,

My soul, wait thou only upon God!

Day 22. Its Certainty of Blessing

Thou shalt know that I am the Lord: for they shall not be ashamed that wait for me.—Isaiah 49:23

Blessed are all they that wait for him.—Isaiah 30:18

What promises! How God seeks to draw us to waiting on Him by the most positive assurance that it never can be in vain; "they shall not be ashamed that wait for me." How strange that, though we should so often have experienced it, we are yet so slow to learn that this blessed waiting must and can be the very breath of our life—a continuous resting in God's presence and His love, an unceasing yielding of ourselves for Him to perfect His work in us. Let us once again listen and meditate, until our heart says with new conviction, "Blessed are all they that wait for him."

We found in the prayer of Psalm 25: "Let none that wait on thee be ashamed"(v. 3). The very prayer shows how we fear that it might be true. Let us listen to God's answer, until every fear is banished, and we send back to heaven the words God speaks, Yes, Lord, we believe what You say: "All they who wait for Me will not be ashamed." "Blessed are all they that wait for him."

The context of each of these two passages points us to times when God's church was in great straits, and to human eyes there were no possibilities of deliverance. But, God interposes with His word of promise, and pledges His almighty power for the deliverance of His people. And it is as the God who has Himself undertaken the work of their redemption that He invites them to wait on Him, and assures them that disappointment is impossible.

We, too, are living in days in which there is much in the state of the church, with its profession and its formalism, that is indescribably sad. Amid all we praise God for, there is, alas, much to mourn over! Were it not for God's promises, we might well despair. But, in His promises the living God has given and bound Himself to us. He calls us to wait on Him. He assures us we will not be put to shame. Oh, that our hearts might learn to wait before Him, until He Himself reveals to us what His promises mean. In the promises, He reveals Himself in His hidden glory! We will be irresistibly drawn to wait on Him alone. May God increase the company of those who say: "Our soul waiteth for the *Lord*: he is our help and our shield" (Ps. 33:20).

This waiting upon God on behalf of His church and people will depend greatly upon the place that waiting on Him has taken in our personal life. The mind may often have beautiful visions of what God has promised to do, and the lips may speak of them in stirring words, but these are not really the measure of our faith or power. No, it is what we really know of God in our personal experience, conquering the enemies within, reigning and ruling, revealing Himself in His holiness and power in our innermost being. It is this that will be the real measure of the spiritual blessing we expect from Him, and bring to our fellow men.

It is as we know how blessed the waiting on God has become to our own souls, that we will confidently hope in the blessing to come on the church around us. The keyword of all our expectations will be, He has said: "All they who wait on Me will not be ashamed." From what He has done in us, we will trust Him to do mighty things around us. "Blessed are all they that wait for him." Yes, blessed even now in the waiting. The promised blessings for ourselves, or for others, may tarry. The unutterable blessedness of knowing and having Him who has promised—the divine Blesser, the living Fountain of the coming blessings—is even now ours. Do let this truth acquire full possession of your souls, that waiting on God is itself the highest privilege of man, the highest blessedness of His redeemed child.

Even as the sunshine enters with its light and warmth, with its beauty and blessing, into every little blade of grass that rises upward out of the cold earth, so the everlasting God meets, in the greatness and the tenderness of His love, each waiting child, to shine in his heart "the light of the knowledge of the glory of God in the face of Jesus Christ" (2 Cor. 4:6). Read these words again, until your heart learns to know what God waits to do to you. Who can measure the difference between the great sun and that little blade of grass? And yet, the grass has all of the sun it can need or hold.

Do believe that in waiting on God, His greatness and your littleness suit and meet each other most wonderfully. Just bow in emptiness and poverty and utter weakness, in humility and meekness, and surrender to His will before His great glory, and be still. As you wait on Him, God draws near. He will reveal Himself' as the God who will mightily fulfill His every promise. And, let your heart continually take up the song: "Blessed are all they that wait for him."

My soul, wait thou only upon God

Day 23. For Unlooked-for Things

For since the beginning of the world men have not heard, nor perceived by the ear, neither hath the eye seen, O God, beside thee, what he hath prepared for him that waiteth for him—Isaiah 64:4

The American Standard Version has the thought: "Neither hath the eye seen a God besides thee, who worketh for him that waiteth for him." In the King James Version, the thought is that no eye has seen the thing that God has prepared. In the American Standard Version, no eye has seen a God, besides our God, who works for him who waits for Him. To both, the two thoughts are common: that our place is to wait upon God, and that what the human heart cannot conceive will be revealed to us. The difference is the following: in the American Standard Version, it is the God who works; in the King James Version, the thing He is to work. In 1 Corinthians 2:9, "But as it is written, Eye hath not seen, nor ear heard, neither have entered into the heart of man, the things which God hath prepared for them that love him," the reference is in regard to the things that the Holy Spirit is to reveal, as in the King James Version, and in this chapter we will keep to that.

The previous verses in Isaiah, especially Isaiah 63:15, refer to the low state of God's people. The prayer has been poured out, "Look down from heaven" (v. 15). "Why hast thou . . . hardened our heart from thy fear? Return for thy servants' sake" (v. 17). And 64:1-2, still more urgent, "Oh that thou wouldest rend the heavens, that thou wouldest come down . . . as when the melting fire burneth . . . to make thy name known to thine adversaries!" Then follows the plea from the past, "When thou didst terrible things which we looked not for, thou camest down, the mountains flowed down at thy presence" (v. 3). "For"—this is now the faith that has been awakened by the thought of things we looked not for, He is still the same God—"neither hath the eye seen, O God, beside thee, what he hath prepared for him that waiteth for him."

God alone knows what He can do for His waiting people. As Paul expounds and applies it: "The things of God knoweth no man, but the Spirit of God" (1 Cor. 2:11). "But God hath revealed them unto us by his Spirit" (v. 10).

The need of God's people, and the call for God's intervention, is as urgent in our days as it was in the time of Isaiah. There is now, as there was then, as there has been at all times, a few who seek after God with their whole hearts. But, if we look at Christendom as a whole, at the state of the church of Christ, there is infinite cause for beseeching God to rend the heavens and come down. Nothing but a special interposition of almighty power will avail. I fear we do not have a proper conception of what the so-called Christian world is in the sight of God. Unless God comes down "as when the melting fire burneth . . . to make [His] name known to [His] adversaries" (Isa. 64:2), our labors are comparatively fruitless.

Look at the ministry: how much it is in the wisdom of man and of literary culture; how little in demonstration of the Spirit and of power. Think of the unity of the body: how little there is of the manifestation of the power of a heavenly love binding God's children into one. Think of holiness—the holiness of Christlike humility and crucifixion to the world. How little the world sees that they have men among them who live in Christ in heaven, in whom Christ and heaven live.

What is to be done? There is only one thing. We must wait upon God. And what for? We must cry, with a cry that never rests, "Oh that thou wouldest rend the heavens . . . [and] come down, that the mountains might flow down at thy presence" (Isa. 64:1). We must desire and believe, we must ask and expect, that God will do unlooked-for things. We must set our faith on a God of whom men do not know what He has prepared for them who wait for Him. The wonder-doing God, who can surpass all our expectations, must be the God of our confidence.

Yes, let God's people enlarge their hearts to wait on a God able to do exceeding abundantly above what we can ask or think (Eph. 3:20). Let us band ourselves together as His elect who cry day and night to Him for things men have not seen. He is able to arise and to make His people a name and a praise in the earth. "The *Lord* will wait, that he may be gracious unto you . . . blessed are all they that wait for him" (Isa. 30:18).

My soul, wait thou only upon God!

Day 24. To Know His Goodness

The Lord is good unto them that wait for him.—Lamentations 3:25

There is none good but God (Matt. 19:17). His goodness is in the heavens. "Oh how great is thy goodness, which thou hast laid up for them that fear thee" (Ps. 31:19). "O taste and see that the *Lord* is good" (Ps. 34:8). And here is now the true way of entering into and rejoicing in this goodness of God—waiting upon Him. The Lord is good—even His children often do not know it, for they do not wait in quietness for Him to reveal it. But, to those who persevere in waiting, whose souls do wait, it will come true. One might think that it is just those who have to wait who might doubt it. But, this is only when they do not wait, but grow impatient. The truly waiting ones will all say, "The *Lord* is good unto them that wait for him." If you want to fully know the goodness of God, give yourself more than ever to a life of waiting on Him.

At our first entrance into the school of waiting upon God, the heart is mainly set on the blessings which we wait for. God graciously uses our needs and desires for help to educate us for something higher than we were thinking of. We were seeking gifts; He, the Giver, longs to give Himself and to satisfy the soul with His goodness. It is just for this reason that He often withholds the gifts, and that the time of waiting is made so long. He is constantly seeking to win the heart of His child for Himself. He wishes that we would not only say, when He bestows the gift, "How good is God!" but that long before it comes, and even if it never comes, we should all the time be experiencing: it is good that a man should quietly wait. "The *Lord* is good unto them that wait for him."

What a blessed life the life of waiting then becomes, the continual worship of faith, adoring, and trusting His goodness. As the soul learns its secret, every act or exercise of waiting becomes just a quiet entering into the goodness of God, to let it do its blessed work and satisfy our every need. And, every experience of God's goodness gives new attractiveness to the work of waiting. Instead of only taking refuge in time of need, there comes a great longing to wait continually and all day. And, however duties and engagements occupy the time and the mind, the soul gets more familiar with the secret art of always waiting. Waiting becomes the habit and disposition, the very second nature and breath of the soul.

Dear Christian, begin to see that waiting is not one among a number of Christian virtues, to be thought of from time to time. But, it expresses that disposition that lies at the very root of the Christian life. It gives a higher value and a new power to our prayers and worship, to our faith and surrender, because it links us, in unalterable dependence, to God Himself. And, it gives us the unbroken enjoyment of the goodness of God: "The *Lord* is good unto them that wait for him."

Let me stress once again that you must take time and trouble to cultivate this much needed element of the Christian life. We get too much secondhand religion from the teaching of men. That teaching has great value, even as the preaching of John the Baptist sent his disciples away from himself to the living Christ, if it leads us to God Himself. What our faith needs is—more of God.

Many of us are too occupied with our work. As with Martha, the very service we want to render the Master separates us from Him. It is neither pleasing to Him nor profitable to ourselves. The more work, the more need of waiting upon God. The doing of God's will would then be, instead of exhausting, our meat and drink, our nourishment and refreshment and strength. "The *Lord* is good unto them that wait for him." How good is known only by those who prove it in waiting on Him. How good none can fully tell but those who have proved Him to the utmost.

My soul, wait thou only upon God!

Day 25. Quietly

It is good that a man should both hope and quietly wait for the salvation of the Lord — Lamentations 3:26

Take heed, and be quiet; fear not, neither be fainthearted" (Isa. 7:4). "In quietness and in confidence shall be your strength" (Isa. 30:15). Such words reveal to us the close connection between quietness and faith. They show us what a deep need there is of quietness, as an element of true waiting upon God. If we are to have our whole heart turned toward God, we must have it turned away from man, from all that occupies and interests, whether of joy or sorrow.

God is a being of such infinite greatness and glory, and our nature has become so estranged from Him, that it requires our whole heart and desires set upon Him, even in some little measure, to know and receive Him. Everything that is not God, that excites our fears or stirs our efforts or awakens our hopes or makes us glad, hinders us in our perfect waiting on Him. The message is one of deep meaning: "Take heed, and be quiet"; "In quietness...shall be your strength"; "It is good that a man should . . . quietly wait."

Scripture abundantly testifies how the very thought of God in His majesty and holiness should silence us: "The *Lord* is in his holy temple: let all the earth keep silence before him" (Hab. 2:20); "Hold thy peace at the presence of the Lord *God*" (Zeph. 1:7); "Be silent, O all flesh, before the *Lord*: for he is raised up out of his holy habitation" (Zech. 2:13).

As long as the waiting on God is chiefly regarded as an end toward more effectual prayer, and the obtaining of our petitions, this spirit of perfect quietness will not be obtained. But, when it is seen that waiting on God is itself an unspeakable blessedness—one of the highest forms of fellowship with the Holy One—the adoration of Him in His glory will of necessity humble the soul into a holy stillness, making way for God to speak and reveal Himself. Then, it comes to the fulfillment of the precious promise, that all of self and self-effort will be humbled: "The haughtiness of men shall be bowed down, and the *Lord* alone shall be exalted in that day" (Isa. 2:11).

Let everyone who wants to learn the art of waiting on God remember the lesson, "Take heed, and be quiet" (Isa. 7:4). "It is good that a man . . . quietly wait." Take time to be separate from all friends and all duties, all cares and all joys; time to be still and quiet before God. Take time not only to secure stillness from man and the world, but from self and its energy. Let the Word and prayer be very precious. But remember, even these may hinder the quiet waiting. The activity of the mind in studying the Word or giving expression to its thoughts in prayer, the activities of the heart, with its desires and hopes and fears, may so engage us that we do not come to the still waiting on the All-glorious One; our whole being is prostrate in silence before Him.

Though at first it may appear difficult to know how thus quietly to wait, with the activities of mind and heart for a time subdued, every effort after it will be rewarded. We will discover that it grows upon us, and the little season of silent worship will bring a peace and a rest that give a blessing not only in prayer, but all day.

"It is good that a man should . . . quietly wait for the salvation of the *Lord*." Yes, it is good. The quietness is the confession of our meekness. It will not be done with all our willing and running (Rom. 9:16), with all our thinking and praying. We must receive it from God. It is the confession of our trust that our God will, in His time, come to our help—the quiet resting in Him alone. It is the confession of our desire to sink into our nothingness and to let Him work and reveal Himself. Do let us wait quietly. In daily life, let there be, in the soul that is waiting for the great God to do His wondrous work, a quiet reverence, an abiding watching against too deep engrossment with the world. Then, the whole character will come to bear the beautiful stamp—quietly waiting for the salvation of God.

My soul, wait thou only upon God!

Day 26. In Holy Expectancy

Therefore I will look unto the Lord; I will wait for the God of my salvation: my God will hear me—Micah 7:7

Have you ever heard of a little book, "Expectation Corners"? It tells of a king who prepared a city for some of his poor subjects. Not far from them were large storehouses, where everything they could need was supplied if they sent in their requests. But, on one condition—that they should be on the lookout for the answer, so that when the king's messengers came with the answer to their petitions, they should always be found waiting and ready to receive them. The sad story is told of one desponding person who never expected to get what he asked, because he was too unworthy. One day, he was taken to the king's storehouses, and there, to his amazement, he saw, with his address on them, all the packages that had been made up for him and sent. There was the garment of praise and the oil of joy and the eye salve and so much more. They had been to his door but found it closed; he was not on the lookout. From that time on, he learned the lesson Micah would teach us today. "I will look unto the *Lord*; I will wait for the God of my salvation: my God will hear me."

We have said more than once: waiting for the answer to prayer is not the whole of waiting, but only a part. Today, I want to take in the blessed truth that it is a part, and a very important one. When we have special petitions, in connection with which we are waiting on God, our waiting must be very definitely in the confident assurance, "My God will hear me."

A holy, joyful expectancy is of the very essence of true waiting. And, this is not only true in reference to the many varied requests every believer has to make, but most especially to the one great petition which ought to be the chief thing every heart seeks for itself—that the life of God in the soul may have full sway, that Christ may be fully formed within, and that we may be filled to all the fullness of God. This is what God has promised. This is what God's people too little seek, very often because they do not believe it possible. This is what we ought to seek and dare to expect, because God is able and waiting to work it in us.

But, God Himself must work it. And for this end our working must cease. We must see how entirely it is to be the faith of the operation of God, who raised Jesus from the dead. Just as much as the resurrection, the perfecting of God's life in our souls is to be directly His work. And, waiting has to become, more than ever, a tarrying before God in stillness of soul, counting upon Him who raises the dead and calls the things that are not as though they were (Rom. 4:17).

Just notice how the threefold use of the name of God in our text points us to Himself as the one from whom alone is our expectation. "I will look unto the *Lord*; I will wait for the God of my salvation: my God will hear me." Everything that is salvation, everything that is good and holy, must be the direct, mighty work of God Himself within us. In every moment of a life in the will of God, there must be the immediate operation of God. And, the one thing I have to do is this: to look to the Lord, to wait for the God of my salvation, to hold fast the confident assurance, "my God will hear me."

God says, "Be still, and know that I am God" (Ps. 46:10).

There is no stillness like that of the grave. In the grave of Jesus, in the fellowship of His death, in death to self with its own will and wisdom, its own strength and energy—there is rest. As we cease from self and our soul becomes still to God, God will arise and show Himself. "Be still, and know"; then you will know "that I am God." There is no stillness like the stillness Jesus gives when He speaks. "Peace, be still" (Mark 4:39). In Christ, in His death, in His life, in His perfected redemption, the soul may be still, and God will come in, take possession, and do His perfect work.

My soul, be thou still only unto God!

Day 27. For Redemption

"Simeon . . . was just and devout, waiting for the consolation of Israel: and the Holy Ghost was upon him. . . Anna, a prophetess . . . spoke of him to all them that looked for redemption in Jerusalem" —Luke 2:25, 36, 38.

Here we have the mark of a waiting believer. "Just," righteous in all his conduct; "devout," devoted to God, ever walking as in His presence; "waiting for the consolation of Israel," looking for the fulfillment of God's promises: "and the Holy Ghost was upon him." In the devout waiting, he had been prepared for the blessing. And Simeon was not the only one. Anna spoke to all who looked for redemption in Jerusalem. This was the one mark, amid surrounding formalism and worldliness, of a godly band of men and women in Jerusalem. They were waiting on God, looking for His promised redemption.

And now that the consolation of Israel has come, and the redemption has been accomplished, do we still need to wait? We do indeed. But, will not our waiting, who look back to it as come, differ greatly from those who looked forward to it as coming? It will, especially in two aspects. We now wait on God in the full power of the redemption, and we wait for its full revelation.

Our waiting is now in the full power of the redemption. Christ said, "In that day you will know that you are in Me. Abide in Me." The Epistles teach us to present ourselves to God as "dead indeed unto sin, but alive unto God through Jesus Christ" (Rom. 6:11), "blessed... with all spiritual blessings in heavenly places in Christ" (Eph. 1:3). Our waiting on God may now be in the wonderful consciousness maintained by the Holy Spirit within us, that we are accepted in the Beloved, that the love that rests on Him rests on us, that we are living in that love, in the very nearness and presence and sight of God.

The old saints took their stand on the Word of God, and waiting, hoping on that Word, we rest on the Word, too—but, oh, under what exceedingly greater privileges, as one with Christ Jesus! In our waiting on God, let this be our confidence: in Christ we have access to the Father. How sure, therefore, we may be that our waiting cannot be in vain.

Our waiting differs, too, in this, that while they waited for a redemption to come, we see it accomplished and now wait for its revelation in us. Christ not only said, "Abide in me" (John 15:4), but also "I in you" (v. 4). The Epistles not only speak of us in Christ, but of Christ in us, as the highest mystery of redeeming love. As we maintain our place in Christ day by day, God waits to reveal Christ in us in such a way that He is formed in us, that His mind and disposition and likeness acquire form and substance in us, so that by each it can in truth be said, "Christ liveth in me" (Gal. 2:20).

My life in Christ up there in heaven and Christ's life in me down here on earth—these two are the complement of each other. And, the more my waiting on God is marked by the living faith, I in Christ, the more the heart thirsts for and claims the Christ in me. The waiting on God, which began with special needs and prayer, will increasingly be concentrated, as far as our personal life is concerned, on this one thing: Lord, reveal Your redemption fully in me; let Christ live in me.

Our waiting differs from that of the old saints in the place we take, and the expectations we entertain. But, at root it is the same: waiting on God, from whom alone is our expectation.

Learn one lesson from Simeon and Anna. How utterly impossible it was for them to do anything toward the great redemption—toward the birth of Christ or His death. It was God's work. They could do nothing but wait. Are we as absolutely helpless in regard to the revelation of Christ in us? We are indeed. God did not work out the great redemption in Christ as a whole and leave its application in detail to us.

The secret thought that it is so is the root of all our feebleness. The revelation of Christ in every individual believer, and in each one the daily revelation, step by step and moment by moment, is as much the work of God's omnipotence as the birth or resurrection of Christ. Until this truth enters and fills us, and we feel that we are just as dependent upon God for each moment of our life in the enjoyment of redemption as they were in their waiting for it, our waiting upon God will not bring its full blessing. The sense of utter and absolute helplessness, the confidence that God can and will do all, are the marks of our waiting as of theirs. As gloriously as God proved Himself to them the faithful and wonder-working God, He will to us, too.

My soul, wait thou only upon God!

Day 28. For the Coming of His Son

"[Be] ye yourselves like unto men that wait for their lord."—Luke 12:36. "Until the appearing of our Lord Jesus Christ: which in its own times he shall show, who is the blessed and only Potentate, the King of kings, and Lord of lords."—1 Timothy 6:14-15 (ASV). "Turned to God from idols to serve the living and true God; and to wait for his Son from heaven."—1 Thessalonians 1:9-10

Waiting on God in heaven, and waiting for His Son from heaven—these two God has joined together, and no man may put them asunder. The waiting on God for His presence and power in daily life will be the only true preparation for waiting for Christ in humility and true holiness. The waiting for Christ coming from heaven to take us to heaven will give the waiting on God its true tone of hopefulness and joy. The Father, who, in His own time, will reveal His Son from heaven, is the God who, as we wait on Him, prepares us for the revelation of His Son. The present life and the coming glory are inseparably connected in God and in us.

There is sometimes a danger of separating them. It is always easier to be engaged with the Christianity of the past or the future than to be faithful in the Christianity of today. As we look to what God has done in the past, or will do in time to come, the personal claim of present duty and present submission to His working may be avoided. Waiting on God must always lead to waiting for Christ as the glorious consummation of His work. And, waiting for Christ must always remind us of the duty of waiting upon God as our only proof that the waiting for Christ is in spirit and in truth.

There is such a danger of our being more occupied with the things that are coming than with Him who is to come. There is such scope in the study of coming events for imagination and reason and human ingenuity, that nothing but deeply humble waiting on God can save us from mistaking the interest and pleasure of intellectual study for the true love of Him and His appearing. All you who say you wait for Christ's coming, be sure that you wait on God now. All you who seek to wait on God now to reveal His Son in you, see to it that you do so as men waiting for the revelation of His Son from heaven. The hope of that glorious appearing will strengthen you in waiting upon God for what He is to do in you now. The same omnipotent love that is to reveal that glory is working in you even now to prepare you for it.

"The blessed hope and appearing of the glory of the great God and our Saviour Jesus Christ" (Titus 2:13 ASV), is one of the great bonds of union given to God's church throughout the ages. "He shall come to be glorified in his saints, and to be marveled at in all them that believed" (2 Thess. 1:10 ASV). Then, we will all meet, and the unity of the body of Christ will be seen in its divine glory. It will be the meeting place and the triumph of divine love. Jesus receiving His own and presenting them to the Father. His own meeting Him and worshiping, in speechless love, that blessed face. His own meeting each other in the ecstasy of God's own love. Let us wait, long for, and love the appearing of our Lord and heavenly Bridegroom. Tender love to Him and tender love to each other is the true and only bridal spirit.

I am very afraid that this is sometimes forgotten. A beloved brother in Holland was speaking about the expectancy of faith being the true sign of the bride. I ventured to express a doubt. An unworthy bride, about to be married to a prince, might only be thinking of the position and the riches that she was to receive. The expectancy of faith might be strong and true love utterly lacking. It is not when we are most occupied with prophetic subjects, but when in humility and love we are clinging close to our Lord and His followers, that we are in the bride's place. Jesus refuses to accept our love except as it is love to His disciples. Waiting for His coming means waiting for the glorious coming manifestation of the unity of the body, while we seek here to maintain that unity in humility and love. Those who love most are the most ready for His coming. Love to each other is the life and beauty of His bride, the church.

And how is this to be brought about? Beloved child of God, if you want to learn how to properly wait for His Son from heaven, live even now waiting on God in heaven. Remember how Jesus lived ever waiting on God. He could do nothing of Himself. It was God who perfected His Son through suffering and then exalted Him. It is God alone who can give you the deep spiritual life of one who is really waiting for His Son: wait on God for it. Waiting for Christ Himself is so different from waiting for things that may come to pass! The latter any Christian can do; the former, God must work in you every day by His Holy Spirit. Therefore, all you who wait on God, look to Him for grace to wait for His Son from heaven in the Spirit which is from heaven. And, you who want to wait for His Son, wait on God continually to reveal Christ in you.

The revelation of Christ in us, as it is given to them who wait upon God, is the true preparation for the full revelation of Christ in glory.

My soul, wait thou only upon God!

Day 29. For the Promise of the Father

"He charged them not to depart from Jerusalem, but to wait for the promise of the Father." Acts1:4 ASV

In speaking of the saints in Jerusalem at Christ's birth—with Simeon and Anna—we saw how the call to waiting is no less urgent now, though the redemption they waited for has come, than it was then. We wait for the full revelation in us of what came to them, but what they could scarcely comprehend. In the same way, it is with waiting for the promise of the Father. In one sense, the fulfillment can never come again as it came at Pentecost. In another sense, and that in as deep a reality as with the first disciples, we need to wait daily for the Father to fulfill His promise in us.

The Holy Spirit is not a person distinct from the Father in the way two persons on earth are distinct. The Father and the Spirit are never without or separate from each other. The Father is always in the Spirit; the Spirit works nothing but as the Father works in Him. Each moment, the same Spirit that is in us is in God, too. And, he who is most full of the Spirit will be the first to wait on God most earnestly to further fulfill His promise and to still strengthen him mightily by His Spirit in the inner man. The Spirit in us is not a power at our disposal. Nor is the Spirit an independent power, acting apart from the Father and the Son. The Spirit is the real, living presence and the power of the Father working in us. Therefore, it is he who knows that the Spirit is in him who waits on the Father for the full revelation and experience of the Spirit's indwelling. It is he who waits for His increase and abounding more and more.

See this in the apostles. They were filled with the Spirit at Pentecost. When they, not long after, on returning from the council where they had been forbidden to preach, prayed afresh for boldness to speak in His name, a fresh coming down of the Holy Spirit was the Father's fresh fulfillment of His promise.

At Samaria, by the Word and the Spirit, many had been converted, and the whole city was filled with joy. At the apostles' prayer, the Father once again fulfilled the promise. (See Acts 8:14-7.) Even so to the waiting company—"We are all here before God"(see Acts 10:33)—in Cornelius' house. And so, too, in Acts 13. It was when men, filled with the Spirit, prayed and fasted, that the promise of the Father was afresh fulfilled, and the leading of the Spirit was given from heaven: "Separate me Barnabas and Saul" (Acts 13:2).

So also we find Paul, in Ephesians, praying for those who have been sealed with the Spirit, that God would grant them the spirit of illumination. And later on, that He would grant them, according to the riches of His glory, to be strengthened with might by the Spirit in the inner man.

The Spirit given at Pentecost was not something that God failed with in heaven, and sent out of heaven to earth. God does not, cannot, give away anything in that manner. When He gives grace or strength or life, He gives it by giving Himself to work it—it is all inseparable from Himself. Much more so is the Holy Spirit. He is God, present and working in us. The true position in which we can count upon that working with an unceasing power is as we, praising for what we have, still unceasingly wait for the Father's promise to be still more mightily fulfilled.

What new meaning and promise does this give to our lives of waiting! It teaches us to continually keep the place where the disciples tarried at the footstool of the throne. It reminds us that, as helpless as they were to meet their enemies, or to preach to Christ's enemies until they were endued with power, we, too, can only be strong in the life of faith, or the work of love, as we are in direct communication with God and Christ. They must maintain the life of the Spirit in us. This assures us that the omnipotent God will, through the glorified Christ, work in us a power that can bring unexpected things to pass, impossible things.

Oh, what the church will be able to do when her individual members learn to live their lives waiting on God—when together, with all of self and the world sacrificed in the fire of love, they unite in waiting with one accord for the promise of the Father, once so gloriously fulfilled, but still unexhausted!

Come and let each of us be still in the presence of the inconceivable grandeur of this prospect: the Father waiting to fill the church with the Holy Spirit. And willing to fill me, let each one say.

With this faith, let a hush and a holy fear come over the soul, as it waits in stillness to take it all in. And, let life increasingly become a deep joy in the hope of the ever fuller fulfillment of the Father's promise.

My soul, wait thou only upon God!

Day 30. Continually

"Therefore turn thou to thy God: keep mercy and judgment, and wait on thy God continually."—Hosea 12:6.

Continuity is one of the essential elements of life. Interrupt it for a single hour in a man, and it is lost; he is dead. Continuity, unbroken and ceaseless, is essential to a healthy Christian life. God wants me to be, and God waits to make me; I want to be, and I wait on Him to make me, every moment, what He expects of me—what is well pleasing in His sight. If waiting on God is the essence of true faith, the maintenance of the spirit of entire dependence must be continuous. The call of God, "wait on thy God continually," must be accepted and obeyed. Although there may be times of special waiting, the disposition and habit of soul must be there unchangeably and uninterrupted.

This continual waiting is indeed a necessity. To those who are content with a feeble Christian life, it appears to be a luxury beyond what is essential to be a good Christian. But, all who are praying the prayer, "Lord, make me as holy as a pardoned sinner can be made! Keep me as near to You as it is possible for me to be! Fill me as full of Your love as You are willing to do!" feel at once that it is something that must be had. They feel that there can be no unbroken fellowship with God, no full abiding in Christ, no maintaining of victory over sin and readiness for service, without waiting continually on the Lord.

The continual waiting is a possibility. Many think that with the duties of life it is out of the question. They cannot always be thinking of it. Even when they wish to, they forget.

They do not understand that it is a matter of the heart and that what the heart is full of, occupies it, even when the thoughts are otherwise engaged. A father's heart may be continuously filled with intense love and longing for a sick wife or child at a distance, even though pressing business requires all his thoughts. When the heart has learned how entirely powerless it is for one moment to keep itself or bring forth any good, when it has learned how surely and truly God will keep it, when it has, in despair of itself, accepted God's promise to do for it the impossible, it learns to rest in God. In the midst of occupations and temptations, it can wait continually.

This waiting is a promise. God's commands are enablings. Gospel precepts are all promises, a revelation of what our God will do for us. When you first begin waiting on God, it is with frequent intermission and failure. But, do believe God is watching over you in love and secretly strengthening you in it. There are times when waiting appears like just losing time, but it is not so. Waiting, even in darkness, is unconscious advance, because it is God you have to do with, and He is working in you. God, who calls you to wait on Him, sees your feeble efforts and works it in you. Your spiritual life is in no respect your own work; as little as you begin it, can you continue it. It is God's Spirit who has begun the work in you of waiting upon God. He will enable you to wait continually.

Waiting continually will be met and rewarded by God Himself working continually. We are coming to the end of our lessons. I hope that you and I might learn one thing: God must, God will work continually. He ever does work continually, but the experience of it is hindered by unbelief. But, He, who by His Spirit teaches you to wait continually, will bring you also to experience how, as the Everlasting One, His work is never ceasing. In the love and the life and the work of God, there can be no break, no interruption.

Do not limit God in this by your thoughts of what may be expected. Do fix your eyes upon this one truth: in His very nature, God, as the only Giver of life, cannot do anything other than work in His child every moment. Do not look only at the one side: "If I wait continually, God will work continually." No, look at the other side. Place God first and say, "God works continually; every moment I may wait on Him continually." Take time until the vision of your God working continually, without one moment's intermission, fills your being. Your waiting continually will then come of itself. Full of trust and joy, the holy habit of the soul will be: "on thee do I wait all the day" (Ps. 25:5). The Holy Spirit will keep you ever waiting.

My soul, wait thou only upon God!

Day 31. Only

"My soul, wait thou only upon God; for my expectation is from him. He only is my rock and my salvation."—Psalm 62:5-6.

It is possible to be waiting continually on God, but not only upon Him. There may be other secret confidences intervening and preventing the blessing that was expected. And so the word only must come to throw its light on the path to the fullness and certainty of blessing. "My soul, wait thou only upon God . . . He only is my rock."

Yes, "my soul, wait thou only upon God." There is but one God, but one source of life and happiness for the heart; "He only is my rock"; "My soul, wait thou only upon God." You desire to be good; "There is none good but . . . God" (Matt. 19:17), and there is no possible goodness but what is received directly from Him. You have sought to be holy; "There is none holy as the *Lord*" (1 Sam. 2:2), and there is no holiness but what He by His Spirit of holiness every moment breathes in you. You would gladly live and work for God and His kingdom, for men and their salvation. Hear how He says: "The everlasting God, the *Lord*, the Creator of the ends of the earth, fainteth not, neither is weary . . . He giveth power to the faint; and to them that have no might he increaseth strength . . . They that wait upon the *Lord* shall renew their strength. (Isa. 40:28-39, 31). He only is God; He only is your Rock: "my soul, wait thou only upon God."

"My soul, wait thou only upon God." You will not find many who can help you in this. There will be enough of your brothers to draw you to put trust in churches and doctrines, in schemes and plans and human appliances, in means of grace and divine appointments. But, "my soul, wait thou only upon God" Himself. His most sacred appointments become a snare when trusted in. The brazen serpent becomes

Nehushtan (see 2 Kings 18:4); the ark and the temple a vain confidence. Let the living God alone, none and nothing but He, be your hope.

"My soul, wait thou only upon God." Eyes and hands and feet, mind and thought, may have to be intently engaged in the duties of this life. "My soul, wait thou only upon God." You are an immortal spirit, created not for this world but for eternity and for God. Oh, my soul, realize your destiny. Know your privilege, and "wait thou only upon God." Let not the interest of spiritual thoughts and exercises deceive you; they very often take the place of waiting upon God. "My soul, wait thou," your very self, your innermost being, with all its power, "wait thou only upon God." God is for you; you are for God. Wait only upon Him.

Yes, "my soul, wait thou only upon God." Beware of two great enemies: the world and self. Beware of allowing any earthly satisfaction or enjoyment, however innocent it appears, keep you back from saying, "I [will] go . . . unto God my exceeding joy" (Ps. 43:4). Remember and study what Jesus said about denying self: "Let [a man] deny himself" (Matt. 16:24). Tersteegen says: "The saints deny themselves in everything." Pleasing self in little things may be strengthening it to assert itself in greater things.

"My soul, wait thou only upon God." Let Him be all your salvation and all your desire. Say continually and with an undivided heart, "From him cometh my [expectation]. He only is my rock . . . I shall not be greatly moved" (Ps. 62:1-2). Whatever your spiritual or temporal needs are, whatever the desire or prayer of your heart, whatever your interest in connection with God's work in the church or the world—in solitude or in the rush of the world, in public worship or other gatherings of the saints, "my soul, wait thou only upon God." Let your expectations be from Him alone. "He only is my rock."

"My soul, wait thou only upon God." Never forget the two foundation truths on which this blessed waiting rests. If you are ever inclined to think this waiting only is too hard or too high, they will recall you at once. They are your absolute helplessness and the absolute sufficiency of your God. Oh, enter deeply into the entire sinfulness of all that is of self, and do not think of letting self have anything to say one single moment. Enter deeply into your utter and unceasing inability to ever change what is evil in you, or to bring forth anything that is spiritually good. Enter deeply into your relationship of dependence on God, to receive from Him every moment what He gives. Enter deeper still into His covenant of redemption, with His promise to restore more gloriously than ever what you have lost. And, by His Son and Spirit, He will unceasingly give you His actual divine presence and power. And thus, wait upon your God continually and only.

"My soul, wait thou only upon God." No words can tell, no heart can conceive, the riches of the glory of this mystery of the Father and of Christ. Our God, in the infinite tenderness and omnipotence of His love, waits to be our life and joy. Oh, my soul, let it no longer be necessary that I repeat the words, "Wait upon God." But, let all that is in me rise and sing, "Truly my soul waiteth upon God" (Ps. 62:1). "On thee do I wait all the day" (Ps. 25:5).

My soul, wait thou only upon God!

Moment by Moment

I the Lord do keep it; I will water it every moment—Isaiah 27:3

Dying with Jesus, by death reckoning mine;
Living with Jesus, a new life divine;
Looking to Jesus till glory doth shine,
Moment by moment, O Lord, I am Thine.

Chorus: Moment by moment I'm kept in His love;
Moment by moment I've life from above;
Looking to Jesus till glory doth shine;
Moment by moment, O Lord, I am Thine.

Never a battle with wrong for the right,
Never a contest that He doth not fight;
Lifting above us His banner so white,
Moment by moment, I'm kept in His sight.

Never a trial that He is not there,

Never a burden that He doth not bear,
Never a sorrow that He doth not share,
Moment by moment, I'm under His care.

Never a heartache, and never a groan,
Never a teardrop, and never a moan;
Never a danger but there on the throne,
Moment by moment, He thinks of His own.

Never a weakness that He doth not feel,
Never a sickness that He cannot heal;
Moment by moment, in woe or in weal,
Jesus, my Saviour, abides with me still.

The Two Covenants

Table of Contents

Introduction

It is often said that the great aim of the preacher ought to be to translate Scripture truth from its Jewish form into the language and the thought of the nineteenth century, and so to make it intelligible and acceptable to our ordinary Christians. It is to be feared that the experiment will do more harm than good. In the course of the translation the force of the original is lost. The scholar who trusts to translations will never become a master of the language he wants to learn. A race of Christians will be raised up, to whom the language of God's Word, and with that the God who spoke it, will be strange. In the Scripture words not a little of Scripture truth will be lost. For the true Christian life nothing is so healthful and invigorating as to have each man come and study for himself the very words in which the Holy Ghost has spoken.

One of the words of Scripture, which is almost going out of fashion, is the word Covenant. There was a time when it was the keynote of the theology and the Christian life of strong and holy men. We know how deep in Scotland it entered into the national life and thought. It made mighty men, to whom God, and His promise and power were wonderfully real. It will be found still to bring strength and purpose to those who will take the trouble to bring all their life under control of the inspiring assurance that they are living in covenant with a God who has sworn faithfully to fulfil in them every promise He has given.

This book is a humble attempt to show what exactly the blessings are that God has covenanted to bestow on us; what the assurance is the Covenant gives that they must, and can, and will be fulfilled; what the hold on God Himself is which it thus gives us; and what the conditions are for the full and continual experience of its blessings. I feel confident that if I can lead any to listen to what God has to say to them of His Covenant, and to deal with Him as a Covenant God, it will bring them strength and joy:

Not long ago I received from one of my correspondents a letter with the following passage in it:—"I think you will excuse and understand me when I say there is one further note of power I would like so much to have introduced into your next book on Intercession. God Himself has, I know, been giving me some direct teaching this winter upon the place the New Covenant is to have in intercessory prayer . . . I know you believe in the Covenant, and the Covenant rights we have on account of it. Have you followed out your views of the Covenant as they bear upon this subject of intercession? Am I wrong in coming to the conclusion that we may come boldly into God's presence, and not only ask, but claim a Covenant right through Christ Jesus to all the spiritual searching, and cleansing, and knowledge, and power promised in the three great Covenant promises? If you would take the Covenant and speak of it as God could enable you to speak, I think that would be the quickest way the Lord could take to make His Church wake up to the power He has put into our hands in giving us a Covenant. I would be so glad if you would tell God's people that they have a Covenant." Though this letter was not the occasion of the writing of the book, and x our Covenant rights have been considered in a far wider aspect than their relation to prayer, I am persuaded that nothing will help us more in our work of intercession, than the entrance for ourselves personally into what it means that we have a Covenant God.

My one great desire has been to ask Christians whether they are really seeking to find out what exactly God wants them to be, and is willing to make them. It is only as they wait, "that the mind of the Lord may be showed them," that their faith can ever truly see, or accept, or enjoy what God calls "His salvation." As long as we expect God to do for us what we ask or think, we limit Him. When we believe that as high as the heavens are above the earth, His thoughts are above our thoughts, and wait on Him as God to do unto us according to His Word, as He means it, we shall be prepared to live the truly supernatural, heavenly life the Holy Spirit can work in us—the true Christ life.

May God lead every reader into the secret of His presence, and "show him His Covenant."

Andrew Murray.

Wellington, South Africa,

A Covenant God

"Know therefore that the Lord thy God, He is God, the faithful God, which keepeth covenant and mercy with them that love Him and keep His commandments."-DEUT. vii. 9.

MEN often make covenants. They know the advantages to be derived from them. As an end of enmity or uncertainty, as a statement of services and benefits to be rendered, as a security for their certain performance, as a bond of amity and goodwill, as a ground for perfect confidence and friendship, a covenant has often been of unspeakable value.

In His infinite condescension to our human weakness and need, there is no possible way in which men pledge their faithfulness, that God has not sought to make use of, to give us perfect confidence in Him, and the full assurance of all that He, in His infinite riches and power as God, has promised to do to us. It is with this view He has consented to bind Himself by covenant, as if He could not be trusted. Blessed is the man who truly knows God as his Covenant God; who knows what the Covenant promises him; what unwavering confidence of expectation it secures, that all its terms will be fulfilled to him; what a claim and hold it gives him on the Covenant-keeping God Himself. To many a man, who has never thought much of the Covenant, a true and living faith in it would mean the transformation of his whole life. The full knowledge of what God wants to do for him; the assurance that it will be done by an Almighty Power; the being drawn to God Himself in personal surrender, and dependence, and waiting to have it done; all this would make the Covenant the very gate of heaven. May the Holy Spirit give us some vision of its glory.

When God created man in His image and likeness, it was that he might have a life as like His own as it was possible for a creature to live. This was to be by God Himself living and working all in man. For this man was to yield himself in loving dependence to the wonderful glory of being the recipient, the bearer, the manifestation of a Divine life. The one secret of man's happiness was to be a trustful surrender of his whole being to the willing and the working of God. When sin entered, this relation to God was destroyed;

when man had disobeyed, he feared God and fled from Him. He no longer knew, or loved, or trusted God.

Man could not save himself from the power of sin. If his redemption was to be effected, God must do it all. And if God was to do it in harmony with the law of man's nature, man must be brought to desire it, to yield his willing consent, and entrust himself to God. All that God wanted man to do was, to believe in Him. What a man believes, moves and rules his whole being, enters into him, and becomes part of his very life. Salvation could only be by faith: God restoring the life man had lost; man in faith yielding himself to God's work and will. The first great work of God with man was to get him to believe. This work cost God more care and time and patience than we can easily conceive. All the dealings with individual men, and with the people of Israel, had just this one object, to teach men to trust Him. Where He found faith He could do anything. Nothing dishonoured and grieved Him so much as unbelief. Unbelief was the root of disobedience and every sin; it made it impossible for God to do His work. The one thing God sought to waken in men by promise and threatening, by mercy and judgment, was faith.

Of the many devices of which God's patient and condescending grace made use to stir up and strengthen faith, one of the chief was—the Covenant. In more than one way God sought to effect this by His Covenant. First of all, His Covenant was always a revelation of His purposes, holding out, in definite promise, what God was willing to work in those with whom the Covenant was made. It was a Divine pattern of the work God intended to do in their behalf, that they might know what to desire and expect, that their faith might nourish itself with the very things, though as yet unseen, which God was working out. Then, the Covenant was meant to be a security and guarantee, as simple and plain and humanlike as the Divine glory could make it, that the very things which God had promised would indeed be brought to pass and wrought out in those with whom He had entered into covenant. Amid all delay and disappointment, and apparent failure of the Divine promises, the Covenant was to be the anchor of the soul, pledging the Divine veracity and faithfulness and unchangeableness for the certain performance of what had been promised. And so the Covenant was, above all, to give man a hold upon God, as the Covenant-keeping God, to link him to God Himself in expectation and hope, to bring him to make God Himself alone the portion and the strength of his soul.

Oh that we knew how God longs that we should trust Him, and how surely His every promise must be fulfilled to those who do so! Oh that we knew how it is owing to nothing but our unbelief that we cannot enter into the possession of God's promises, and that God cannot—yes, cannot—do His mighty works in us, and for us, and through us! Oh that we knew how one of the surest remedies for our unbelief—the divinely chosen cure for it—is the Covenant into which God has entered with us! The whole dispensation of the Spirit, the whole economy of grace in Christ Jesus, the whole of our spiritual life, the whole of the health and growth and strength of the Church, has been laid down and provided for, and secured in the New Covenant. No wonder that, where that Covenant, with its wonderful promises, is so little thought of, its plea for an abounding and unhesitating confidence in God so little understood, its claim upon the faithfulness of the Omnipotent God so little tested; no wonder that Christian life should miss the joy and the strength, the holiness and the heavenliness which God meant and so clearly promised that it should have.

Let us listen to the words in which God's Word calls us to know, and worship, and trust our Covenant-keeping God—it may be we shall find what we have been looking for: the deeper, the full experience of all God's grace can do in us. In our text Moses says: "Know therefore that the Lord thy God, He is God, the faithful God, which keepeth covenant with them that love Him." Hear what God says in Isaiah: "The mountains shall depart, and the hills be removed; but My kindness shall not depart from thee, neither shall My covenant of peace be removed, saith the Lord that hath mercy on thee." More sure than any mountain is the fulfilment of every Covenant promise. Of the New Covenant, in Jeremiah, God speaks: "I will make an everlasting covenant with them, that I will not turn away from them, to do them good; but I will put My fear in their hearts, that they shall not depart from Me." The Covenant secures alike that God will not turn from us, nor we depart from Him: He undertakes both for Himself and us.

Let us ask very earnestly whether the lack in our Christian life, and specially in our faith, is not owing to the neglect of the Covenant. We have not worshipped nor trusted the Covenant-keeping God. Our soul has not done what God called us to—"to take hold of His Covenant," "to remember the Covenant"; is it wonder that our faith has failed and come short of the blessing? God could not fulfil His promises in us. If we will begin to examine into the terms of the Covenant, as the title-deeds of our inheritance, and the riches we are to possess even here on earth; if we will think of the certainty of their fulfilment, more sure than the foundations of the everlasting mountains; if we will turn to the God who has engaged to do all for us, who keepeth covenant for ever, our life will become different from what it has been; it can, and will be, all that God would make it.

The great lack of our religion is—we need more of God. We accept salvation as His gift, and we do not know that the only object of salvation, its chief blessing, is to fit us for, and bring us back to, that close intercourse with God for which we were created, and in which our glory in eternity will be found. All that God has ever done for His people in making a covenant was always to bring them to Himself as their chief, their only good, to teach them to trust in Him, to delight in Him, to be one with Him. It cannot be otherwise. If God indeed be nothing but a very fountain of goodness and glory, of beauty and blessedness, the more we can have of His presence, the more we conform to His will, the more we are engaged in His service, the more we have Him ruling and working all in us, the more truly happy shall we be. If God indeed be thereby Owner and Author of life and strength, of holiness and happiness, and can alone give and work it in us, the more we trust Him, and depend and wait on Him, the stronger and the holier and the happier we shall be. And that only is a true and good religious life, which brings us every day nearer to this God, which makes us give up everything to have more of Him. No obedience can be too strict, no dependence too absolute, no submission too complete, no confidence too implicit, to a soul that is learning to count God Himself its chief good, its exceeding joy.

In entering into covenant with us, God's one object is to draw us to Himself, to render us entirely dependent upon Himself, and so to bring us into the right position and disposition in which He can fill us with Himself, His love, and His blessedness. Let us undertake our study of the New Covenant, in which, if we are believers, God is at this moment living and walking with us, with the honest purpose and surrender, at any price, to know what God wishes to be to us, to do in us, and to have us be and do to Him. The New Covenant may become to us one of the windows of heaven through which we see into the face, into the very heart, of God.

The Two Covenants: Their Relation

"It is written, that Abraham had two sons, one by the bondmaid, and one by the freewoman. Howbeit, the one by the bondmaid is born after the flesh; but the son by the freewoman is born through promise. Which things contain an allegory: for these women are two covenants." —GAL. iv. 22-24.

There are two covenants, one called the Old, the other the New. God speaks of this very distinctly in Jeremiah, where He says: "The days come, that I will make a new covenant with the house of Israel, not after the covenant I made with their fathers" (Jer. xxxi.). This is quoted in Hebrews, with the addition: "In that He saith a new covenant, He hath made the first old." Our Lord spoke Himself of the New Covenant in His blood. In His dealings with His people, in His working out His great redemption, it has pleased God that there should be two covenants.

It has pleased Him, not as an arbitrary appointment, but for good and wise reasons, which made it indispensably necessary that it should be so, and no otherwise. The clearer our insight into the reasons, and the Divine reasonableness, of there thus being two covenants, and into their relation to each other, the more full and true can be our own personal apprehension of what the New Covenant is meant to be to us. They indicate two stages in God's dealing with man; two ways of serving God, a lower or elementary one of preparation and promise, a higher or more advanced one of fulfilment and possession. As that in which the true excellency of the second consists is opened up to us, we can spiritually enter into what God has prepared for us. Let us try and understand why there should have been two, neither less nor more.

The reason is to be found in the fact that, in religion, in all intercourse between God and man, there are two parties, and that each of these must have the opportunity to prove what their part is in the Covenant. In the Old Covenant man had the opportunity given him to prove what He could do, with the aid of all the means of grace God could bestow. That Covenant ended in man proving his own unfaithfulness and failure. In the New

Covenant, God is to prove what He can do with man, all unfaithful and feeble as he is, when He is allowed and trusted to do all the work. The Old Covenant was one dependent on man's obedience, one which he could break, and did break (Jer. xxxi. 32). The New Covenant was one which God has engaged shall never be broken; He Himself keeps it and ensures our keeping it: so He makes it an Everlasting Covenant.

It will repay us richly to look a little deeper into this. This relation of God to fallen man in covenant is the same as it was to unfallen man as Creator. And what was that relation? God proposed to make a man in His own image and likeness. The chief glory of God is that He has life in Himself; that He is independent of all else, and owes what He is to Himself alone. If the image and likeness of God was not to be a mere name, and man was really to be like God in the power to make himself what he was to be, he must needs have the power of free will and self-determination. This was the problem God had to solve in man's creation in His image. Man was to be a creature made by God, and yet he was to be, as far as a creature could be, like God, self-made. In all God's treatment of man these two factors were ever to be taken into account. God was ever to take the initiative, and be to man the source of life. Man was ever to be the recipient, and yet at the same time the disposer of the life God bestowed.

When man had fallen through sin, and God entered into a covenant of salvation, these two sides of the relationship had still to be maintained intact. God was ever to be the first, and man the second. And yet man, as made in God's image, was ever, as second, to have full time and opportunity to appropriate or reject what God gave, to prove how far he could help himself, and indeed be self-made. His absolute dependence upon God was not to be forced upon him; if it was really to be a thing of moral worth and true blessedness, it must be his deliberate and voluntary choice. And this now is the reason why there was a first and a second covenant, that in the first, man's desires and efforts might be fully awakened, and time given for him to make full proof of what his human nature, with the aid of outward instruction and miracles and means of grace, could accomplish. When his utter impotence, his hopeless captivity under the power of sin had been discovered, there came the New Covenant, in which God was to reveal how man's true liberty from sin and self and the creature, his true nobility and God-likeness, was to be found in the most entire and absolute dependence, in God's being and doing all within him.

In the very nature of things there was no other way possible to God than this in dealing with a being whom He had endowed with the Godlike power of a will. And all the weight this reason for the Divine procedure has in God's dealing with His people as a whole, it equally has in dealing with the individual. The two covenants represent two stages of God's education of man and of man's seeking after God. The progress and transition from the one to the other is not merely chronological or historical; it is organic and spiritual. In greater or lesser degree it is seen in every member of the body, as well as in the body as a whole. Under the Old Covenant there were men in whom, by anticipation, the powers of the coming redemption worked mightily. In the New Covenant there are men in whom the spirit of the Old still makes itself manifest. The New Testament proves, in some of its most important epistles,—especially those to the Galatians, Romans, and Hebrews,—how possible it is within the New Covenant still to be held fast in the bondage of the Old.

This is the teaching of the passage from which our text is taken. In the home of Abraham, the father of the faithful, Ishmael and Isaac are both found—the one born of a slave, the other of a free woman; the one after the flesh and the will of man, the other through the promise and the power of God; the one only for a time, then to be cast out, the other to be heir of all. A picture held up to the Galatians of the life they were leading, as they trusted to the flesh and its religion, making a fair show, and yet proved, by their being led captive to sin, to be, not of the free but of the bond woman. Only through faith in the promise and the mighty quickening power of God could they, could any of them, be made truly and fully free, and stand in the freedom with which Christ has made us free.

As we proceed to study the two covenants in the light of this and other scriptures, we shall see how they are indeed the Divine revelation of two systems of religious worship, each with its spirit or life-principle ruling every man who professes to be a Christian. We shall see how the one great cause of the feebleness of so many Christians is just this, that the Old Covenant spirit of bondage still has the mastery. And we shall see that nothing but a spiritual insight, with a whole-hearted acceptance, and a living experience, of all the New Covenant engages that God will work in us, can possibly fit for walking as God would have us do.

This truth of there being two stages in our service of God, two degrees of nearness in our worship, is typified in many things in the Old Covenant worship; perhaps nowhere more clearly than in the difference between the Holy Place and the Most Holy Place in the temple, with the veil separating them. Into the former the priests might always enter to draw near to God. And yet they might not come too near; the veil kept them at a distance. To enter within that, was death. Once a year the High Priest might enter, as a promise of the time when the veil should be taken away and the full access to dwell in God's presence be given to His people. In Christ's death the veil of the temple was rent, and His blood gives us boldness and power to enter into the Holiest of all and live there day by day in the immediate presence of God. It is by the Holy Spirit, who issued forth from that Holiest of all, where Christ had entered, to bring its life to us, and make us one with it, that we can have the power to live and walk always with the consciousness of God's presence in us.

It is thus not only in Abraham's home that there were the types of the two covenants, the spirit of bondage and the spirit of liberty, but even in God's home in the temple. The priests had not yet the liberty of access into the Father's presence. Not only among the Galatians, but everywhere throughout the Church, there are to be found two classes of Christians. Some are content with the mingled life, half flesh and half spirit, half self-effort and half grace. Others are not content with this, but are seeking with their whole heart to know to the full what the deliverance from sin and what the abiding full power for a walk in God's presence is, which the New Covenant has brought and can give. God help us all to be satisfied with nothing less.

The First Covenant

"Now therefore, if ye will obey My voice, and keep My covenant, ye shall be a peculiar treasure unto Me."—EX. xix. 5.

"He declared unto you His covenant, which He commanded you to perform, even ten commandments."—DEUT. iv. 13.i

"If ye keep these judgments, the Lord thy God shall keep unto thee the covenant,"—DEUT. vii. 12.

"I will make a new covenant with the house of Israel, not according to the covenant which I made with their fathers, which My covenant they brake."—JER. xxxi. 31, 32.

We have seen how the reason for there being two Covenants is to be found in the need of giving the Divine and the human will, each their due place in the working out of man's destiny. God ever takes the initiative. Man must then have the opportunity to do his part, and to prove either what he can do, or needs to have done for him. The Old Covenant was on the one hand indispensably necessary to waken man's desires, to call forth his efforts, to deepen the sense of dependence on God, to convince of his sin and impotence, and so to prepare him to feel the need of the salvation of Christ. In the significant language of Paul, "The law was our schoolmaster unto Christ." "We were kept under the law, shut up unto the faith, which should afterwards be revealed." To understand the Old Covenant aright we must ever remember its two great characteristics —the one, that it was of Divine appointment, fraught with much true blessing, and absolutely indispensable for the working out of God's purposes; the other, that it was only provisional and preparatory to something higher, and therefore absolutely insufficient for giving that full salvation which man needs if his heart or the heart of God is to be satisfied.

Note now the terms of this first Covenant. "If ye will obey My voice and keep My covenant, ye shall be unto Me a holy nation." Or, as it is expressed in Jeremiah (vii. 23, xi. 4), "Obey My voice, and I will be your God." Obedience everywhere, especially in the Book of Deuteronomy, appears as the condition of blessing. "A blessing if ye obey" (xi. 27). Some may ask how God could make a covenant of which He knew that man could not keep it. The answer opens up to us the whole nature and object of the Covenant. All education, Divine or human, ever deals with its pupils on the principle—faithfulness in the less is essential to the attainment of the greater. In taking Israel into His training, God dealt with them as men in whom, with all the ruin sin had brought, there still was a conscience to judge of good and evil, a heart capable of being stirred to long after God, and a will to choose the good and to choose Himself. Before Christ and His salvation could be revealed and understood and truly appreciated, these faculties of man had to be stirred and wakened. The law took men into its training, and sought, if I may use the expression, to make the very best that could be made of them by external instruction. In the provision made in the law for a symbolical atonement and pardon, in all God's revelation of Himself through priest and prophet and king, in His interposition in providence and grace, everything was done that He could do, to touch and win the heart of His people and to give force to the appeal to their self-interest or their gratitude, their fear or their love.

Its work was not without fruit. Under the law, administered by the grace that ever accompanied it, there was trained up a number of men whose great mark was the fear of God, and a desire to walk blameless in all His commandments. And yet, as a whole, Scripture represents the Old Covenant as a failure. The law had promised life; but it could not give it (Deut. iv. 1; Gal. iii. 21). The real purpose for which God had given it was the very opposite: it was meant by Him as "a ministration of death." He gave it that it might convince man of his sin, and might so waken the confession of his impotence, and of his need of a New Covenant and a true redemption. It is in this view that Scripture uses such strong expressions—"By the law is the knowledge of sin: that every mouth may be stopped, and the whole world may become guilty before God." "The law worketh wrath." "The law entered, that the offence might abound." "That sin by the commandment might appear exceeding sinful." "As many as are of the works of the law are under the curse." "We were kept under the law, shut up to the faith, which should afterwards be revealed." "Wherefore the law was our schoolmaster to bring us to Christ, that we might be justified by faith." The great work of the law was to discover what sin was: its hatefulness as accursed of God; its misery, working temporal and eternal ruin; its power, binding man down in hopeless slavery; and the need of a Divine interposition as the only hope of deliverance.

In studying the Old Covenant we ought ever to keep in mind the twofold aspect under which we have seen that Scripture represents it. It was God's grace that gave Israel the law, and wrought with the law to make it work out its purpose in individual believers and in the people as a whole. The whole of the Old Covenant was a school of grace, an elementary school, to prepare for the fulness of grace and truth in Christ Jesus. A name is generally given to an object according to its chief feature. And so the Old Covenant is called a ministration of condemnation and death, not because there was no grace in it—it had its own glory (2 Cor. iii. 10-12)—but because the law with its curse was the predominating element. The combination of the two aspects we find with especial clearness in Paul's epistles. So he speaks of all who are of the works of the law as under the curse (Gal. iii. 10). And then almost immediately after he speaks of the law as being our benefactor, a schoolmaster unto Christ, into whose charge, as to a tutor or governor, we had been given, till the time appointed of the Father. We are everywhere brought back to what we said above. The Old Covenant is absolutely indispensable for the preparation work it had to do; utterly insufficient to work for us a true or a full redemption.

The two great lessons God would teach us by it are very simple. The one is the lesson of *sin*, the other the lesson of *holiness*. The Old Covenant attains its object only as it brings men to a sense of their utter sinfulness and their hopeless impotence to deliver themselves. As long as they have not learnt this, no offer of the New Covenant life can lay hold of them. As long as an intense longing for deliverance from sinning has not been wrought, they will naturally fall back into the power of the law and the flesh. The holiness which the New Covenant offers will rather terrify than attract them; the life in the spirit of bondage appears to make more allowance for sin, because obedience is declared to be impossible.

The other is the lesson of Holiness. In the New Covenant the Triune God engages to do all. He undertakes to give and keep the new heart, to give His own Spirit in it, to give the will and the power to obey and do His will. As the one demand of the first Covenant was the sense of sin, the one great demand of the New is faith that that need, created by the discipline of God's law, will be met in a Divine and supernatural way. The law cannot work out its purpose, except as it brings a man to lie guilty and helpless before the holiness of God. There the New finds him, and reveals that same God, in His grace accepting him and making him partaker of His holiness.

This book is written with a very practical purpose. Its object is to help believers to know that wonderful New Covenant of grace which God has made with them, and to lead them into the living and daily enjoyment of the blessed life it secures them. The practical lesson taught us by the fact that there was a first Covenant, that its one special work was to convince of sin, and that without it the New Covenant could not come, is just what many Christians need. At conversion they were convinced of sin by the Holy Spirit. But this had chiefly reference to the guilt of sin and, in some degree, to its hatefulness. But a real knowledge of the power of sin, of their entire and utter impotence to cast it out, or to work in themselves what is good, is what they did not learn at once. And until they have learned this, they cannot possibly enter fully into the blessing of the New Covenant. It is when a man sees that, as little as he could raise himself from the dead, can he make or keep his own soul alive, that he becomes capable of appreciating the New Testament promise, and is made willing to wait on God to do all in him.

Do you, my reader, feel that you are not fully living in the New Covenant, that there is still somewhat of the Old-Covenant spirit of bondage in you?—do come, and let the Old Covenant finish its work in you. Accept its teaching, that all your efforts are failures. As, at conversion, you were content to fall down as a condemned, death-deserving sinner, be content now to sink down before God in the confession that, as His redeemed child, you still feel yourself utterly impotent to do and be what you see He asks of you. And begin to ask whether the New Covenant has not perhaps a provision you have never yet understood for meeting your impotence and giving you the strength to do what is well-pleasing to God. You will find the wonderful answer in the assurance that God, by His Holy Spirit, undertakes to work everything in you. The longing to be delivered from the life of daily sinning, and the extinction of all hope to secure this by our efforts as Christians, will prepare us for understanding and accepting God's new way of salvation—Himself working in us all that is pleasing in His sight.

The New Covenant

"But this is the covenant that I will make with the house of Israel; After those days, saith the Lord, I will put My law in their inward parts, and write it in their hearts; and will be their God, and they shall be My people. And they shall teach no more every man his neighbour, saying, Know the Lord: for they shall all know Me, from the least of them unto the greatest of them, for I will forgive their iniquity, and I will remember their sin no more."—JER. xxxi. 33, 34.

Isaiah has often been called the evangelical prophet, for the wonderful clearness with which he announces the coming Redeemer, both in His humiliation and suffering, and in the glory of the kingdom He was to establish. And yet it was given to Jeremiah, in this passage, and to Ezekiel, in the parallel one, to foretell what would actually be the outcome of the Redeemer's work and the essential character of the salvation He was to effect, with a distinctness which is nowhere found in the older prophet. In words which the New Testament (Hebrews viii.) takes as the divinely inspired revelation of what the New Covenant is of which Christ is the Mediator, God's plan is revealed and we are shown what it is that He will do in us, to make us fit and worthy of being the people of which He is the God. Through the whole of the Old Covenant there was always one trouble: man's heart was not right with God. In the New Covenant the evil is to be remedied. Its central promise is a heart delighting in God's law and capable of knowing and holding fellowship with Him. Let us mark the fourfold blessing spoken of.

1. "I will put My law in their inward parts, and write it in their hearts." Let us understand this well. In our inward parts, or in our heart, there are no separate chambers in which the law can be put, while the rest of the heart can be given up to other things; the heart is a unity. Nor are the inward parts and the heart like a house, which can be filled with things of an entirely different nature from what the walls are made of, without any living organic connection. No; the inward parts, the heart, are the disposition, the love, the will, the life. Nothing can be put into the heart, and especially by God, without entering and taking possession of it, without securing its affection

and controlling its whole being. And this is what God undertakes to do in the power of His divine life and operation, to breathe the very spirit of His law into and through the whole inward being. "I will put it into their inward parts, and write it in their hearts." At Sinai the tables of the Covenant, with the law written on them, were of stone, as a lasting substance. It is easy to know what that means. The stone was wholly set apart for this one thing—to carry and show this Divine writing. The writing and the stone were inseparably connected. And so the heart in which God gets His way, and writes His law in power, lives only and wholly to carry that writing, and is unchangeably identified with it. So alone can God realise His purpose in creation, and have His child of one mind and one spirit with Himself, delighting in doing His will. When the Old Covenant with the law graven on stone had done its work in the discovering and condemning of *sin*, the New Covenant would give in its stead the life of obedience and true holiness of heart. The whole of the Covenant blessing centres in this—the heart being put right and fitted to know God: "I will give them an heart to know Me, that I am the Lord; and they shall be My people, and I will be their God; for they shall return unto Me with their whole heart" (Jer. xxiv. 7).

2. "And I will be their God, and they shall be My people." Do not pass these words lightly. They occur chiefly in Jeremiah and Ezekiel in connection with the promise of the everlasting Covenant. They express the very highest experience of the Covenant relationship. It is only when His people learn to love and obey His law, when their heart and life are together wholly devoted to Him and His will, that He can be to them the altogether inconceivable blessing which these words express, "I will be your God." All I am and have as God shall be yours. All you can need or wish for in a God, I will be to you. In the fullest meaning of the word, I, the Omnipresent, will be ever present with you, in all My grace and love. I, the Almighty One, will each moment work all in you by My mighty power. I, the Thrice-Holy One, will reveal My sanctifying life within you. I will be your God. And ye shall be My people, saved and blessed, ruled and guided and provided for by Me, known and seen to be indeed the people of the Holy One, the God of glory. Only let us give our hearts time to meditate and wait for the Holy Spirit to work in us all that these words mean.

3. "And they shall teach no more every man his neighbour, and every man his brother, saying, Know the Lord, for they shall all know Me, from the least of them unto the greatest of them, saith the Lord." Individual personal fellowship with God, for the feeblest and the least, is to be the wonderful privilege of every member of the New Covenant people. Each one will know

the Lord. That does not mean the knowledge of the mind,—that is not the equal privilege of all, and that in itself may hinder the fellowship more than help it,—but with that knowledge which means appropriation and assimilation, and which is eternal life. As the Son knew the Father because He was one with Him and dwelt in Him, the child of God will receive by the Holy Spirit that spiritual illumination which will make God to him the One he knows best, because he loves Him most and lives in Him. The promise, "They shall be all taught of God," will be fulfilled by the Holy Spirit's teaching. God will speak to each out of His Word what he needs to know.

4. "For I will forgive their iniquities, and I will remember their sin no more." The word for shows that this is the reason of all that precedes. Because the blood of this New Covenant was of such infinite worth, and its Mediator and High Priest in heaven of such Divine power, there is promised in it such a Divine blotting out of sin that God cannot remember it. It is this entire blotting out of sin that cleanses and sets us free from its power, so that God can write His law in our hearts, and show Himself in power as our God, and by His Spirit reveal to us His deep things—the deep mystery of Himself and His love. It is the atonement and redemption of Jesus Christ wrought without us and for us, that has removed every obstacle and made it meet for God, and made us meet, that the law in the heart, and the claim on our God, and the knowledge of Him, should now be our daily life and our eternal portion.

Here we now have the Divine summary of the New Covenant inheritance. The last-named blessing, the pardon of sin, is the first in order, the root of all. The second, having God as our God, and the third, the Divine teaching, are the fruit. The tree itself that grows on this root, and bears such fruit, is what is named first—the law in the heart.

The central demand of the Old Covenant, Obey My voice, and I will be your God, has now been met. With the law written in the heart, He can be our God, and we shall be His people. Perfect harmony with God's will, holiness in heart and life, is the only thing that can satisfy God's heart or ours. And it is this the New Covenant gives in Divine power, "I wil give them an heart to know Me; and I will be their God, and they shall be My people; for they shall turn to Me with their whole heart." It is on the state of the heart, it is on the new heart, as given by God, that the New Covenant life hinges.

But why, if all this is meant to be literally and exactly true of God's people, why do we see so little of this life, experience so little in ourselves? There is but one answer: Because of your unbelief! We have spoken of the relation of

God and man in creation as what the New Covenant is meant to make possible and real. But the law cannot be repealed that God will not compel. He can only fulfil His purpose as the heart is willing and accepts His offer. In the New Covenant all is of faith. Let us turn away from what human wisdom and human experience may say, and ask God Himself to teach us what His Covenant means. If we persevere in this prayer in a humble and teachable spirit, we can count most certainly on its promise: "They shall no more every man teach his neighbour: Know the Lord, for they shall all know Me." The teaching of God Himself, by the Holy Spirit, to make us understand what He says to us in His Word, is our Covenant right. Let us count upon it. It is only by a God-given faith that we can appropriate these God-given promises. And it is only by a God-given teaching and inward illumination that we can see their meaning, so as to believe them. When God teaches us the meaning of His promises in a heart yielded to His Holy Spirit, then alone we can believe and receive them in a power which makes them a reality in our life.

But is it really possible, amid the wear and tear of daily life, to walk in the experience of these blessings? Are they really meant for all God's children? Let us rather ask the question, Is it possible for God to do what He has promised? The one part of the promise we believe—the complete and perfect pardon of sin. Why should we not believe the other part—the law written in the heart, and the direct Divine fellowship and teaching? We have been so accustomed to separate what God has joined together, the objective, outward work of His Son, and the subjective, inward work of His Spirit, that we consider the glory of the New Covenant above the Old to consist chiefly in the redeeming work of Christ for us, and not equally in the sanctifying work of the Spirit in us. It is owing to this ignorance and unbelief of the indwelling of the Holy Spirit, as the power through whom God fulfils the New Covenant promises, that we do not really expect them to be made true to us.

Do let us turn our hearts away from all past experience of failure, as caused by nothing but unbelief; do let us admit fully and heartily, what failure has taught us, the absolute impossibility of even a regenerate man walking in God's law in his own strength, and then turn our hearts quietly and trustfully to our own Covenant God. Let us hear what He says He will do for us, and believe Him; let us rest on His unchangeable faithfulness and the surety of the Covenant, on His Almighty power and the Holy Spirit working in us; and let us give up ourselves to Him as our God. He will prove that what He has done for us in Christ is not one whit more wonderful than what He will do in us every day by the Spirit of Christ.

The Two Covenants in Christian Experience

"These women are two covenants: one from Mount Sinai, bearing children unto bondage, which is Hagar. Now this Hagar answereth to Jerusalem that now is, for she is in bondage with her children. But the Jerusalem which is above is free, which is our mother. So then, brethren, we are not children of the bondwoman, but of the free. With freedom did Christ set us free. Stand fast, therefore, and be not entangled again in a yoke of bondage."-GAL. iv. 24-81, v. 1.

The house of Abraham was the Church of God of that age. The division in his house, one son, his own son, but born after the flesh, the other after the promise, was a divinely-ordained manifestation of the division there would be in all ages between the children of the bondwoman, those who served God in the spirit of bondage, and those who were children of the free, and served Him in the Spirit of His Son. The passage teaches us what the whole Epistle confirms: that the Galatians had become entangled with a yoke of bondage, and were not standing fast in the freedom with which Christ makes free indeed. Instead of living in the New Covenant, in the Jerusalem which is from above, in the liberty which the Holy Spirit gives, their whole walk proved that, though Christians, they were of the Old Covenant, which bringeth forth children unto bondage. The passage teaches us the great truth, which it is of the utmost consequence for us to apprehend thoroughly, that a man, with a measure of the knowledge and experience of the grace of God, may prove, by a legal spirit, that he is yet practically, to a large extent, under the Old Covenant. And it will show us, with wonderful clearness; what the proofs are of the absence of the true New Covenant life.

A careful study of the Epistle shows us that the difference between the two Covenants is seen in three things. The law and its works is contrasted with the hearing of faith, the flesh and its religion with the flesh crucified, the impotence to good with a walk in the liberty and the power of the Spirit. May the Holy Spirit reveal to us this twofold life.

The first antithesis we find in Paul's words, "Received ye the Spirit by the works of the law, or the hearing of faith?" These Galatians had indeed been born into the New Covenant; they had received the Holy Spirit. But they had been led away by Jewish teachers, and, though they had been justified by faith, they were seeking to be sanctified by works; they were looking for the maintenance and the growth of their Christian life to the observance of the law. They had not understood that, equally with the beginning, the progress of the Divine life is alone by faith, day by day receiving its strength from Christ alone; that in Jesus Christ nothing avails but faith working by love.

Almost every believer makes the same mistake as the Galatian Christians. Very few learn at conversion at once that it is only by faith that we stand, and walk, and live. They have no conception of the meaning of Paul's teaching about being dead to the law, freed from the law—about the freedom with which Christ makes us free. "As many as are led by the Spirit are not under the law." Regarding the law as a Divine ordinance for our direction, they consider themselves prepared and fitted by conversion to take up the fulfilment of the law as a natural duty. They know not that, in the New Covenant, the law written in the heart needs an unceasing faith in a Divine power, to enable us by a Divine power to keep it. They cannot understand that it is not to the law, but to a Living Person, that we are now bound, and that our obedience and holiness are only possible by the unceasing faith in His power ever working in us. It is only when this is seen, that we are prepared truly to live in the New Covenant.

The second word, that reveals the Old Covenant spirit, is the word "flesh." Its contrast is, the flesh crucified. Paul asks: "Are ye so foolish? Having begun in the Spirit, are ye made perfect in the flesh?" Flesh means our sinful human nature. At his conversion the Christian has generally no conception of the terrible evil of his nature, and the subtlety with which it offers itself to take part in the service of God. It may be most willing and diligent in God's service for a time; it may devise numberless observances for making His worship pleasing and attractive; and yet this may be all only what Paul calls "making a fair show in the flesh," "glorying in the flesh," in man's will and man's efforts. This power of the religious flesh is one of the great marks of the Old Covenant religion; it misses the deep humility and spirituality of the true worship of God—a heart and life entirely dependent upon Him.

The proof that our religion is very much that of the religious flesh, is that the sinful flesh will be found to flourish along with it. It was thus with the Galatians. While they were making a fair show in the flesh, and glorying in it, their daily life was full of bitterness and envy and hatred, and other sins.

They were biting and devouring one another. Religious flesh and sinful flesh are one: no wonder that, with a great deal of religion, temper and selfishness and worldliness are so often found side by side. The religion of the flesh cannot conquer sin.

What a contrast to the religion of the New Covenant! What is the place the flesh has there? "They that are Christ's have crucified the flesh, with its desires and affections." Scripture speaks of the will of the flesh, the mind of the flesh, the lust of the flesh; all this the true believer has seen to be condemned and crucified in Christ: he has given it over to the death. He not only accepts the Cross, with its bearing of the curse, and its redemption from it, as his entrance into life; he glories in it as his only power day by day to overcome the flesh and the world. "I am crucified with Christ." "God forbid that I should glory save in the cross of my Lord Jesus Christ, by which I am crucified to the world." Even as nothing less than the death of Christ was needed to inaugurate the New Covenant, and the resurrection life that animates it, there is no entrance into the true New Covenant life other than by a partaking of that death.

"Fallen from grace." This is a third word that describes the condition of these Galatians in that bondage in which they were really impotent to all true good. Paul is not speaking of a final falling away here, for he still addresses them as Christians, but of their having wandered from that walk in the way of enabling and sanctifying grace, in which a Christian can get the victory over sin. As long as grace is principally connected with pardon and the entrance to the Christian life, the flesh is the only power in which to serve and work. But when we know what exceeding abundance of grace has been provided, and how God "makes all grace abound, that we may abound to all good works," we know that, as it is by faith, so too it is by grace alone that we stand a single moment or take a single step.

The contrast to this life of impotence and failure is found in the one word, "the Spirit." "If ye be led of the Spirit, ye are not under the law," with its demand on your own strength. "Walk in the Spirit, and ye shall not"—a definite, certain promise—"ye shall not fulfil the lusts of the flesh." The Spirit gives liberty from the law, from the flesh, from sin. "The fruit of the Spirit is love, peace, joy." Of the New Covenant promise, "I will put My Spirit within you, and I will cause you to walk in My statutes, and ye shall keep My judgments," the Spirit is the centre and the sum. He is the power of the supernatural life of true obedience and holiness.

And what would have been the course that the Galatians would have taken if they had accepted this teaching of St. Paul? As they hear his question, "Now that ye have come to know God, how turn ye back again into the weak and beggarly rudiments, whereunto ye desire to be in bondage again?" they would have felt that there was but one course. Nothing else could help them but at once to turn back again to the path they had left. At the point where they had left it, they could enter again. With any one of them who wished to do so, this turning away from the Old Covenant legal spirit, and the renewed surrender to the Mediator of the New Covenant, could be the act of a moment—one single step. As the light of the New Covenant promise dawned upon him, and he saw how Christ was to be all, and faith all, and the Holy Spirit in the heart all, and the faithfulness of a Covenant-keeping God all in all, he would feel that he had but one thing to do—in utter impotence to yield himself to God, and in simple faith to count upon Him to perform what He had spoken. In Christian experience there may be still the Old Covenant life of bondage and failure. In Christian experience there may be a life that gives way entirely to the New Covenant grace and spirit. In Christian experience, when the true vision has been received of what the New Covenant means, a faith that rests fully on the Mediator of the New Covenant can enter at once into the life which the Covenant secures.

I cannot too earnestly beg all believers who long to know to the utmost what the grace of God can work in them, to study carefully the question as to whether the acknowledgment that our being in the bondage of the Old Covenant is the reason of our failure, and whether a clear insight into the possibility of an entire change in our relation to God, is not what is needed to give us the help we seek. We may be seeking for our growth in a more diligent use of the means of grace, and a more earnest striving to live in accordance with God's will, and yet entirely fail. The reason is, that there is a secret root of evil which must be removed. That root is the spirit of bondage, the legal spirit of self-effort, which hinders that humble faith that knows that God will work all, and yields to Him to do it. That spirit may be found amidst very great zeal for God's service, and very earnest prayer for His grace; it does not enjoy the rest of faith, and cannot overcome sin, because it does not stand in the liberty with which Christ has made us free, and does not know that where the Spirit of the Lord is, there is liberty. There the soul can say: "The law of the Spirit of life in Christ Jesus bath made me free from the law of sin and death." When once we admit heartily, not only that there are failings in our life, but that there is something radically wrong that can be changed, we shall turn with a new interest, with a deeper confession of ignorance and impotence, with a hope that looks to God alone for teaching and strength, to find that in the New Covenant there is an actual provision for every need.

The Everlasting Covenant of the Spirit

"They shall be My people, and l will be their God. And I will make an everlasting covenant with them, that I will not turn away from them, to do them good; but I will put My fear in their hearts, that they shall not depart from Me."—JER. xxxii. 38, 40.

"A new heart also will I give you, and a new spirit will I put within you: and I will take the stony heart out of your flesh, and I will give you an heart of flesh. And I will put my Spirit within you, and cause you to walk in My statutes, and ye shall keep My judgments, and do them. Moreover, I will make a covenant of peace with them: it shall be an everlasting covenant with them."—EZEK. xxxvi. 26, 27, xxxvii. 26.

We have had the words of the institution of the New Covenant. Let us listen to the further teaching we have concerning it in Jeremiah and Ezekiel, where God speaks of it as an everlasting Covenant. In every covenant there are two parties. And the very foundation of a covenant rests on the thought that each party is to be faithful to the part it has undertaken to perform. Unfaithfulness on either side breaks the covenant.

It was thus with the Old Covenant. God had said to Israel, Obey My voice, and I will be your God (Jer. vii. 23, xi. 4). These simple words contained the whole Covenant. And when Israel disobeyed, the Covenant was broken. The question of Israel being able or not able to obey was not taken into consideration: disobedience forfeited the privileges of the Covenant.

If a New Covenant were to be made, and if that was to be better than the Old, this was the one thing to be provided for. No New Covenant could be of any profit unless provision were made for securing obedience. Obedience there must be. God as Creator could never take His creatures into His favour and fellowship, except they obeyed Him. The thing would have been an impossibility. If the New Covenant is to be better than the Old, if it is to be an everlasting Covenant, never to be broken, it must make some sufficient provision for securing the obedience of the Covenant people. And this is indeed the glory of the New Covenant, the glory that excelleth, that this provision has been made. In a way that no human thought could have devised, by a stipulation that never entered into any human covenant, by an undertaking in which God's infinite condescension and power and faithfulness are to be most wonderfully exhibited, by a supernatural mystery of Divine wisdom and grace, the New Covenant provides a guarantee, not only for God's faithfulness, but for man's too! And this in no other way than by God Himself undertaking to secure man's part as well as His own. Do try and get hold of this.

It is just because this, the essential part of the New Covenant, so exceeds and confounds all human thoughts of what a covenant means, that Christians, from the Galatians downwards, have not been able to see and believe what the New Covenant really brings. They have thought that human unfaithfulness was a factor permanently to be reckoned with as something utterly unconquerable and incurable, and that the possibility of a life of obedience, with the witness from within of a good conscience, and from above of God's pleasure, was not to be expected. They have therefore sought to stir the mind to its utmost by arguments and motives, and never realised how the Holy Spirit is to be the unceasing, universal, all-sufficient worker of everything that has to be wrought by the Christian.

Let us beseech God earnestly that He would reveal to us by the Holy Spirit the things that He hath prepared for them that love Him; things that have not entered into the heart of man; the wonderful life of the New Covenant. All depends upon our knowledge of what God will work in us. Listen to what God says in Jeremiah of the two parts of His everlasting Covenant, shortly after He had announced the New Covenant, and in further elucidation of it. The central thought of that, that the heart is to be put right, is here reiterated and confirmed. "I will make an everlasting covenant with them, that I will not turn away from them, to do them good." That is, God will be unchangeably faithful. He will not turn from us. "But I will put My fear into their heart, that they shall not depart from Me." This is the second half: Israel will be unchangeably faithful too. And that because God will so put His fear in their heart, that they shall not depart from Him. As little as God will turn from them, will they depart from Him! As faithfully as He undertakes for the fulfilment of His part, will He undertake for the fulfilment of their part, that they shall not depart from Him!

Listen to God's word in Ezekiel, in regard to one of the terms of His Covenant of peace, His everlasting Covenant. (Ezek. xxxiv. 25, xxxvi. 27, xxxvii. 26): "I will put My Spirit within you, and cause you to walk in My statutes, and ye shall keep My judgments, and do them." In the Old Covenant we have nothing of this sort. You have, on the contrary, from the story of the golden calf and the breaking of the Tables of the Covenant onward, the sad fact of continual departure from God. We find God longing for what He would so fain have seen, but was not to be found. "O that there were such an heart in them, that they would fear Me, and keep all My commandments always" (Deut. v. 29). We find throughout the Book of Deuteronomy, a thing without parallel in the history of any religion or religious lawgiver, that Moses most distinctly prophesies their forsaking of God, with the terrible curses and dispersion that would come upon them. It is only at the close of his threatenings (Deut. xxx. 6) that he gives the promise of the new time that would come: "The Lord thy God will circumcise thine heart, to love the Lord thy God with all thine heart, and with all thy soul, and thou shalt obey the voice of the Lord thy God." The whole Old Covenant was dependent on man's faithfulness: "The Lord thy God keepeth covenant with them that keep His commandments." God's keeping the Covenant availed little, if man did not keep it. Nothing could help man until the "If ye shall diligently keep" of the law, was replaced by the word of promise, "I will put My Spirit in you, and ye shall keep My judgments, and do them." The one supreme difference of the New Covenant; the one thing for which the Mediator, and the Blood, and the Spirit were given; the one fruit God sought and Himself engaged to bring forth was this: a heart filled with His fear and love, a heart to cleave unto Him and not depart from Him, a heart in which His Spirit and His law dwells, a heart that delights to do His will.

Here is the inmost secret of the New Covenant. It deals with the heart of man in a way of Divine power. It not only appeals to the heart by every motive of fear or love, of duty or gratitude. That the law also did. But it reveals God Himself, cleansing our heart and making it new, changing it entirely from a stony heart into a heart of flesh, a tender, living, loving heart, putting His Spirit within it, and so, by His Almighty Power and Love, breathing and working in it, making the promise true, "I will cause you to walk in My statutes, and ye shall keep My judgments." A heart in perfect harmony with Himself, a life and walk in His way—God has engaged in Covenant to work this in us. He undertakes for our part in the Covenant as much as for His own.

This is nothing but the restoration of the original relation between God and the man He had made in His likeness. He was on earth to be the very image of God, because God was to live and to work all in him, and he to find his glory and blessedness in thus owing all to God. This is the exceeding glory of the New Covenant, of the Pentecostal dispensation, that by the Holy Spirit God could now again be the indwelling life of His people, and so make the promise a reality: "I will cause you to walk in My statutes."

With God's presence secured to us every moment of the day—"I will not turn away from them"; with God's "fear put into our heart" by His own Spirit, and our heart thus responding to His holy presence; with our hearts thus made right with God, we can, we shall walk in His statutes, and keep His judgments.

My brethren, the great sin of Israel under the Old Covenant, that by which they greatly grieved Him, was this: "they limited the Holy One of Israel." Under the New Covenant there is no less danger of this sin. It makes it impossible for God to fulfil His promises. Let us seek, above everything, for the Holy Spirit's teaching, to show us exactly what God has established the New Covenant for, that we may honour Him by believing all that His love has prepared for us.

And if we ask for the cause of the unbelief, that prevents the fulfilment of the promise, we shall find that it is not far to seek. It is, in most cases, the lack of desire for the promised blessing. In all who came to Jesus on earth the intensity of their desire for the healing they needed made them ready and glad to believe in His word. Where the law has done its full work, where the actual desire to be freed from every sin is strong, and masters the heart, the promise of the New Covenant, when once really understood, comes like bread to a famishing man. The subtle unbelief, that thinks it impossible to be kept from sinning, cuts away the power of accepting the provision of the everlasting Covenant. God's Word, "I will put My fear in their heart, that they shall not depart from Me"; "I will put My Spirit within you, and ye shall keep My judgment," is understood in some feeble sense, according to our experience, and not according to what the Word and what God means. And the soul settles down into a despair, or a self-contentment, that says it can never be otherwise, and makes true conviction for sin impossible.

Let me say to every reader who would fain be able to believe fully all that God says: Cherish every whisper of the conscience and of the Spirit that convinces of sin. Whatever it be, a hasty temper, a sharp word, an unloving or impatient thought, anything of selfishness or self-will—cherish that which condemns it in you, as part of the schooling that is to bring you to Christ and the full possession of His salvation. The New Covenant is meant to meet the need for a power of not sinning, which the Old could not give. Come with that need; it will prepare and open the heart for all the everlasting Covenant secures you. It will bring you to that humble and entire dependence upon God in His Omnipotence and His Faithfulness, in which He can and will work all He has promised.

The New Covenant: A Ministration of the Spirit

"Ye are an epistle of Christ, ministered by us, written not with ink, but with the Spirit of the living God; not on tables of stone, but on tables that are hearts of flesh . . . Our sufficiency is of God; who also made us sufficient as ministers of the New Covenant; not of the letter, but of the Spirit: for the letter killeth, but the Spirit giveth life. For if the ministration of death came with glory, how shall not rather the ministration of the Spirit be with glory? For if the ministration of condemnation is glory, much rather doth the ministration of righteousness exceed in glory."—2 COR. *iii. 3, 6-10.*

In this wonderful chapter Paul reminds the Corinthians, in speaking of his ministry among them, of what its chief characteristics were. As a ministry of the New Covenant he contrasts it, and the whole dispensation of which it is part, with that of the Old. The Old was graven in stone, the New in the heart. The Old could be written in ink, and was in the letter that killeth; the New, of the Spirit that maketh alive. The Old was a ministration of condemnation and death; the New, of righteousness and life. The Old indeed bad its glory, for it was of Divine appointment, and brought its Divine blessing; but it was a glory that passed away, and had no glory by reason of the glory that excelleth, the exceeding glory of that which remaineth. With the Old there was the veil on the heart; in the New, the veil is taken away from the face and the heart, the Spirit of the Lord gives liberty, and, reflecting with unveiled face the glory of the Lord, we are changed from glory to glory, into the same image, as by the Spirit of the Lord. The glory that excelleth proved its power in this, that it not only marked the dispensation on its Divine side, but so exerted its power in the heart and life of its subjects, that it was seen in them too, as they were changed by the Spirit into Christ's image, from glory to glory.

Think a moment of the contrast. The Old Covenant was of the letter that killeth. The law came with its literal instruction, and sought by the knowledge it gave of God's will to appeal to man's fear and his love, to his natural powers of mind and conscience and will. It spoke to him as if he could obey, that it might convince him of what he did not know, that he could not obey. And so it fulfilled its mission: "The commandment which was unto life, this I found to be unto death." In the New, on the contrary, how different was everything. Instead of the letter, the Spirit that giveth life, that breathes the very life of God, the life of heaven into us. Instead of a law graven in stone, the law written in the heart, worked into the heart's affection and powers, making it one with them. Instead of the vain attempt to work from without inward, the Spirit and the law are put into the inward parts, thence to work outward in life and walk.

This passage brings into view that which is the distinctive blessing of the New Covenant. In working out our salvation God bestowed upon us two wonderful gifts. We read: "God sent forth His Son, that He might redeem them that were under the law, that we might receive the adoption of sons. And because ye are sons, God sent forth the Spirit of His Son into your hearts, crying, Abba, Father." Here we have the two parts of God's work in salvation. The one, the more objective, what He did that we might become His children—He sent forth His Son. The second, the more subjective, what He did that we might live like His children: He sent forth the Spirit of His Son into our hearts. In the former we have the external manifestation of the work of redemption; in the other, its inward appropriation; the former for the sake of the latter. These two halves form one great whole, and may not be separated.

In the promises of the New Covenant, as we find them in Jeremiah and Ezekiel, as well as in our text and many other passages of Scripture, it is manifest that God's great object in salvation is to get possession of the heart. The heart is the real life; with the heart a man loves, and wills, and acts; the heart makes the man. God made man's heart for His own dwelling, that in it He might reveal His love and His glory. God sent Christ to accomplish a redemption by which man's heart could be won back to Him; nothing but that could satisfy God. And that is what is accomplished when the Holy Spirit makes the heart of God's child what it should be. The whole work of Christ's redemption—His Atonement and Victory, His Exaltation and Intercession, His glory at the right hand of God—all these are only preparatory to what is the chief triumph of His grace: the renewal of the heart to be the temple of God. Through Christ God gives the Holy Spirit to glorify Him in the heart, by working there all that He has done and is doing for the soul.

In a great deal of our religious teaching a fear, lest we should derogate from the honour of Christ, has been alleged as the reason for giving His work for us, on the Cross or in heaven, a greater prominence than His work in our heart by the Holy Spirit. The result has been that the indwelling of the Holy Spirit, and His mighty work as the life of the heart, as very little known in true power. If we look carefully at what the New Covenant promises mean, we shall see how the "sending forth of the Spirit of His Son into our hearts" is indeed the consummation and crown of Christ's redeeming work. Let us just think of what these promises imply.

In the Old Covenant man had failed in what he had to do. In the New, God is to do everything in him. The Old could only convict of sin. The New is to put it away and cleanse the heart from its filthiness. In the Old it was the heart that was wrong; for the New a new heart is provided, into which God puts His fear and His law and His love. The Old demanded, but failed to secure obedience; in the New, God causes us to walk in His judgments. The New is to fit man for a true holiness, a true fulfilment of the law of loving God with the whole heart, and our neighbours as ourselves, a walk truly well-pleasing to God. The New changes a man from glory to glory after the image of Christ. All because the Spirit of God's Son is given into the heart. The Old gave no power: in the New all is by the Spirit, the mighty power of God. As complete as the reign and power of Christ on the throne of heaven, is His dominion on the throne of the heart by His Holy Spirit given to us.

It is as we bring all these traits of the New Covenant life together into one focus, and look at the heart of God's child as the object of this mighty redemption, that we shall begin to understand what is secured to us, and what it is that we are to expect from our Covenant God. We shall see wherein the glory of the ministration of the Spirit consists, even in this, that God can fill our heart with His love, and make it His abode.

We are accustomed to say, and truly so, that the worth of the Son of God, who came to die for us, is the measure of the worth of the soul in God's sight, and of the greatness of the work that had to be done to save it. Let us even so see, that the Divine glory of the Holy Spirit, the Spirit of the Father and the Son, is the measure of God's longing to have our heart wholly for Himself, of the glory of the work that is to be wrought within us, of the power by which that work will be accomplished.

We shall see how the glory of the ministration of the Spirit is no other than the glory of the Lord, as it is not only in heaven, but resting upon us and dwelling in us, and changing us into the same image from glory to glory. The inconceivable glory of our exalted Lord in heaven has its counterpart here on earth in the exceeding glory of the Holy Spirit who glorifies Him in us, who lays His glory on us, as He changes us into His likeness.

The New Covenant has no power to save and to bless except as it is a ministration of the Spirit. That Spirit works in lesser or greater degree, as He is neglected and grieved, or yielded to and trusted. Let us honour Him, and give Him His place as the Spirit of the New Covenant, by expecting and accepting all He waits to do for us.

He is the great gift of the Covenant. His coming from heaven was the proof that the Mediator of the Covenant was on the throne in glory, and could now make us partakers of the heavenly life.

He is the only teacher of what the Covenant means: dwelling in our heart, He wakens there the thought and the desire for what God has prepared for us.

He is the Spirit of faith, who enables us to believe the otherwise incomprehensible blessing and power in which the New Covenant works, and to claim it as our own.

He is the Spirit of grace and of power, by whom the obedience of the Covenant and the fellowship with God can be maintained without interruption.

He Himself is the Possessor and the Bearer and the Communicator of all the Covenant promises, the Revealer and the Glorifier of Jesus, its Mediator and Surety.

To believe fully in the Holy Spirit, as the present and abiding and all-comprehending gift of the New Covenant, has been to many a one an entrance into its fulness of blessing.

Begin at once, child of God, to give the Holy Spirit the place in thy religion He has in God's plan. Be still before God, and believe that He is within thee, and ask the Father to work in thee through Him. Regard thyself, thy spirit as well as thy body, with holy reverence as His temple. Let the consciousness of His holy presence and working fill thee with holy calm and fear. And be sure that all that God calls thee to be, Christ through His Spirit will work in thee.

The Two Covenants: the Transition

"Now the God of peace, who brought again from the dead the great Shepherd of the sheep, in the blood of the everlasting covenant, even our Lord Jesus, make you perfect in every good thing to do His will, working in us that which is well-pleasing in His sight, through Jesus Christ."—HEB. xiii. 20, 21.

The transition from the Old Covenant to the New was not slow or gradual, but by a tremendous crisis. Nothing less than the death of Christ was the close of the Old. Nothing less than His resurrection from the dead, through the blood of the everlasting Covenant, the opening of the New. The path of preparation that led up to the crisis was long and slow; the rending of the veil, that symbolised the end of the old worship, was the work of a moment. By a death, once for all, Christ's work, as fulfiller of law and prophets, as the end of the law, was for ever finished. By a resurrection in the power of an endless life, the Covenant of Life was ushered in.

These events have an infinite significance, as revealing the character of the Covenants they are related to. The death of Christ shows the true nature of the Old Covenant. It is elsewhere called "a ministration of death" (2 Cor. iii. 7). It brought forth nothing but death. It ended in death; only by death could the life that had been lived under it be brought to an end. The New was to be a Covenant of Life; it had its birth in the omnipotent resurrection power that brought Christ from the dead; its one mark and blessing is, that all it gives comes, not only as a promise, but as an experience, in the power of an endless life. The Death reveals the utter inefficacy and insufficiency of the Old; the Life brings nigh and imparts to us for ever all that the New has to offer. An insight into the completeness of the transition, as seen in Christ, prepares us for apprehending the reality of the change in our life, when, "like as Christ was raised from the dead by the glory of the Father, so we also walk in newness of life." The complete difference between the life in the Old and the New is remarkably illustrated by a previous passage in the Epistle (Heb. ix. 16). After having said that a death for the redemption of transgressions had to take place ere the New Covenant could be established, the writer adds, "Where a testament is, there must of necessity be the death of him that made it." Before any heir can obtain the legacy, its first owner, the testator, must have died. The old proprietorship, the old life, must disappear entirely before the new heir, the new life, can enter upon the inheritance. Nothing but death can work the transference of the property. It is even so with Christ, with the Old and the New Covenant life, with our own deliverance from the Old and our entrance on the New. Now, having been made dead to the law by the body of Christ, we have been discharged from the law, having died to that wherein we were holden—here is the completeness of the deliverance from Christ's side; "so that we serve "—here is the completeness of the change in our experience—"in newness of the spirit, and not in oldness of the letter."

The transition, if it is to be real and whole, must take place by a death. As with Christ the Mediator of the Covenant, so with His people, the heirs of the Covenant. In Him we are dead to sin; in Him we are dead to the law. Just as Adam died to God, and we inherit a nature actually and really dead in sin, dead to God and His kingdom, so in Christ we died to sin, and inherit a nature actually dead to sin and its dominion. It is when the Holy Spirit reveals and makes real to us this death to sin and to the law too, as the one condition of a life to God, that the transition from the Old to the New Covenant can be fully realised in us. The Old was, and was meant to be, a "ministration of death "; until it has completely done its work in us there is no complete discharge from its power. The man who sees that self is incurably evil and must die; who gives self utterly to death as he sinks before God in utter impotence and the surrender to His working; who consents to death with Christ on the cross as his desert, and in faith accepts it as his only deliverance; he alone is prepared to be led by the Holy Spirit into the full enjoyment of the New Covenant life. He will learn to understand how completely death makes an end to all self-effort, and how, as he lives in Christ to God, everything henceforth is to be the work of God Himself.

See how beautifully our text brings out this truth, that just as much as Christ's resurrection out of death was the work of God Himself, is our life equally to be wholly God's own work too. Not more direct and wonderful than was in Christ the transition from death to life, is to be in us the experience of what the New Covenant life is to bring. Notice the subject of the two verses. In ver. we have what God has done in raising Christ from the dead; in ver. , what God is to do in us, working in us what is pleasing to Him. "The God of peace, who brought from the dead that great Shepherd of the sheep, even our Lord Jesus, Make you perfect in every good thing to do His will, working in you that which is pleasing in His sight, through Jesus Christ." We have the name of our Lord Jesus twice. In the first case it refers to what God has done to Christ for us, raising Him; in the second, to what God is doing through Christ in us, working His pleasure in us. Because it is the same God continuing in us the work He began in Christ, it is in us just what it was in Christ. In Christ's death we see Him in utter impotence allowing and counting upon God to work all and give Him life. God wrought the wonderful transition. In us we see the same; it is only as we give ourself unto that death too, as we entirely cease from self and its works, as we lie, as in the grave, waiting for God to work all, that the God of resurrection life can work in us all His good pleasure.

It was "through the blood of the everlasting Covenant," with its atonement for sin, and its destruction of sin's power, that God effected that resurrection. It is through that same blood that we are redeemed and freed from the power of sin, and made partakers of Christ's resurrection life. The more we study the New Covenant, the more we shall see that its one aim is to restore man, out of the Fall, to the life in God for which he was created. It does this first, by delivering him from the power of sin in Christ's death, and then by taking possession of his heart, his life, for God to work all in him by the Holy Spirit. The whole argument of the Epistle to the Hebrews as to the Old and New Covenants is here summed up in these concluding verses. Just as He raised Christ from the dead, the God of the everlasting Covenant can and will now make you perfect in every good thing to do His will, working in you that which is well-pleasing in His sight through Jesus Christ. Your doing His will is the object of creation and redemption. God's working it all in you is what redemption has made possible. The Old Covenant of law and effort and failure has ended in condemnation and death. The New Covenant is coming to give, in all whom the law has slain and brought to bow in their utter impotence, the law written in the heart, the Spirit dwelling there, and God working all, both to will and to do, through Jesus Christ.

Oh for a Divine revelation that the transition from Christ's death, in its impotence, to His life in God's power, is the image, the pledge, the power of our transition out of the Old Covenant, when it has slain us, to the New, with God working in us all in all!

The transition from Old to New, as effected in Christ, was sudden. Is it so in the believer? Not always. In us it depends upon a revelation. There have been cases in which a believer, sighing and struggling against the yoke of bondage, has in one moment had it given to him to see what a complete salvation the New Covenant brings to the heart and the inner life, through the ministration of the Spirit, and by faith he has entered at once into his rest. There have been other cases in which, gradual as the dawn of day, the light of God has risen upon the heart. God's offer of entrance into the enjoyment of our New Covenant privileges is always urgent and immediate. Every believer is a child of the New Covenant, and heir of all its promises. The death of the Testator gives him full right to immediate possession. God longs to bring us into the land of promise; let us not come short through unbelief.

There may be someone who can hardly believe that such a mighty change in his life is within his reach, and yet who would fain know what he is to do if there is to be any hope of his attaining it. I have just said, the death of the testator gives the heir immediate right to the inheritance. And yet the heir, if he be a minor, does not enter on the possession. A term of years ends the stage of minority on earth, and he is no longer under guardians. In the spiritual life the state of pupilage ends, not with the expiry of years, but the moment the minor proves his fitness for being made free from the law, by accepting the liberty there is in Christ Jesus. The transition, as with the Old Testament, as with Christ, as with the disciples, comes when the time is fulfilled and all things are now ready.

But what is one to do who is longing to be thus made ready? Accept your death to sin in Christ, and act it out. Acknowledge the sentence of death on everything that is of nature: take and keep the place before God of utter unworthiness and helplessness; sink down before Him in humility, meekness, patience, and resignation to His will and mercy. Fix your heart upon the great and mighty God, who in His grace will work in you above what you can ask or think, and will make you a monument of His mercy. Believe that every blessing of the Covenant of grace is yours; by the death of the Testator you are entitled to it all—and on that faith act, knowing that all is yours. The new heart is yours, the law written in the heart is yours, the Holy Spirit, the seal of the Covenant, is yours. Act on thie faith, and count upon God as Faithful and Able, and oh! so Loving, to reveal in you, to make true in you, all the power and glory of His everlasting Covenant.

May God reveal to us the difference between the two lives under the Old and the New; the resurrection power of the New, with God working all in us; the power of the transition secured to us in death with Christ and life in Him. And may He teach us at once to trust Christ Jesus for a full participation in all the New Covenant secures.

The Blood of the Covenant

"Behold the blood of the covenant, which the Lord hath made with you."—*EX. xxiv. 8; HEB. ix. 20.*

"This cup is the new covenant in My blood."—*1 COR. xi. 25; MATT. xxvi. 28.*

"The blood of the covenant, wherewith he was sanctified."—*HEB. x. 29.*

"The blood of the everlasting covenant."—*HEB. xiii.21.*

The blood is one of the strangest, the deepest, the mightiest, and the most heavenly of the thoughts of God. It lies at the very root of both Covenants, but specially of the New Covenant. The difference between the two Covenants is the difference between the blood of beasts, and the blood of the Lamb of God! The power of the New Covenant has no lesser measure than the worth of the blood of the Son of God! Your Christian experience ought to know of no standard of peace with God, and purity from sin, and power over the world, than the blood of Christ can give! If we would enter truly and fully into all the New Covenant is meant to be to us, let us beseech God to reveal to us the worth and the power of the blood of the Covenant, the precious blood of Christ!

The First Covenant was not brought in without blood. There could be no Covenant of friendship between a holy God and sinful men without atonement and reconciliation; and no atonement without a death as the penalty of sin. God shake: "I have given you the blood upon the altar to make an atonement for your souls; for it is the blood that maketh an atonement for the soul." The blood shed in death meant the death of a sacrifice slain for sin of man; the blood sprinkled on the altar meant that vicarious death accepted of God for the sinful one. No forgiveness, no covenant without blood-shedding.

All this was but type and shadow of what was one day to become a mysterious reality. What no thought of man or angel could have conceived, what even now passeth all understanding, the Eternal Son of God took flesh and blood, and then shed that blood as the blood of the New Covenant, not merely to ratify it, but to open the way for it and to make it possible. Yea, more, to be, in time and eternity, the living power by which entrance into the Covenant was to be obtained, and all life in it be secured. Until we learn to form our expectation of a life in the New Covenant, according to the inconceivable worth and power of the blood of God's Son, we never can have even an insight into the entirely supernatural and heavenly life that a child of God may live. Let us think for a moment on the threefold light in which Scripture teaches us to regard it.

In the passage from Hebrews ix. we read "For this cause Christ is the Mediator of a new covenant, that a death having taken place for the redemption of the transgressions that were under the first covenant, they that have been called may receive the promise of the eternal inheritance." The sins of the ages, of the First Covenant, which had only figuratively been atoned for, had gathered up before God. A death was needed for the redemption of these: In that death and blood-shedding of the Lamb of God not only were these atoned for, but the power of all sin was for ever broken.

The blood of the New Covenant is redemption blood, a purchase price and ransom from the power of Sin and the Law. In any purchase made on earth the transference of property from the old owner to the new is complete. Its worth may be ever so great and the hold on it ever so strong, if the price be paid, it is gone for ever from him who owned it. The hold sin had on us was terrible. No thought can realise its legitimate claim on us under God's law, its awful tyrant power in enslaving us. But the blood of God's Son has been paid. "Ye were redeemed, not with corruptible things as silver and gold, from your vain manner of life handed down from your fathers, but with precious blood, as of a lamb without spot, even the blood of Christ." We have been rescued, ransomed, redeemed out of our old natural life under the power of sin, utterly and eternally. Sin has not the slightest claim on us, nor the slightest power over us, except as our ignorance or unbelief or half-heartedness allows it to have dominion. Our New Covenant birthright is to stand in the freedom with which Christ has made us free. Until the soul sees, and desires and accepts, and claims the redemption and the liberty which has the blood of the Son of God for its purchase price, and its measure, and its security, it never can fully live the New Covenant life.

As wonderful as the blood-shedding for our redemption is the blood-sprinkling for our cleansing. Here is indeed another of the spiritual mysteries of the New Covenant, which lose their power when understood in human wisdom, without the ministration of the Spirit of life. When Scripture speaks of "having our hearts sprinkled from an evil conscience," of "the blood of Christ cleansing our conscience," of our singing here on earth (Rev. i. 5), "To Him that washed us from our sins in His blood," it brings this mighty, quickening blood of the Lamb into direct contact with our hearts. It gives the assurance that that blood, in its infinite worth, in its Divine sin-cleansing power, can keep us clean in our walk in the sight and the light of God. It is as this blood of the New Covenant is known, and trusted, and waited for, and received from God, in the Spirit's mighty operation in the heart, that we shall begin to believe that the blessed promise of a New Covenant life and walk can be fulfilled.

There is one more thing Scripture teaches concerning this blood of the New Covenant. When the Jews contrasted Moses with our Lord Jesus, He spake: "Except ye eat the flesh of the Son of man, and drink His blood, ye have not life in yourselves. He that eateth My flesh, and drinketh My blood, abideth in Me, and I in him." As if the redeeming, and sprinkling, and washing, and sanctifying does not sufficiently express the intense inwardness of its action and its power to permeate our whole being, the drinking of this precious blood is declared to be indispensable to having life. If we would enter deep into the Spirit and power of the New Covenant, let us, by the Holy Spirit, drink deep of this cup—the cup of the New Covenant in His blood.

On account of sin there could be no covenant between man and God without blood. And no New Covenant without the blood of the Son of God. As the cleansing away of sins was the first condition in making a covenant, so it is equally the first condition of an entrance into it. It has ever been found that a deeper appropriation of the blessings of the Covenant must be preceded by a new and deeper cleansing from sin. We know how in Ezekiel the words about God's causing us to walk in His statutes are preceded by "From all your filthiness will I cleanse you." And then later we read (xxxvii. 23, 25), "Neither shall they defile themselves any more with any of their transgressions; I will cleanse them: so shall they be My people, and I will be their God. Moreover, I will make a Covenant of peace with them; it shall be an everlasting Covenant with them." The confession and casting away, and the cleansing away of sin in the blood, are the indispensable, but all-sufficient, preparation for a life in everlasting Covenant with God.

Many feel that they do not understand or realise this wonderful power of the blood. Much thought does not help them; even prayer does not appear to bring the light they seek. The blood of Christ is a Divine mystery that passes all thought. Like every spiritual and heavenly blessing, this too, but this especially, needs to be imparted to us by the Holy Spirit. It was "through the Eternal Spirit" that Christ offered the sacrifice in which the blood was shed. The blood had the life of Christ, the life of the Spirit, in it. The outpouring of the blood for us was to prepare the way for the outpouring of the Spirit on us. It is the Holy Spirit, and He alone, who can minister the blood of the everlasting Covenant in power. Just as He leads the soul to the initial faith in the pardon that blood has purchased, and the peace it gives, He leads further to the knowledge and experience of its cleansing power. Here again, too, by faith—a faith in a heavenly power, of which it does not fully understand, and cannot define, the action, but of which it knows that it is an operation of God's mighty power, and effects a cleansing that does give a clean heart. A clean heart, first known and accepted by the same faith, apart from signs or feelings, apart from sense or reason, and then experienced in the joy and the fellowship with God it brings. Oh! let us believe in the blood of the everlasting Covenant, and the cleansing the Holy Spirit ministers. Let us believe in the ministration of the Holy Spirit, until our whole life in the New Covenant becomes entirely His work, to the glory of the Father and of Christ.

The blood of the Covenant, O mystery of mysteries! O grace above all grace! O mighty power of God, opening the way, into the holiest, and into our hearts, and into the New Covenant, where the Holy One and our heart meet! Let us ask God much, by His Holy Spirit, to make us know what it is and works. The transition from the death of the Old Covenant to the life of the New was, in Christ, "through the blood of the Everlasting Covenant." No otherwise will it be with us.

Jesus, the Mediator of the New Covenant

"I give thee for a covenant of the people."—ISA. xlii. 6, xlix. 8.

"The Lord shall suddenly come to His temple, even the Messenger of the covenant, whom ye delight in."—MAL. iii. 1.

"Jesus was made Surety of a better covenant."—HEB. vii. 22.

"The Mediator of the Better Covenant, established upon better promises . . . The Mediator of the New Covenant. . . Ye are come to Jesus, the Mediator of the New Covenant."—HEB. viii. 6, ix. 15, xii. 24.

We have here four titles given to our Lord Jesus in connection with the New Covenant. He is Himself called a Covenant. The union between God and man, which the Covenant aims at, was wrought out in Him personally; in Him the reconciliation between the human and Divine was perfectly effected; in Him His people find the Covenant with all its blessings; He is all that God has to give, and is the assurance that it is given. . . He is called the Messenger of the Covenant, because He came to establish and to proclaim it. . . He is the Surety of the Covenant, not only because He paid our debt, but as He is Surety to us for God, that God will fulfil His part; and Surety for us with God, that we will fulfil our part. . . And He is Mediator of the Covenant, because as the Covenant was established in His atoning blood, is administered and applied by Him, is entered upon alone by faith in Him, so it is experimentally known only through the power of His resurrection life, and His never-ceasing intercession. All these names point to the one truth, that in the New Covenant Christ is all in all.

The subject is so large that it would be impossible to enter upon all the various aspects of this precious truth. Christ's work in atonement and intercession, in His bestowal of pardon and the Holy Spirit, in His daily communication of grace and strength, are truths which lie at the very foundation of the faith of Christians. We need not speak of them here. What specially needs to be made clear to many is how, by faith in Christ as the Mediator of the New Covenant, we actually have access to and enter into the enjoyment of all its promised blessings. We have already seen, in studying the New Covenant, how all these blessings culminate in the one thing—that the heart of man is to be put right, as the only possible way of his living in the favour of God, and God's love finding its satisfaction in him. That he is to receive a heart to fear God, to love God with all his strength, to obey God, and to keep all His statutes. All that Christ did and does has this for its aim; all the higher blessings of peace and fellowship flow from this. In this God's saving power and love find the highest proof of their triumph over sin. Nothing so reveals the grace of God, the power of Jesus Christ, the reality of salvation, the blessedness of the New Covenant, as the heart of a believer, where sin once abounded, with grace now abounding more exceedingly within it.

I do not know how I can better set forth the glory of our Blessed Lord Jesus as He accomplishes this, the real object of His redeeming work, and as He takes entire possession of the heart He has bought and won and cleansed as a dwelling for His Father, than by pointing out the place He takes, and the work He does, in the case of a soul who is being led out of the Old Covenant bondage with its failure, into the real experience of the promise and power of the New Covenant. In thus studying the work of the Mediator in an individual, we may get a truer conception of the real glory and greatness of the work He actually accomplishes, than when we only think of the work He has done for all. It is in the application of the redemption here in the life of earth, where sin abounded, that its power is seen. Let us see how the entrance into the New Covenant blessing is attained.

The first step towards it, in one who has been truly converted and assured of his acceptance with God, is the sense of sin. He sees that the New Covenant promises are not made true in his experience. There is not only indwelling sin, but he finds that he gives way to temper, and self-will, and worldliness, and other known transgressions of God's law. The obedience to which God calls and will fit him, the life of abiding in Christ's love which is his privilege, the power for a holy walk, well-pleasing to God,—in all this his conscience condemns him. It is in this conviction of sin that any thought or desire of the full New Covenant blessing must have its rise. Where the thought that obedience is an impossibility, and that nothing but a life of failure and self-condemnation is to be looked for, has wrought a secret despair of deliverance, or contentment with our present state, it is vain to speak of God's promise or power. The heart does not respond: it knows well enough, it is sure, the liberty spoken of is a dream. But where the dissatisfaction with our state has wrought a longing for something better, the heart is open to receive the message.

The New Covenant is meant to be the deliverance from the power of sin; a keen longing for this is the indispensable preparation for entering fully into the Covenant.

Now comes the second step. As the mind is directed to the literal meaning of the terms of the New Covenant, in its promises of cleansing from sin, and a heart filled with God's fear and God's law, and a power to keep God's commands and never to depart from Him; as the eye is fixed on Jesus the Surety of the Covenant, who will Himself make it all true; and as the voice is heard of witnesses who can declare how, after years of bondage, all this has been fulfilled in them—the longing begins to grow into a hope, and the inquiry is made, as to what is needed to enter this blessed life.

Then follows another step. The heart-searching question comes whether we are willing to give up every evil habit, all our own self-will, all that is of the spirit of the world, and surrender ourselves to be wholly and exclusively for Jesus. God cannot take so complete possession of a man, and bless him so wonderfully, and work in him so mightily, unless He has him very completely, yea, wholly for Himself. Happy the man who is ready for any sacrifice.

Now comes the last, the simplest, and yet often the most difficult step. And here it is we need to know Jesus as Mediator of the Covenant. As we hear of the life of holiness, and obedience, and victory over sin, which the Covenant promises, and hear that it will be to us according to our faith, so that if we claim it in faith it will surely be ours, the heart often fails for fear. I am willing, but have I the power to make, and what is more, to maintain this full surrender? Have I the power, the strong faith, so to grasp and hold this offered blessing, that it shall indeed be and continue mine? How such questions perplex the soul until it finds the answer to them in the one word: Jesus! It is He who will bestow the power to make the surrender and to believe. This is as surely and as exclusively His work, as atonement and intercession are His alone. As sure as it was His to win and ascend the throne, it is His to prove His dominion in the individual soul. It is He, the Living One, who is in Divine power to work and maintain the life of communion and victory within us. He is the Mediator and Surety of the Covenant—He, the God-man, who has undertaken not only for all that God requires, but for all that we need too.

When this is seen, the believer learns that here, just as at conversion, it is all of faith. The one thing needed now is, with the eye definitely fixed on some promise of the New Covenant, to turn from self and anything it could or need do, to let go self, and fall into the arms of Jesus. He is the Mediator of the New Covenant: it is His to lead us into it. In the assurance that Jesus, and every New Covenant blessing, is already ours in virtue of our being God's children; with the desire now to appropriate and enjoy what we have hitherto allowed to lie unused; in the faith that Jesus now gives us the needed strength in faith to claim and accept our heritage as a present possession; the will dares boldly to do the deed, and to take the heavenly gift—a life in Christ according to the better promises. By faith in Jesus you have seen and received Him as to you, in full truth, the Mediator of the New Covenant, both in heaven arid in your heart. He is the Mediator who makes it true between God and you, as your experience.

The fear has sometimes been expressed that, if we press so urgently the work that Christ through the Spirit does in the heart, we may be drawn off from trusting in what He has done and ever is doing, to what we are experiencing of its working. The answer is simple. It is with the heart alone that Christ can be truly known or honoured. It is in the heart the work of grace is to be done, and the saving power of Christ to be displayed. It is in the heart alone the Holy Spirit has His sphere of work; there He is to work Christ's likeness; it is there alone He can glorify Christ. The Spirit can only glorify Christ by revealing His saving power in us. If we were to speak of what we are to do in cleansing our heart and keeping it right, the fear would be well-grounded. But the New Covenant calls us to the very opposite. What it tells us of the Atonement, and the Righteousness of God it has won for us, will be our only glory even amid the highest holiness of heaven: Christ's work of holiness here in the heart can only deepen the consciousness of that Righteousness as our only plea. The sanctification of the Spirit, as the fulfilment of the New Covenant promises, is all a taking of the things of Christ and revealing and imparting them to us. The deeper our entrance into and our possession of the New Covenant gift of a new heart, the fuller will be our knowledge and our love of Him who is its Mediator; the more we shall glory in Him alone. The Covenant deals with the heart, just that Christ may be found there, may dwell there by faith. As we look at the heart, not in the light of feeling or experience, but in the light of the faith of God's Covenant, we shall learn to think and speak of it as God does, and begin to know what it is, that there Christ manifests Himself and there He and the Fatlier come to make their abode.

Jesus, the Surety of a Better Covenant

"And inasmuch as it is not without the taking of an oath: by so much also hath Jesus become the Surety of a better covenant. Wherefore also He is able to save completely them that draw near unto God through Him, seeing He ever liveth to make intercession for them."-HEB. vii. 20, 22, 25.

A surety is one who stands good for another, that a certain engagement will be faithfully performed. Jesus is the Surety of the New Covenant. He stands surety with us for God—, that God's part in the Covenant will faithfully be performed. And He stands surety with God for us, that our part will be faithfully performed too. If we are to live in covenant with God, everything depends upon our knowing aright what Jesus secures to us. The more we know and trust Him, the more assured will our faith be that its every promise and every demand will be fulfilled, that a life of faithful keeping of God's Covenant is indeed possible, because Jesus is the Surety of the Covenant. He makes God's faithfulness and ours equally sure.

We read that it was because His priesthood was confirmed by the oath of God, that He became the Surety of a so much better Covenant. The oath of God gives us the security that His suretyship will secure all the better promises. The meaning and infinite value of God's oath had been explained in the previous chapter. "In every dispute the oath is final for confirmation. Wherein God, being minded to show more abundantly unto the heirs of the promise the immutability of His counsel, interposed with an oath, that by two immutable things, in which it is impossible for God to lie, we may have a strong encouragement." We thus have not only a Covenant, with certain definite promises; we have not only Jesus, the Surety of the Covenant; but at the back of that again, we have the living God, with a view to our having perfect confidence in the unchangeableness of His counsel and promise, coming in between with an oath. Do we not begin to see that the one thing God aims at in this Covenant, and asks with regard to it, is an absolute confidence that He is going to do all He has promised, however difficult or wonderful it may appear? His oath is an end of all fear or doubt. Let no one think of understanding the Covenant, of judging or saying what may be expected from it, much less of experiencing its blessings, until he meets God with an Abrahamlike faith, that gives Him the glory, and is fully assured that what He has promised He is able to perform. The Covenant is a sealed mystery, except to the soul who is going without reserve to trust God, and abandon itself to His word and work.

Of the work of Christ, as the Surety of the better Covenant, our passage tells us that, because of this priesthood confirmed by oath, He is able to save completely those who draw near to God through Him. And this, because "He ever liveth to make intercession for them." As Surety of the Covenant, He is ceaselessly engaged in watching their needs, and presenting them to the Father, in receiving His answer, and imparting its blessing. It is because of this never-ceasing mediation, receiving and transmitting from God to us the gifts and powers of the heavenly world, that He is able to save completely—to work and maintain in us a salvation as complete as God is willing it should be, as complete as the Better Covenant has assured us it shall be, in the better promises upon which it was established. These promises are expounded (ch. viii. 7-13) as being none other than those of the New Covenant of Jeremiah, with the law written in the heart by the Spirit of God as our experience of the power of that salvation.

Jesus, the Surety of a better Covenant, Jesus is to be our assurance that everything connected with the Covenant is unchangeably and eternally sure. In Jesus the keynote is given of all our intercourse with God, of all our prayers and desires, of all our life and walk, that with full assurance of faith and hope we may look for every word of the Covenant to be made fully true to us by God's own power. Let us look at some of these things of which we are to be fully assured, if we are to breathe the spirit of children of the New Covenant. There is the love of God. The very thought of a Covenant is an alliance of friendship. And it is as a means of assuring us of His love, of drawing us close to His heart of love, of getting our hearts under the power of His love, and filled with it—it is because God loves us with an infinite love, and wants us to know it, and to give it complete liberty to bestow itself on us, and bless us, that the New Covenant has been made, and God's own Son been made its Surety. This love of God is an infinite Divine energy, doing its utmost to fill the soul with itself and its blessedness. Of this love God's Son is the Messenger; of the Covenant in which God reveals it to us He is the Surety; let us learn that the chief need in studying the Covenant and keeping it, in seeking and claiming its blessings, is the exercise of a strong and confident assurance in God's love.

Then there is the assurance of the sufficiency of Christ's finished redemption. All that was needed to put away sin, to free us entirely and for ever from its power, has been accomplished by Christ. His blood and death, His resurrection and ascension, have taken us out of the power of the world and transplanted us into a new life in the power of the heavenly world. All this is Divine reality; Christ is Surety that the Divine righteousness, and the Divine acceptance, that all-sufficient Divine grace and strength, are ever ours. He is Surety that all these can and will be communicated to us in unbroken continuance.

It is even so with the assurance of what is needed on our part to enter into this life in the New Covenant. We shrink back, either from the surrender of all, because we know not whether we have the power to let it go, or from the faith for all, because we fear ours will never be so strong or so bold as to take all that is offered us in this wonderful Covenant. Jesus is Surety of a better Covenant. The better consists just in this very thing, that it undertakes to provide the children of the Covenant with the very dispositions they need, to accept and enjoy it. We have seen how the heart is just the central object of the Covenant promise. A heart circumcised to love God with all the heart, a heart into which God's law and fear have been put, so that it will not depart from Him—it is of all this Jesus is the Surety under the oath of God. Let us say it once more: Surely the one thing God asks of us, and has given the Covenant and its Surety to secure—the confident trust that all will be done in us that is needed—is what we dare not withhold.

I think some of us are beginning to see what has been our great mistake. We have thought and spoken great things of what Christ did on the Cross, and does on the Throne, as Covenant Surety. And we have stopped there. But we have not expected Him to do great things in our hearts. And yet it is there, in our heart, that the consummation takes place of the work on the Cross and the Throne; in the heart the New Covenant has its full triumph; the Surety is to be known not by what the mind can think of Him in heaven, but by what he does to make Himself known in the heart. There is the place where His love triumphs and is enthroned. Let us with the heart believe and receive Him as the Covenant Surety. Let us, with every desire we entertain in connection with it, with every duty it calls us to, with every promise it holds out, look to Jesus, under God's oath the Surety of the Covenant. Let us believe that by the Holy Spirit the heart is His home and His throne. Let us, if we have not done it yet, in a definite act of faith, throw ourselves utterly on

Him, for the whole of the New Covenant life and walk. No surety was ever so faithful to his undertaking as Jesus will be to His on our behalf, in our hearts.

And now, notwithstanding the strong confidence and consolation the oath of God and the Surety of the Covenant gives, there are some still looking wistfully at this blessed life, and yet afraid to trust themselves to this wondrous grace. They have a conception of faith as something great and mighty, and they know and feel that theirs is not such. And so their feebleness remains an insuperable barrier to their inheriting the promise. Let me try and say once again: Brother, the act of faith, by which you accept and enter this life in the New Covenant, is not commonly an act of power, but often of weakness and fear and much trembling. And even in the midst of all this feebleness, it is not an act in your strength, but in a secret and perhaps unfelt strength, which Jesus the Surety of the Covenant gives you. God has made Him Surety, with the very object of inspiring us with courage and confidence. He longs, He delights to bring you into the Covenant. Why not bow before Him, and say meekly: He does hear prayer; He brings into the Covenant; He enables a soul to believe; I may trust Him confidently. And just begin quietly to believe that there is an Almighty Lord, given by the Father, to do everything needed to make all Covenant grace wholly true in you. Bow low, and look up out of your low estate to your glorified Lord, and maintain your confidence that a soul, that in its nothingness trusts in Him, will receive more than it can ask or think.

Dear believer, come and be a believer. Believe that God is showing you how entirely the Lord Jesus wants to have you and your life for Himself; how entirely He is willing to take charge of you and work all in you; how entirely you may even now commit your trust, and your surrender, and your faithfulness to the Covenant, with all you are and are to be, to Him, your Blessed Surety. If thou believest, thou shalt see the glory of God. What Christ has undertaken, you may confidently count upon His performing.

In a sense, and measure, and power that passeth knowledge, Jesus Christ is Himself all that God can either ask or give, all that God wants to see in us. "He that believeth in me, out of him shall flow rivers of living water."

The Book of the Covenant

"And Moses took the book of the covenant, and read in the audience of the people: and they said, All that the Lord hath said will we do and be obedient. And Moses took the blood, and sprinkled it on the people, and said, Behold the blood of the covenant, which the Lord hath made with you concerning all these words."-EX. xxiv. 7, 8; comp. HEB. ix. 18-20.

Here is a new aspect in which to regard God's blessed Book. Before Moses sprinkled the blood, he read the Book of the Covenant, and obtained the people's acceptance of it. And when he had sprinkled it, he said, "Behold the blood of the covenant, which the Lord hath made concerning all these words." The Book contained all the conditions of the Covenant; only through the Book could they know all that God asked of them, and all that they might ask of Him. Let us consider what new light may be thrown both upon the Covenant and upon the Book, by the one thought, that the Bible is the Book of the Covenant.

The very first thought suggested will be this, that in nothing will the spirit of our life and experience, as it lives either in the Old or the New Covenant, be more manifest than in our dealings with the Book. The Old had a book as well as the New. Our Bible contains both. The New was enfolded in the Old; the Old is unfolded in the New. It is possible to read the Old in the spirit of the New; it is possible to read the New as well as the Old in the spirit of the Old.

What this spirit of the Old is, we cannot see so clearly anywhere as just in Israel when the Covenant was made. They were at once ready to promise: "All that the Lord hath said will we do and be obedient." There was so little sense of their own sinfulness, or of the holiness and glory of God, that with perfect self-confidence they considered themselves able to undertake to keep the Covenant. They understood little of the meaning of that blood with which they were sprinkled, or of that death and redemption of which it was the symbol. In their own strength, in the power of the flesh, they were ready to engage to serve God. It is just the spirit in which many Christians regard the Bible; as a system of laws, a course of instruction to direct us in the way God would have us go. All He asks of us is, that we should do our utmost in seeking to fulfil them; more we cannot do; this we are sincerely ready to do. They know little or nothing of what the death means through which the Covenant is established, or what the life from the dead is through which alone a man can walk in covenant with the God of heaven.

This self-confident spirit in Israel is explained by what had happened just previously. When God had come down on Mount Sinai in thunderings and lightnings to give the law, they were greatly afraid. They said to Moses: "Let not God speak with us, lest we die; speak thou with us, and we will hear." They thought it was simply a matter of hearing and knowing; they could for certain obey. They knew not that it is only the presence, and the fear, and the nearness, and the power of God humbling us and making us afraid, that can conquer the power of sin and give the power to obey. It is so much easier to receive the instruction from man, and live, than to wait and hear the voice of God and die to all our own strength and goodness. It is no otherwise that many Christians seek to serve God without ever seeking to live in daily contact with Him, and without the faith that it is only His presence can keep from sin. Their religion is a matter of outward instruction from man: the waiting to hear God's voice that they may obey Him, the death to the flesh and the world that comes with a close walk with God, are unknown. They may be faithful and diligent in the study of their Bible, in reading or hearing Bible teaching; to have as much as possible of that intercourse with the Covenant God Himself which makes the Christian life possible—this they do not seek.

If you would be delivered from all this, learn ever to read the Book of the New Covenant in the New Covenant Spirit. One of the very first articles of the New Covenant has reference to this matter. When God says, I will put My law in their inward parts, and write it in their hearts, He engages that the words of His Holy Book shall no longer be mere outward teaching, but that what they command shall be our very disposition and delight, wrought in us as a birth and a life by the Holy Spirit. Every word of the New Covenant then becomes a Divine assurance of what may be obtained by the Holy Spirit's working. The soul learns to see that the letter killeth, that the flesh profiteth nothing. The study, and knowledge of, the delight in, Bible words and thoughts, cannot profit, except as the Holy Spirit is waited on to make them life. The acceptance of Holy Scripture in the letter, the reception of it in the human understanding, is seen to be as fruitless as was Israel's at Sinai. But as the Word of God, spoken by the Living God through the Spirit into the heart that waits on Him, it is found to be quick and powerful. It then is a word that worketh effectually in them that believe, giving within the heart the actual possession of the very grace of which the Word has spoken.

The New Covenant is a ministration of the Spirit (see Chap. VII). All its teaching is meant to be teaching by the Holy Spirit. The two most remarkable chapters in the Bible on the preaching of the gospel are those in which Paul expounds the secret of this teaching (1 Cor. ii.; 2 Cor. iii.). Every minister ought to see whether he can pass his examination in them. They tell us that in the New Covenant the Holy Spirit is everything. It is the Holy Spirit entering the heart, writing, revealing, impressing upon it God's law and truth, that alone works true obedience. No excellency of speech or human wisdom can in the least profit: God must reveal by His Holy Spirit to preacher and hearer the things He hath prepared for us. What is true of the preacher is equally true of the hearer. One of the great reasons that so many Christians never come out of the Old Covenant, never even know that they are in it, and have to come out of it, is that there is so much head knowledge, without the power of the Spirit in the heart being waited for. It is only when preachers and hearers and readers believe that the Book of the New Covenant needs the Spirit of the New Covenant, to explain and apply it, that the Word of God can do its work.

Learn the double lesson. What God hath joined together, let no man put asunder. The Bible is the Book of the New Covenant. And the Holy Spirit is the only minister of what belongs to the Covenant. Expect not to understand or profit by thy Bible knowledge without seeking continually the teaching of the Holy Spirit. Beware lest thy earnest Bible study, thy excellent books, or thy beloved teachers take the place of the Holy Spirit! Pray daily, and perseveringly, and believingly for His teaching. He will write the Word in thy heart.

The Bible is the Book of the New Covenant. Ask the Holy Spirit specially to reveal to thee the New Covenant in it. It is inconceivable what loss the Church of our day is suffering because so few believers truly live as its heirs, in the true knowledge and enjoyment of its promises. Ask God, in humble faith, to give thee in all thy Bible reading, the spirit of wisdom and revelation, enlightened eyes of thine heart, to know what the promises are which the Covenant reveals; and what the Divine security in Jesus, the Surety of the Covenant, that every promise will be fulfilled in thee in Divine power; and what the intimate fellowship to which it admits thee with the God of the Covenant. The ministration of the Spirit, humbly waited for and listened to, will make the Book of the Covenant shine with new light—even the light of God's countenance and a full salvation.

All this applies specially to the knowledge of what actually the New Covenant is meant to work. Amid all we hear, and read, and understand of the different promises of the New Covenant, it is quite possible that we never yet have had that heavenly vision of it as a whole, that with its overmastering power compels acceptance. Just hear once again what it really is. True obedience, and fellowship with God, for which man was created, which sin broke off, which the law demanded, but could not work, which God's own Son came from heaven to restore in our lives, is now brought within our reach and offered us. Our Father tells us in the Book of the New Covenant that He now expects us to live in full and unbroken obedience and communion with Him. He tells us that by the mighty power of His Son and Spirit He Himself will work this in us: everything has been arranged for it. He tells us that such a life of unbroken obedience is possible because Christ, as the Mediator, will live in us and enable us each moment to live in Him. He tells us that all He wants is simply the surrender of faith, the yielding ourselves to Him to do His work. Oh! let us look, and see this holy life, with all its powers and blessings, coming down from God in heaven, in the Son and His Spirit. Let us believe that the Holy Spirit can give us a vision of it, as a prepared Gift, to be bestowed in living power, and take possession of us. Let us look upward and look inward, in the faith of the Son and the Spirit, and God will show us that every word written in the Book of the Covenant is not only true, but that it can be made spirit and truth within us, and in our daily life. This can indeed be.

New Covenant Obedience

"Now therefore, if ye will obey My voice indeed, and keep My covenant, then ye shall be a holy nation unto Me."-EX. xix. 5.

"And the Lord Thy God will circumcise thine heart, and the heart of thy seed, to love the Lord thy God with all thy heart, and with all thy soul. And thou shalt obey the voice of the Lord, and do all His commandments."—DEUT.xxx. 6, 8.

"And I will put My Spirit within you, and cause you to walk in My statutes, and ye shall keep My judgments."—EZEK.xxxvi. 27.

In making the New Covenant, God said very definitely, "Not after the covenant I made with your fathers." We have learnt what the fault was with that Covenant: it made God's favour dependent upon the obedience of the people. "If ye obey, I will be your God." We have learnt how the New Covenant remedied the defect: God Himself provided for the obedience. It changes "If ye keep My judgments" into "I will put My Spirit within you, and ye shall keep." Instead of the Covenant and its fulfilment depending on man's obedience, God undertakes to ensure the obedience. The Old Covenant proved the need, and pointed out the path, of holiness: the New inspires the love, and gives the power, of holiness.

In connection with this change, a serious and most dangerous mistake is often made. Because in the New Covenant obedience no longer occupies the place it had in the Old, as the condition of the Covenant, and free grace has taken its place, justifying the ungodly, and bestowing gifts on the rebellious, many are under the impression that obedience is now no longer as indispensable as it was then. The error is a terrible one. The whole Old Covenant was meant to teach the lesson of the absolute and indispensable necessity of obedience for a life in God's favour. The New Covenant comes, not to provide a substitute for that obedience in faith, but through faith to secure the obedience, by giving a heart that delights in it and has the power for it. And men abuse the free grace, that without our own obedience accepts us for a life of new obedience, when they rest content with the grace, without the obedience it is meant for. They boast of the higher privileges of the New Covenant, while its chief blessing, the power of a holy life, a heart delighting in God's law, and a life in which God causes and enables us, by his indwelling Spirit, to keep His commandments, is neglected. If there is one thing we need to know well, it is the place obedience takes in the New Covenant.

Let our first thought be: Obedience is essential. At the very root of the relation of a creature to his God, and of God admitting the creature to His fellowship, lies the thought of obedience. It is the one only thing God spoke of in Paradise when "the Lord God commanded the man" not to eat of the forbidden fruit. In Christ's great salvation it is the power that redeemed us: "By the obedience of one shall many be made righteous." In the promise of the New Covenant it takes the first place. God engages to circumcise the hearts of His people—in the putting off of the body of the flesh, in the circumcision of Christ—to love God with all their heart, and to obey His commandments. The crowning gift of Christ's exaltation was the Holy Ghost, to bring salvation to us as an inward thing. The first Covenant demanded obedience, and failed because it could not find it. The New Covenant was expressly made to provide for obedience. To a life in the full experience of the New Covenant blessing, obedience is essential.

It is this indispensable necessity of obedience that explains why so often the entrance into the full enjoyment of the New Covenant has depended upon some single act of surrender. There was something in the life, some evil or doubtful habit, in regard to which conscience had often said that it was not in perfect accord with God's perfect will. Attempts were made to push aside the troublesome suggestion. Or unbelief said it would be impossible to overcome the habit, and maintain the promise of obedience to the Voice within. Meantime, all our prayer appeared of no avail. It was as if faith could not lay hold of the blessing which was full in sight, until at last the soul consented to regard this little thing as the test of its surrender to obey in everything, and of its faith that in everything the Surety of the Covenant would give power to maintain the obedience. With the evil or doubtful thing given up, with a good conscience restored, and the heart's confidence before God assured, the soul could receive and possess what it sought. Obedience is essential.

Obedience is possible. The thought of a demand which man cannot possibly render, cuts at the very root of true hope and strength. The secret thought, "No man can obey God," throws thousands back into the Old Covenant life, and into a false peace that God does not expect more than that we do our best. Obedience is possible: the whole New Covenant promises and secures this.

Only understand aright what obedience means. The renewed man has still the flesh, with its evil nature, out of which there arise involuntary evil thoughts and dispositions. These may be found in a truly obedient man. Obedience deals with the doing of what is known to be God's will, as taught by the Word, and the Holy Spirit, and conscience. When George Muller spoke of the great happiness he had had for more than sixty years in God's service, he attributed it two things—He had loved God's Word, and "he had maintained a good conscience, not wilfully going on in a course he knew to be contrary to the mind of God." When the full light of God broke in upon Gerhard Tersteegen, he wrote: "I promise, with Thy help and power, rather to give up the last drop of my blood, than knowingly and willingly in my heart or my life be untrue and disobedient to Thee." Such obedience is an attainable degree of grace.

Obedience is possible. When the law is written in the heart; when the heart is circumcised to love the Lord with all our heart, and to obey Him; when the love of God is shed abroad in the heart; it means that the love of God's law and of Himself has now become the moving power of our life. This love is no vague sentiment, in man's imagination of something that exists in heaven, but a living, mighty power of God in the heart, working effectually according to His working, which worketh in us mightily. A life of obedience is possible.

This obedience is of faith. "By faith, Abraham obeyed." By faith the promises of the Covenant, the presence of the Surety of the Covenant, the hidden inworking of the Holy Spirit, and the love of God in His infinite desire and power to make true in us all His love and promises, must live in us. Faith can bring them nigh, and make us live in the very midst of them. Christ and His wonderful redemption need not remain at a distance from us in heaven, but can become our continual experience. However cold or feeble we may feel, faith knows that the new heart is in us, that the love of God's law is our very nature, that the teaching and power of the Spirit are within us. Such faith knows it can obey. Let us hear the voice of our Saviour, the Surety of the Covenant, as He says, with a deeper, fuller meaning than when He was on earth: "Only believe. If thou canst believe, all things are possible to him that believeth."

And last of all, let us understand: Obedience is blessedness. Do not regard it only as the way to the joy and blessings of the New Covenant, but as itself, in its very nature, joy and happiness. To have the voice of God teaching and guiding you, to be united to God in willing what He wills, in working out what He works in you by His Spirit, in doing His Holy Will, and pleasing Him,—surely all this is joy unspeakable and full of glory.

To a healthy man it is a delight to walk or work, to put forth his strength and conquer difficulties. To a slave or a hireling it is bondage and weariness. The Old Covenant demanded obedience with an inexorable must, and the threat that followed it. The New Covenant changes the must to can and may. Do ask God, by the Holy Spirit, to show you how "you have been created in Christ Jesus unto good works, "and how, as fitted as a vine is for bearing grapes, your new nature is perfectly prepared for every good work. Ask Him to show you that He means obedience, not only to be a possible thing, but the most delightful and attractive gift He has to bestow, the entrance into His love and all its blessedness.

In the New Covenant the chief thing is not the wonderful treasure of strength and grace it contains, nor the Divine security that that treasure never can fail, but this, that the living God gives Himself, and makes Himself known, and takes possession of us as our God. For this man was created, for this He was redeemed again, for this, that it maybe our actual experience, the Holy Spirit has been given and is dwelling in us. Between what God has already wrougbt in us, and what He waits to work, obedience is the blessed link. Let us seek to walk before Him in the confidence that we are of those who live in the noble and holy consciousness: my one work is to obey God.In a volume just published, The School of Obedience, the thoughts of this chapter are more fully worked out. What can be the reason, I ask once again, that so many believers have seen so little of the beauty of this New Covenant life, with its power of holy and joyful obedience? "Their eyes were holden that they knew Him not." The Lord was with the disciples, but their hearts were blind. It is so still. It is as with Elisha's servant, all heaven is around him and he knows it not. Nothing will help but the prayer, "Lord, open his eyes, that he may see." Lord, is there not someone who may be reading this, who just needs one touch to see it all? Oh! give that touch!

Just listen, my brother. Thy Father loves thee with an infinite love, and longs to make thee, even to-day, His holy, happy, obedient child. Hear His message: He has for thee an entirely different life from what thou art living. A life in which His grace shall actually work in thee every moment all He asks thee to be. A life of simple childlike obedience, doing for the day just what the Father shows thee to be His will. A life in which the abiding love of thy Father, and the abiding presence of thy Saviour, and the joy of the Holy Spirit, can keep thee, and make thee glad and strong. This is His message.

This life is for thee. Fear not to accept this life, to give up thyself to it and its entire obedience. In Christ it is possible, it is sure.

Now, my brother, just turn heavenward and ask the Father, by the Holy Spirit, to show thee the beautiful heavenly life. Ask and expect it. Keep thine eyes fixed upon it. The great blessing of the New Covenant is obedience; the wonderful power to will and do as God wills. It is indeed the entrance to every other blessing. It is paradise restored and heaven opened—the creature honouring his Creator, the Creator delighting in His creature; the child glorifying the Father, the Father glorifying the child, as He changes him, from glory to glory, into the likeness of His Son.

The New Covenant: a Covenant of Grace

"Sin shall not have dominion over you: for ye are not under the law, but under grace."-ROM. vi. 14.

The words, Covenant of grace, though not found in Scripture, are the correct expression of the truth it abundantly teaches, that the contrast between the two covenants is none other than that of law and grace. Of the New Covenant, grace is the great characteristic: "The law came in, that the offence might abound; but where sin abounded, grace did abound more exceedingly." It is to bring the Romans away entirely from under the Old Covenant, and to teach them their place in the New, that Paul writes: "Ye are not under the law, but under grace." And he assures them that if they believe this, and live in it, their experience would confirm God's promise: "Sin shall not have dominion over you." What the law could not do—give deliverance from the power of sin over us—grace would effect. The New Covenant was entirely a Covenant of grace. In the wonderful grace of God it had its origin; it was meant to be a manifestation of the riches and the glory of that grace; of grace, and by grace working in us, all its promises can be fulfilled and experienced.

The word grace is used in two senses. It is first the gracious disposition in God which moves Him to love us freely without our merit, and to bestow all His blessings upon us. Then it also means that power through which this grace does its work in us. The redeeming work of Christ, and the righteousness He won for us; equally with the work of the Spirit in us, as the power of the new life, are spoken of as Grace. It includes all that Christ has done and still does, all He has and gives, all He is for us and in us. John says, "We beheld His glory, the glory of the Only Begotten of the Father, full of grace and truth." "The law was given by Moses grace and truth came by Jesus Christ." "And of His fulness have all we received, and grace for grace." What the law demands, grace supplies.

The contrast which John pointed out is expounded by Paul: "The law came in, that the offence might abound," and the way be prepared for the abounding of grace more exceedingly. The law points the way, but gives no strength to walk in it. The law demands, but makes no provision for its demands being met. The law burdens and condemns and slays. It can waken desire, but not satisfy it. It can rouse to effort, but not secure success. It can appeal to motives, but gives no inward power beyond what man himself has. And so, while warring against sin, it became its very ally in giving the sinner over to a hopeless condemnation. "The strength of sin is the law."

To deliver us from the bondage and the dominion of sin, grace came by Jesus Christ. Its work is twofold. Its exceeding abundance is seen in the free and full pardon there is of all transgression, in the bestowal of a perfect righteousness, and in the acceptance into God's favour and friendship. "In Him we have redemption through His blood, the forgiveness of sin according to the riches of His grace." It is not only at conversion and our admittance into God's favour, but throughout all our life, at each step of our way, and amid the highest attainments of the most advanced saint; we owe everything to grace, and grace alone. The thought of merit and work and worthiness is for ever excluded.

The exceeding abundance of grace is equally seen in the work which the Holy Spirit every moment maintains within us. We have found that the central blessing of the New Covenant, flowing from Christ's redemption and the pardon of our sins, is the new heart in which God's law and fear and love have been put. It is in the fulfilment of this promise, in the maintenance of the heart in a state of meetness for God's indwelling, that the glory of grace is specially seen. In the very nature of things this must be so. Paul writes: "Where sin abounded, grace did more exceedingly abound." And where, as far as I was concerned, did sin abound? All the sin in earth and hell could not harm me, were it not for its presence in my heart. It is there it has exercised its terrible dominion. And it is there the exceeding abundance of grace must be proved, if it is to benefit me. All grace in earth and heaven could not help me; it is only in the heart it can be received, and known, and enjoyed. "Where sin abounded," in the heart, there "grace did more exceedingly abound; that as sin reigned in death," working its destruction in the heart and life, "even so might grace reign," in the heart too, "through righteousness into eternal life, through Jesus Christ our Lord." As had been said just before, "They that receive the abundance of grace shall reign in life through Jesus Christ."

Of this reign of grace in the heart Scripture speaks wondrous things. Paul speaks of the grace that fitted him for his work, of "the gift of that grace of God which was given me according to the working of His power." "The grace of our Lord was exceeding abundant, with faith and love." "The grace which was bestowed upon me was not found vain, but I laboured more abundantly than they all; yet not I, but the grace of God which was with me." "He said unto me, My grace is sufficient for thee; My strength is made perfect in weakness." He speaks in the same way of grace as working in the life of believers, when he exhorts them to "be strong in the grace that is in Christ Jesus"; when he tells us of "the grace of God" exhibited in the liberality of the Macedonian Christians, and "the exceeding grace of God" in the Corinthians; when he encourages them: "God is able to make all grace abound in you, that ye may abound unto every good work." Grace is not only the power that moves the heart of God in its compassion towards us, when He acquits and accepts the sinner and makes him a child, but is equally the power that moves the heart of the saint, and provides it each moment with just the disposition and the power which it needs to love God and do His will.

It is impossible to speak too strongly of the need there is to know that, as wonderful and free and alone sufficient as is the grace that pardons, is the grace that sanctifies; we are just as absolutely dependent upon the latter as the former. We can do as little to the one as the other. The grace that works in us must as exclusively do all in us and through us as the grace that pardons does all for us. In the one case as the other, everything is by faith alone. Not to apprehend this brings a double danger. On the one hand, people think that grace cannot be more exalted than in the bestowal of pardon on the vile and unworthy; and a secret feeling arises that, if God be so magnified by our sins more than anything else, we must not expect to be freed from them in this life. With many this cuts at the root of the life of true holiness. On the other hand, from not knowing that grace is always and alone to do all the work in our sanctification and fruit-bearing, men are thrown upon their own efforts, their life remains one of feebleness and bondage under the law, and they never yield themselves to let grace do all it would.

Let us listen to what God's Word says: "By grace have ye been saved, through faith; not of works, lest any man should glory. For we are His workmanship, created in Christ Jesus for good works, which God afore prepared that we should walk in them." Grace stands in contrast to good works of our own not only before conversion, but after conversion too. We are created in Christ Jesus for good works, which God had prepared for us. It is grace alone can work them in us and work them out through us. Not only the commencement but the continuance of the Christian life is the work of grace. "Now if it is by grace it is no more of works, otherwise grace is no more grace; therefore it is of faith that it may be according to grace." As we see that grace is literally and absolutely to do all in us, so that all our actings are the showing forth of grace in us, we shall consent to live the life of faith—a life in which, every moment, everything is expected from God. It is only then that we shall experience that sin shall not, never, not for a moment, have dominion over us.

"Ye are not under the law, but under grace." There are three possible lives. One entirely under the law; one entirely under grace; one a mixed life, partly law, partly grace. It is this last against which Paul warns the Romans. It is this which is so common, and works such ruin among Christians. Let us find out whether this is not our position, and the cause of our low state. Let us beseech God to open our eyes by the Holy Spirit to see that in the New Covenant everything, every movement, every moment of our Christian life, is of grace, abounding grace; grace abounding exceedingly, and working mightily. Let us believe that our Covenant God waits to cause all grace to abound toward us. And let us begin to live the life of faith that depends upon, and trusts in, and looks to, and ever waits for God, through Jesus Christ, by the Holy Spirit, to work in us that which is pleasing in His sight.

Grace unto you, and peace be multiplied!

The Covenant of an Everlasting Priesthood

"That My covenant might be with Levi. My covenant was with him of life and peace; and I gave them to him for the fear wherewith he feared Me, and was afraid before My name. The law of truth was in his mouth, and iniquity was not found in his lips; he walked with Me in peace and equity, and did turn many away from iniquity."—MAL. ii. 4-6.

Israel was meant by God to be a nation of priests. In the first making of the Covenant this was distinctly stipulated. "If ye will obey My voice, and keep My covenant, ye shall be unto Me a kingdom of priests." They were to be the stewards of the oracles of God; the channels through whom God's knowledge and blessing were to be communicated to the world; in them all nations were to be blessed.

Within the people of Israel one tribe was specially set apart to embody and emphasise the priestly idea. The first-born sons of the whole people were to have been the priests. But to secure a more complete separation from the rest of the people, and the entire giving up of any share in their possessions and pursuits, God chose one tribe to be exclusively devoted to the work of proving what constitutes the spirit and the power of priesthood. Just as the priesthood of the whole people was part of God's Covenant with them, so the special calling of Levi is spoken of as God's Covenant of Life and Peace being with Him, as the Covenant of an everlasting priesthood. All this was to be a picture to help them and us, in some measure, to apprehend the priesthood of His own Blessed Son, the Mediator of the New Covenant.

Like Israel, all God's people, under the New Covenant, are a royal priesthood. The right of free and full access to God, the duty and power of mediating for our fellowmen and being God's channel of blessing to them, is the inalienable birthright of every believer. Owing to the feebleness and incapacity of many of God's children, their ignorance of the mighty grace of the New Covenant, they are utterly impotent to take up and exercise their priestly functions. To make up for this lack of service, to show forth the exceeding riches of His grace in the New Covenant, and the power He gives men of becoming, just as the priests of old were the forerunners of the Great High Priest, His followers and representatives, God still allows and invites those of His redeemed ones who are willing, to offer their lives to this blessed ministry. To him who accepts the call, the New Covenant brings in special measure what God has said: "My Covenant of Life and Peace shall be with him"; it becomes to him in very deed "the Covenant of an everlasting priesthood." As the Covenant of Levi's priesthood issued and culminated in Christ's, ours issues from that again, and receives from it its blessing to dispense to the world.

To those who desire to know the conditions on which, as part of the New Covenant, the Covenant of an everlasting priesthood can be received and carried out, a study of the conditions on which Levi received the priesthood will be most instructive. We are not only told that God chose that tribe, but what there specially was in that tribe that fitted it for the work. Malachi says: "I gave him My covenant for the fear wherewith he feared Me, and was afraid before My name." The reference is to what took place at Sinai when Israel had made the molten calf. Moses called all who were on the Lord's side, who were ready to avenge the dishonour done to God, to come to him. The tribe of Levi did so, and at his bidding took their swords, and slew three thousand of the idolatrous people (Ex. xxxii. 26-29). In the blessing with which Moses blessed the tribes before his death, their absolute devotion to God, without considering relative or friend, is mentioned as the proof of their fitness for God's service (Deut. xxxiii. 5-11): "Let Thy Thummim and Thy Urim be with Thy holy one, who said unto his father and to his mother, I have not known thee; neither did he acknowledge his own brethren, nor know his own children: for they have observed Thy word and kept Thy covenant."

The same principle is strikingly illustrated in the story of Aaron's grandson, Phineas, where he, in his zeal for God, executed judgment on disobedience to God's command. The words are most suggestive. "And the Lord apake unto Moses, saying, Phineas, the son of Eleazar, the son of Aaron, hath turned away My wrath from the children of Israel, in that he was jealous with My jealousy among them, so that I consumed them not in My jealousy. Wherefore say, Behold, I give unto him My covenant of peace: and it shall be unto him, and his seed after him, the covenant of an everlasting priesthood; because he was jealous for his God, and made an atonement for the children of Israel" (Num. xxv. 10-13). To be jealous with God's jealousy, to be jealous for God's honour, and rise up against sin, is the gate into the Covenant of an everlasting priesthood, is the secret of being entrusted by God with the sacred work of teaching His people, and burning incense before Him, and turning many from iniquity (Deut. xxxiii. 10; Mal. ii. 6).

Even the New Covenant is in danger of being abused by the seeking of our own happiness or holiness, more than the honour of God or the deliverance of men. Even where these are not entirely neglected, they do not always take the place they are meant to have—that first place that makes everything, the dearest and best, secondary and subordinate to the work of helping and blessing men. A reckless disregard of everything that would interfere with God's will and commands, a being jealous with God's jealousy against sin, a witnessing and a fighting against it at any sacrifice —this is the school of training for the priestly office.

It is this the world needs nowadays—men of God in whom the fire of God burns, men who can stand and speak and act in power on behalf of a God who, amid His own people, is dishonoured by the worship of the golden calf. Understand that as you will, of the place given to money and rich men in the church, of the prevalence of worldliness and luxury, or of the more subtle danger of a worship meant for the true God, under forms taken from the Egyptians, and suited to the wisdom and the carnal life of this world. A religion God cannot approve is often found even where the people still profess to be in covenant with God. "Consecrate yourselves to-day unto the Lord, even every man upon his brother." This call of Moses is as much needed to-day as ever. To each one who responds there is the reward of the priesthood.

Let all who would know to the full what the New Covenant means, remember God's Covenant of Life and Peace with Levi. Accept of the holy calling to be an intercessor, and to burn incense before the Lord continually. Love, work, pray, believe, as one whom God has sought and found to stand in the gap before Him. The New Covenant was dedicated by a sacrifice and a death: reckon it your most wonderful privilege, your fullest entrance into its life, as you reflect the glory of the Lord, and are changed into the same image from glory to glory, as by the Spirit of the Lord, to let the Spirit of that sacrifice and death be the moving power in all your priestly functions. Sacrifice yourself, live and die for your fellowmen.

One of the great objects with which God has made a Covenant with us, is, as we have said so often, to waken strong confidence in Himself and His faithfulness to His promise. And one of the objects that He has in wakening and so strengthening the faith in us, is that He may use us as His channels of blessing to the world. In the work of saving men, He wants intercessory prayer to take the first place. He would have us come to Him to receive, from Him in heaven, the spiritual life and power which can pass out from us to them. He knows how difficult and hopeless it is in many cases to deal with sinners; He knows that it is no light thing for us to believe that in answer to our prayer the mighty power of God will move to save those around us; He knows that it needs strong faith to persevere patiently in prayer in cases in which the answer is long delayed, and every year appears farther off than ever. And so He undertakes, in our own experience, to prove what faith in His Divine power can do, in bringing down all the blessings of the New Covenant on ourselves, that we may be able to expect confidently what we ask for others.

In our priestly life there is still another aspect. The priests had no inheritance with their brethren; the Lord God was their inheritance. They had access to His dwelling and His presence, that there they might intercede for others, and thence testify of what God is and wills. Their personal privilege and experience fitted them for their work. If we would intercede in power, do let us live in the full realisation of New Covenant life. It gives us not only liberty and confidence with God, and power to persevere; it gives us power with men, as we can testify to and prove what God has done to us. Herein is the full glory of the New Covenant, that, like Christ, its Mediator, we have the fire of the Divine love dwelling in us, and consuming us in the service of men. May to each of us the chief glory of the New Covenant be that it is the Covenant of an everlasting priesthood.

The Ministry of the New Covenant

"Ye are our epistle, written in our hearts, known and read of all men; being made manifest that ye are an epistle of Christ, ministered by us, written not with ink, but with the Spirit of the living God: not in tables of stone, but in tables that are hearts of flesh. And such confidence have we through Christ Godward: not that we are sufficient of ourselves, to account anything as from ourselves; but our sufficiency is from God: who also made us sufficient as ministers of a new covenant; not of the letter, but of the Spirit; for the letter killeth, but the Spirit giveth fife."—2 COR. iii. 2-6.

We have seen that the New Covenant is a ministration of the Spirit. The Holy Spirit ministers all its grace and blessing in Divine power and life. He does this through men, who are called ministers of a New Covenant, ministers of the Spirit. The Divine ministration of the Covenant to men, and the earthly ministry of God's servants, are equally to be in the power of the Holy Spirit. The ministry of the New Covenant has its glory and its fruit in this, that it is all to be a demonstration of the Spirit and of power.

What a contrast this to the Old Covenant. Moses had indeed received of the glory of God shining upon him, but had to put a veil on his face. Israel was incapable of looking on it. In hearing and reading Moses, there was a veil on their hearts. From Moses they might receive knowledge and thoughts and desires,—the power of God's Spirit, to enable them to see the glory of what God speaks, was not yet given. This is the exceeding glory of the New Covenant, that it is a ministration of the Spirit; that its ministers have their sufficiency from God, who makes them ministers of the Spirit, and makes them able so to speak the words of God in the Spirit, that they are written in the heart, and that the hearers become legible, living epistles of Christ, showing the law written in their heart and life.

The ministry of the Spirit! What a glory there is in it! What a responsibility it brings! What a sufficiency of grace there is provided for it! What a privilege, to be a minister of the Spirit!

What tens of thousands we have throughout Christendom who are called ministers of the gospel. What an inconceivable influence they exert for life or for death over the millions who depend upon them for their knowledge and participation of the Christian life. What a power there would be if all these were ministers of the Spirit! Let us study the word, until we see what God meant the ministry to be, and learn to take our part in praying and labouring to have it nothing less.

God hath made us ministers of the Spirit. The first thought is that a minister of the New Covenant must be a man personally possessed of the Holy Spirit. There is a twofold work of the Spirit: one in giving a holy disposition and character, the other in qualifying and empowering a man for work. The former must always come first. The promise of Christ to His disciples, that they should receive the Holy Spirit for their service, was very definitely given to those who had followed and loved Him, and kept His commandments. It is by no means enough that a man have been born of the Spirit. If he is to be a "sufficient minister" of the New Covenant, he must know what it is to be led by the Spirit, to walk in the Spirit, and to say, "The law of the Spirit of life in Christ Jesus hath made me free from the law of sin and death." Who that wants to learn Greek or Hebrew would accept a professor who hardly knows the elements of these languages? And how can a man be a minister of the New Covenant, which is so entirely "a ministration of the Spirit," a ministration of heavenly life and power, unless he knows by experience what it is to live in the Spirit? The minister must, before everything, be a personal proof and witness of the truth and power of God in the fulfilment of what the New Covenant promises. Ministers are to be picked men; the best specimens and examples of what the Holy Spirit can do to sanctify a man, and by the working of God's power in him to fit him for His service.

God hath made us ministers of the Spirit. Next to this thought, of being personally possessed by the Spirit, comes the truth that all their work in the ministry can be done in the power of the Spirit. What an unspeakably precious assurance—Christ sends them to do a heavenly work, to do His work, to be the instruments in His hands, by which He works: He clothes them with a heavenly power. Their calling is "to preach the gospel with the Holy Ghost sent down from heaven." As far as feelings are concerned, they may have to say as Paul: "I was with you in weakness, and in fear, and in much trembling." That does not prevent their adding, nay rather, that may just be the secret of their being able to add: "My preaching was in demonstration of the Spirit and of power." If a man is to be a minister of the

New Covenant, a messenger and a teacher of its true blessing, so as to lead God's children to live in it, nothing less will do than a full experience of its power in himself, as the Spirit ministers it. Whether in his feeding on God's word himself, or his seeking in it for God's message for his people, whether in secret or intercessory prayer, whether in private intercourse with souls or public teaching, he is to wait upon, to receive, to yield to the energising of the Holy Spirit, as the mighty power of God working with him. This is his sufficiency for the work. He may every day afresh claim and receive the anointing with fresh oil, the new inbreathing from Christ of His own Spirit and life.

God hath made us ministers of the Spirit. There is something still, of no less importance. The Minister of the Spirit must especially see to it that he lead men to the Holy Spirit. Many will say, If he be led of the Spirit in teaching men, is not that enough? By no means. Men may become too dependent on him; men may take his Scripture teaching at second-hand, and, while there is power and blessing in his ministry, have reason to wonder that the results are not more definitely spiritual and permanent. The reason is simple. The New Covenant is: they shall no longer every man teach his brother, know the Lord, for all shall know Me, from the least even to the greatest. The Father wants every child, from the least, to live in continual personal intercourse with Himself. This cannot be, except as he is taught and helped to know and wait on the Holy Spirit. Bible study and prayer, faith and love and obedience, the whole daily walk must be taught as entirely dependent on the teaching and working of the indwelling Spirit.

The minister of the Spirit, very definitely and perseveringly, points away from himself to the Spirit. This is what John the Baptist did. He was filled with the Holy Spirit from his birth, but sent men away from himself to Christ, to be by Him baptized with the Spirit. Christ did the same. In His farewell discourse He called His disciples to turn from His personal instruction to the inward teaching of the Holy Spirit, who should dwell in them, and guide them into the truth and power of all He had taught them.

There is nothing so needed in the Church to-day. All its feebleness and formalities and worldliness, the lack of holiness, of personal devotion to Christ, of enthusiasm for His cause and kingdom, is owing to one thing—the Holy Spirit is not known and honoured and yielded to, as the one only, as the one all-sufficient source of a holy life. The New Covenant is not known as a ministration of the Spirit in the heart of every believer. The one thing needful for the Church is—the Holy Spirit in His power dwelling and ruling in the lives of God's saints. And as one of the chief means to this there are needed ministers of the Spirit, themselves living in the enjoyment and power of this great gift, who persistently labour to bring their brethren into the possession of their birthright: the Holy Spirit in the heart, maintaining, in Divine power, an unceasing communion with the Son and with the Father. The ministration of the Spirit makes the ministry of the Spirit possible and effectual. And the ministry of the Spirit again makes the ministration of the Spirit an actual experimental reality in the life of the Church.

We know how dependent the Church is on its ministry. The converse is no less true. The ministers are dependent on the Church. They are its children; they breathe its atmosphere; they share its health or sickliness; they are dependent upon its fellowship and intercession. Let none of us think that all that the New Covenant calls us to is to see that we personally accept and rejoice in its blessings. No, indeed; God wants everyone who enters into it to know that its privileges are for all His children, and to give himself to make this known. And there is no more effectual way of doing this than taking thought for the ministry of the Church. Compare the ministry around you with its pattern in God's word (see specially 1 Cor. ii.; 2 Cor. iii.). Join with others who know how the New Covenant is nothing, if it be not a ministration of the Spirit, and cry to God for a spiritual ministry. Ask the leading of God the Holy Ghost to teach you what can be done, what you can do, to have the ministry of your Church become a truly spiritual one. Human condemnation will do as little good as human approbation. It is as the supreme place of the Holy Spirit, as the representative and revealer of the Father and the Son, is made clear to us, that the one desire of our heart, and our continual prayer, will be, that God would so discover to all the ministers of His word their heavenly calling, that they may, above everything, seek this one thing,—to be sufficient ministers of the New Covenant, not of the letter, but of the Spirit.

His Holy Covenant

"To remember His Holy Covenant; to grant unto us that we, being delivered out of the hands of our enemies, should serve Him without fear, in holiness and righteousness before Him, all our days."-LUKE i. 68-75.

When Zacharias was filled with the Holy Spirit and prophesied, he spoke of God's visiting and redeeming His people, as a remembering of His Holy Covenant. He speaks of what the blessings of that Covenant would be, not in words that had been used before, but in what is manifestly a Divine revelation to him by the Holy Spirit; and gathers up all the former promises in these words: "That we should serve Him without fear, in holiness and righteousness before Him all the days of our life." Holiness in life and service is to be the great gift of the Covenant of God's Holiness. As we have seen before, the Old Covenant proclaimed and demanded holiness; the New provides it; holiness of heart and life is its great blessing.

There is no attribute of God so difficult to define, so peculiarly a matter of Divine revelation, so mysterious, incomprehensible, and inconceivably glorious, as His Holiness. It is that by which He is specially worshipped in His majesty on the throne of heaven (Isa. vi. 2; Rev. iv. 8, xv. 4). It unites His righteousness, that judges and condemns, with His love, that saves and blesses. As the Holy One He is a consuming fire (Isa. x. 17); as the Holy One He loves to dwell among His people (Isa. xii. 6). As the Holy One He is at an infinite distance from us; as the Holy One He comes inconceivably near, and makes us one with, makes us like Himself. The one purpose of His holy Covenant is to make us holy as He is holy.

As the Holy One He says: "I am holy; be ye holy; I am the Lord which hallow you, which make you holy." The highest conceivable summit of blessedness is our being partakers of the Divine nature, of the Divine holiness.

This is the great blessing Christ, the Mediator of the New Covenant, brings. He has been made unto us "both righteousness and sanctification"—righteousness in order to, as a preparation for, sanctification or holiness. He prayed to the Father: "Sanctify them; for their sakes I sanctify Myself, that they themselves may also be sanctified in truth." In Him we are sanctified, saints, holy ones (Rom. i. 7; 1 Cor. i. 2). We have put on the new man which after God is created in righteousness and holiness. Holiness is our very nature.

We are holy in Christ. As we believe it, as we receive it, as we yield ourselves to the truth, and draw nigh to God to have the holiness drawn forth and revealed in fellowship with Him, its fountain, we shall know how divinely true it is.

It is for this the Holy Spirit has been given in our hearts. He is the "Spirit of Holiness." His every working is in the power of holiness. Paul says : "God hath chosen us unto salvation, in sanctification of the Spirit and belief of the truth." As simple and entire as is our dependence on the word of truth, as the external means, must our confidence be in the hidden power for holiness which the working of the Spirit brings. The connection between God's electing purpose, and the work of the Spirit, with the word we obey, comes out with equal clearness in Peter: "Elect, in sanctification of the Spirit, unto obedience." The Holy Spirit is the Spirit of the life of Christ; as we know, and honour, and trust Him, we shall learn and also experience that, in the New Covenant, as the ministration of the Spirit, the sanctification, the holiness of the Holy Spirit is our covenant right. We shall be assured that, as God has promised, so He will work it in us, that we "should serve Him without fear, in righteousness and holiness before Him, all the days of our life." With a treasure of holiness in Christ, and the very Spirit of holiness in our hearts, we can live holy lives. That is, if we believe Him "who worketh in us both to will and to work."

In the light of this Covenant promise, with the Blessed Son and the Holy Spirit to work it out in us, what new meaning is given to the teaching of the New Testament. Take the first epistle St. Paul ever wrote. It was directed to men who had only a few months previously been turned from idols to serve the Living God, and to wait for His Son from heaven. The words he speaks in regard to the holiness they might aim at and expect, because God was going to work it in them, are so grand that many Christians pass them by, as practically unintelligible (1 Thess. iii. 13): "The Lord make you to increase and abound in love, to the end He may stablish your hearts unblamable in holiness at the coming of our Lord Jesus with all His saints." That promises holiness, unblamable holiness, a heart unblamable in holiness, a heart stablished in all this by God Himself. Paul might indeed say of a word like this: "Who hath believed our report?" He had written of himself (ii. 10) : "Ye know how holily and righteously and unblamably we behaved ourselves." He assures them that what God has done for him He will do for them—give them hearts unblameable in holiness. The Church believes so little in the mighty power of God, and the truth of His Holy Covenant, that the grace of such heart-holiness is hardly spoken of. The verse is often quoted in connection with "the coming of our Lord Jesus with His saints"; but its real point and glory,—that when He comes we may meet Him with hearts stablished unblamable in holiness by God Himself: all too little this is understood or proclaimed or expected.

Or take another verse in the Epistle (v. 21), also spoken to these young converts from heathenism, in reference to the coming of our Lord. Some think that to speak much of the coming of the Lord will make us holy. Alas! how little it has done so in many .cases. It is the New Covenant Holiness, wrought by God Himself in us, believed in and waited for from Him, that can make our waiting differ from the carnal expectations of the Jews or the disciples. Listen-"*the god of peace himself* "—that is the keynote of the New Covenant—what you never can do God will work in you—"*sanctify you wholly*"; this you may ask and expect,—"and may your spirit and soul and body be preserved entire, *unblamable*, at the coming of our Lord Jesus Christ." And now, as if to meet the doubt that will arise: "Faithful is He that calleth You, *Who will also do it*." Again it is the secret of the New Covenant—what hath not entered into the heart of man,—*God will work* in them that wait for Him. Until the Church.awakes to see and believe that our holiness is to be the immediate almighty working of the Three-One God in us, and that our whole religion must be an unceasing dependence to receive it direct from Himself, these promises remain a sealed book.

Let us now return to the prophecy of the Holy Spirit by Zacharias, of God's remembering the Covenant of His Holiness, to make us holy, to stablish our hearts unblamable in holiness, that we should serve Him *in holiness and righteousness*. Note how every word is significant.

To grant us. It is to be a gift from above. The promise given with the Covenant was: "I the Lord have spoken it; I will perform it." We need to beseech God to show us both what He will do, and that He will do it. When our faith expects all from Him, the blessing will be found.

"That we, being delivered out of the hands of our enemaes." He had just before said: He hath raised up an horn of salvation for us; salvation from our enemies and the hand of all that hate us. It is only a free people can serve a Holy God, or be holy. It is only as the teaching of Rom. vi.-viii. is experienced, and I know what it is that we are "freed from sin," and "freed from the law," and that "the Spirit of life in Christ Jesus hath made me free from the law of sin and death," that in the perfect liberty from every power that could hinder, I can expect God to do His mighty work in me.

Should serve Him. My servant does not serve me by spending all his time in getting himself ready for work, but in doing my work. The Holy Covenant sets us free, and endows us with Divine grace, that God may have us for His work,—the same work Christ began, and we now carry on.

Without fear. In childlike confidence and boldness before God. And before men too. A freedom from fear in every difficulty, because having learnt to know that God works all in us we can trust Him to work all for us and through us.

Before Him. With His continued unceasing presence all the day, as the unceasing security of our obedience and our fearlessness, the neverfailing secret of our being sanctified wholly.

All our days. Not only all the day for one day, but for every day, because Jesus is a High Priest in the power of an endless life, and the mighty operation of God as promised in the Covenant is as unchanging as is God Himself. Is it not as if you begin to see that God's word does appear to mean more than you have ever conceived of or expected? It is well that it should be so. It is only when you begin to say, Glory to Him who is able to do exceeding abundantly above all we can ask or think, and expect God's almighty, supernatural, altogether immeasurable power and grace to work out the New Covenant life in you, and to make you holy, that you will really come to the place of helplessness and dependence where God can work.

I pray you, my Brother, do believe that God's word is true, and say with Zacharias, "Blessed be the Lord, the God of Israel, who bath visited His people, to remember *His holy covenant*, and to grant us, that we, being delivered from the hand of our enemies, should serve Him without fear, in holiness rind righteousness before Him, all our days."

Entering the Covenant: with all the Heart

"And they entered into the covenant to seek the Lord God of their fathers with all their heart, and all their soul."—2 CHRON. *xv. 12 (see xxxiv. 31, and 2 Kings xxiii. 3).*

"The Lord thy God will circumcise thine heart, to love the Lord thy God with all thine heart, and with all thy soul."—DEUT. *xxx. 6.*

"And I will give them an heart to know Me, that I am the Lord; and they shall be My people, and I will be their God: for they shall turn to Me with their whole heart."—JER. *xxiv. 7 (see xxix. 13).*

"I will make an everlasting covenant with them, that I will not turn away from them, to do them good; but I will put My fear in their hearts, that they shall not depart from Me. Yea, I will rejoice over them to do them good, with My whole heart and My whole soul."—JER. *xxxii. 40.*

In the days of Asa, Hezekiah, and Josiah, we read of Israel entering into "the Covenant" with their whole heart, "to perform the words of the Covenant which are written in the book." Of Asa's day, we read: "They sware unto the Lord; and all Judah rejoiced at the oath, for they had sworn with their whole heart, and sought Him with their whole desire; and He was found of them." Wholeheartedness is the secret of entering the Covenant, and God being found of us in it. Wholeheartedness is the secret of joy in religion—a full entrance into all the blessedness the Covenant brings. God rejoices over His people to do them good, with His whole heart and His whole soul: it needs, on our part, our whole heart and our whole soul to enter into and enjoy this joy of God in doing us good with His whole heart and His whole soul. With what measure we mete, it shall be measured unto us again.

If we have at all understood the teaching of God's word in regard to the New Covenant, we know what it reveals in regard to the two parties who meet in it. On God's side there is the promise to do for us and in us all that we need to serve and enjoy Him. He will rejoice in doing us good, with His whole heart. He will be our God, doing for us all that a God can do, giving Himself as God to be wholly ours. And on our side there is the prospect held out of our being able, in the power of what He engages to do, to "turn to Him with our whole heart," "to love Him with all our heart and all our strength." The first and great commandment, the only possible terms on which God can fully reveal Himself, or give Himself to His creature to enjoy, is, "Thou shalt love the Lord thy God with all thy heart." That law is unchangeable. The New Covenant comes and brings us the grace to obey, by lifting us into the love of God as the air we breathe, and enabling us, in the faith of that grace, to rise and be of good courage, and with our whole heart to yield ourselves to the God of the Covenant, and the life in His service.

Wholeheartedness in the love and the service of God! how shall I speak of it? Of its imperative necessity? It is the one unalterable condition of true communion with God, of which nothing can supply the want. Of its infinite reasonableness? With such a God, a very Fountain of all that is loving and lovely, of all that is good and blessed, the All-glorious God: surely there cannot for a moment be a thought of anything else being His due, or of our consenting to offer Him anything less, than the love of the whole heart. Of its unspeakable blessedness? To love Him with the whole heart, this is the only possible way of receiving His great love into our heart and rejoicing in it—yielding oneself to that mighty love, and allowing God Himself, just as an earthly love enters into us and makes us glad, to give us the taste and the joy of the heavenliness of that love. Of its terrible lack? Yes, what shall I speak of this ? Where find words to open the eyes and reach the heart, and show how almost universal is the lack of true wholeheartedness in the faith and love of God, in the desire to love Him with the whole heart, in the sacrifice of everything to possess Him, to please Him, to be wholly possessed of Him? And then of the blessed certainty of its attainableness? The Covenant has provided for it. The Triune God will work it by taking possession of the heart, and dwelling there. The Blessed Mediator of the Covenant undertakes for all we have to do. His constraining love shed abroad in our hearts by the Holy Spirit can bring it and maintain it. Yes, I ask how shall I speak of all this?

Have we not spoken enough of it already in this book? Do we not need something more than words and thoughts? Is not what we need rather this—quietly to turn to the Holy Spirit who dwells in us, and in the faith of the light and the strength our Lord gives through Him, accept and act out what God tells us of the God-given heart He has placed within us, the God-wrought wholeheartedness He works? Surely the new heart which has been given us to love God with, with God's Spirit in it, is wholly for God. Let our faith accept and rejoice in the wondrous gift, and not fear to say: I will love Thee, O Lord, with my whole heart. Just think for a moment of what it means that God has given us such a heart.

We know what God's giving means. His giving depends on our taking. He does not force upon us spiritual possessions. He promises, and gives, in such measure as desire and faith are ready to receive. He gives in Divine power; as faith yields itself to that power, and accepts the gift, it becomes consciously and experimentally our possession.

As spiritual gifts God's bestowings are not recognised by sense or reason. "Ear hath not heard, neither have entered into the heart of man, the things which God hath prepared for them that love Him. But God hath revealed them unto us by His Spirit. We have received the Spirit which is of God, that we might know the things which are freely given us of God." It is as you yield yourself to be led and taught by the Spirit, that your faith will be able, despite of all lack of feeling, to rejoice in the possession of the new heart, and all that is given with it.

Then, this Divine giving is continuous. I bestow a gift on a man; he takes it, and I never see him again. So God bestows temporal gifts on men, and they never think of Him. But spiritual gifts are only to be received and enjoyed in unceasing communication with God Himself. The new heart is not a power I have in myself, like the natural endowments of thinking or loving. No, it is only in unceasing dependence upon, in close contact with God, that the heavenly gift of a new heart can be maintained uninjured, can day by day become stronger. It is only in God's immediate presence, in unbroken direct dependence on Him, that spiritual endowments are preserved.

Then, further, spiritual gifts can only be enjoyed by acting them out in faith. None of the graces of the Christian life, like love, or meekness, or boldness, can be felt or known, much less strengthened, until we begin to exercise them, We must not wait to feel them, or to feel the strength for them; we must, in the obedience of the faith that they are given us, and hidden within us, practise them. Whatever we read of the new heart, and of all God has given into it in the New Covenant, must be boldly believed and carried out into action.

All this is especially true of wholeheartedness, and loving God with all our heart. You may at first be very ignorant of all it implies. God has planted the new heart in the midst of the flesh, which, with its animating Principle, *self*, has to be denied, to be kept crucified, and by the Holy Spirit to be mortified. God has placed you in the midst of a world, from which, with all that is of it and its spirit, you are to come out and be entirely separate. God has given you your work in His kingdom, for which He asks all your interest, and time, and strength. In all these three respects you need wholeheartedness, to enable you to make the sacrifices that may be required. If you take the ordinary standard of Christian life around you, you will find that wholeheartedness, intense devotion to God and His service, is hardly thought of. How to make the best of both worlds, innocently to enjoy as much as possible of this present life, is the ruling principle, and, as a natural consequence, the present world secures the larger share of interest. To please self is considered legitimate, and the Christlike life of not pleasing self has little place. Wholeheartedness will lead you, and. enable you too, to accept Christ's command and sell all for the pearl of great price. Though at first afraid of what it may involve, do not hesitate to speak the word frequently in the ear of your Father: with my whole heart. You may count on the Holy Spirit to open up its meaning, to show you to what service or what sacrifice God calls you in it, to increase its power, to reveal its blessedness, to make it the very spirit of your life of devotion to your Covenant God.

And now, who is ready to enter into this New and Everlasting Covenant with his whole heart? Let each of us do it.

Begin by asking God very humbly to give you by the Spirit, who dwells in you, the vision of the heavenly life of wholehearted love and obedience, as it has actually been prepared for you in Christ. It is an existing reality, a spiritual endowment out of the life of God which can come upon you. It is secured to you in the Covenant, and in Christ Jesus, its Surety. Ask earnestly, definitely, believingly, that God reveal this to you. Rest not till you know fully what your Father means you to be, and has provided for your most certainly being.

When you begin to see why the New Covenant was given, and what it promises, and how divinely certain its promises are, offer yourself to God unreservedly to be taken up into, it. Offer, if He will take you in, to love Him with your whole heart, and to obey Him with all your strength. Hold not back, be not afraid. God has sworn to do you good with His whole heart: do say, do not hesitate to say, that into this Covenant, in which He promises to cause you to turn to Him and to love Him with your whole heart, you now with your whole heart enter. If there be any fear, just ask again and believingly for a vision of the Covenant life: God swearing to do you good with His whole heart; God undertaking to make and enable you to love and obey Him with your whole heart. The vision of this life will make you bold to say: Into this Covenant of a wholehearted love in God and in me I do with my whole heart now enter: here will I dwell.

Let us close and part with this one thought. A redeeming God, rejoicing with His whole heart and whole soul to do us good, and to work in us all that is well-pleasing in His sight: this is the one side. Such is the God of the Covenant. Gaze upon Him. Believe Him. Worship Him. Wait upon Him, until the fire begin to burn, and your heart be drawn out with all its might to love this God. Then the other side. A redeemed soul, rejoicing with all its heart and all its soul in the love of this God, entering into the covenant of wholehearted love, and venturing, ere it knows, to say to Him: With my whole heart I do love Thee, God, my exceeding joy. Such are the children of the Covenant.

Beloved reader! rest not till you have entered in, through the Gate Beautiful, through Christ the door, into this temple of the love, of the heart, of God.

The Second Blessing

In the life of the believer there sometimes comes a crisis, as clearly marked as his conversion, in which he passes out of a life of continual feebleness and failure to one of strength, and victory, and abiding rest. The transition has been called the Second Blessing. Many have objected to the phrase, as being unscriptural, or as tending to make a rule for all, what was only a mode of experience in some. Others have used it as helping to express clearly in human words what ought to be taught to believers as a possible deliverance from the ordinary life of the Christian, to one of abiding fellowship with God, and entire devotion to His service. In introducing it into the title of this book, I have indicated my belief that, rightly understood, the words express a scriptural truth, and may be a help to believers in putting clearly before them what they may expect from God. Let me try and make clear how I think we ought to understand it.

I have connected the expression with the two Covenants. Why was it that God made two Covenants—not one, and not three? Because there were two parties concerned. In the First Covenant man was to prove what he could do, and what he was. In the Second, God would show what He would do. The former was the time of needed preparation; the latter, the time of Divine fulfilment. The same necessity as there was for this in the race, exists in the individual too. Conversion makes of a sinner a child of God, full of ignorance and weakness, without any conception of what the whole-hearted devotion is that God asks of him, or the full possession God is ready to take of him. In some cases the transition from the elementary stage is by a gradual growth and enlightenment. But experience teaches, that in the great majority of cases this healthy growth is not found. To those who have never found the secret of a healthy growth, of victory over sin and perfect rest in God, and have possibly despaired of ever finding it, because all their efforts have been failures, it has often been a wonderful help to learn that it is possible by a single decisive step, bringing them into a right relationship to Christ, His Spirit, and His strength, to enter upon an entirely new life.

What is needed to help a man to take that step is very simple. He must see and confess the wrongness, the sin, of the life he is living, not in harmony with God's will. He must see and believe in the life which Scripture holds out, which Christ Jesus promises to work and maintain in him. As he sees that his failure has been owing to his striving in his own strength, and believes that our Lord Jesus will actually work all in him in Divine power, he takes courage, and dares surrender himself to Christ anew. Confessing and giving up all that is of self and sin, yielding himself wholly to Christ and His service, he believes and receives a new power to live his life by the faith of the Son of God. The change is in many cases as clear, as marked, as wonderful, as conversion. For lack of a better name, that of A Second Blessing came most naturally.

When once it is seen how greatly this change is needed in the life of most Christians, and how entirely it rests on faith in Christ and His power, as revealed in the Word, all doubt as to its scripturalness will be removed. And when once its truth is seen, we shall be surprised to find how, throughout Scripture, in history and teaching, we find what illustrates and confirms it.

Take the twofold passage of Israel through water, first out of Egypt, then into Canaan. The wilderness journey was the result of unbelief and disobedience, allowed by God to humble them, and prove them, and show what was in their heart. When this purpose had been accomplished, a second blessing led them through Jordan as mightily into Canaan, as the first had brought them through the Red Sea out of Egypt.

Or take the Holy Place and the Holiest of All, as types of the life in the two covenants, and equally in the two stages of Christian experience. In the former, very real access to God and fellowship with Him, but always with a veil between. In the latter, the full access, through a rent veil, into the immediate presence of God, and the full experience of the power of the heavenly life. As the eyes are opened to see how terribly the average Christian life comes short of God's purpose, and how truly the mingled life can be expelled by the power of a new revelation of what God waits to do, the types of Scripture will shine with a new meaning.

Or look to the teachings of the New Testament. In Romans, Paul contrasts the life of the Christian under the law with that under grace, the spirit of bondage with the Spirit of adoption. What does this mean but that Christians may still be living under the law and its bondage, that they need to come out of this into the full life of grace and liberty through the Holy Spirit, and that, when first they see the difference, nothing is needed but the surrender of faith, to accept and experience what grace will do by the Holy Spirit.

To the Corinthians, Paul writes of some being carnal, and still babes, walking as men after the flesh; others being spiritual, with spiritual discernment and character. To the Galatians, he speaks of the liberty with which Christ, by the Spirit, makes free from the law, in contrast to those who sought to perfect in the flesh, what was begun in the Spirit, and who gloried in the flesh;—all to call them to recognise the danger of the carnal, divided life, and to come at once to the life of faith, the life in the Spirit, which alone is according to God's will.

Everywhere we see in Scripture, what the state of the Church at the present day confirms, that conversion is only the gate that leads into the path of life, and that within that gate there is still great danger of mistaking the path, of turning aside, or turning back, and that where this has taken place we are called at once, and with our whole heart, to turn and give ourselves to nothing less than all that Christ is willing to work in us. Just as there are many who have always thought that conversion must be slow, and gradual, and uncertain, and cannot understand how it can be sudden and final, because they only take man's powers into account, so many cannot see how the revelation of the true life of holiness, and the entrance on it by faith out of a life of self-effort and failure, may be immediate and permanent. They look too much to man's efforts, and know not how the second blessing is nothing more nor less than a new vision of what Christ is willing to work in us, and the surrender of faith that yields all to Him.

I would fain hope that what I have written in this book may help some to see that the second blessing is just what they need, is what God by His Spirit will work in them, is nothing but the acceptance of Christ in all His saving power as our strength and life, and is what will bring them into, and fit them for, that full life in the New Covenant, in which God works all in all.

Let me close this note with a quotation from the introduction to a little book just published, Dying to Self: A Golden Dialogue, by William Law, with notes by A.M.: "A great deal has been said against the use of the terms, the Higher Life, the Second Blessing. In Law one finds nothing of such language, but of the deep truth of which they are the, perhaps defective, expression, his book is full. The points on which so much stress is laid in what is called Keswick teaching, stand prominently out in his whole argument. The low state of the average life of believers, the cause of all failure as coming from self-confidence, the need of an entire surrender of the whole being to the operation of God, the call to turn to Christ as the One and Sure Deliverer from the power of self, the Divine certainty of a better life for all who will in self-despair trust Christ for it, and the heavenly joy of a life in which the

Spirit of Love fills the heart—these truths are common to both. What makes Law's putting of the truth of special value is the way in which he shows how humility and utter self-despair, with the resignation to God's mighty working in simple faith, is the infallible way to be delivered from self, and have the Spirit of Love born in the heart."

The Law written in the Heart

The thought of the law written in the heart sometimes causes difficulty and discouragement, because believers do not see or feel in themselves anything corresponding to it. An illustration may help to remove the difficulty. There are fluids by which you can write so that nothing is visible, either at once or later, unless the writing be exposed to the sun or the action of some chemical. The writing is there, but one who is ignorant of the process cannot think it is there, and knows not how to make it readable. The faith of a man who is in the secret believes in it though he see it not.

It is even thus with the new heart. God has put His law into it, "Blessed are the people in whose heart is God's law." But it is there invisibly. He that takes God's promise in faith, knows that it is in his own heart. As long. as there is not clear faith on this point, all attempts to find it, or to fulfil that law, will be vain. But when by a simple faith the promise is held fast, the first step is taken to realise it. The soul is then prepared to receive instruction as to what the writing of the law in the heart means. It means, first, that God has implanted in the new heart a love of God's law, and a readiness to do all His will. You may not feel this disposition there, but it is there. God has put it there. Believe this, and be assured that there is in you a Divine nature that says—and you therefore do not hesitate to say it—"I delight to do Thy will, O God!" In the name of God, and in faith, say it.

This writing of the law means, further, that in planting this principle in you, God has taken all that you know of God's will already, and inspired that new heart with the readiness to obey it. It may as yet be written there with invisible writing, and you are not conscious of it. That does not matter. You have here to deal with a Divine and hidden work of the Holy Spirit. Be not afraid to say: Oh, how love I Thy law! God has put the love of it into your heart, the new heart. He has taken away the stony heart; it is by the new heart you have to live.

The next thing implied in this writing of the law, is that you have accepted all God's will, even what you do not yet know, as the delight of your heart. In giving yourself up to God, you gave yourself wholly to His will. That was the one condition of your entering the Covenant; Covenant grace will now provide for teaching you to know, and strengthening you to do, all your Father would have you do.

The whole life in the New Covenant is a life of faith. Faith accepts every promise of the Covenant, is certain that it is being fulfilled, looks confidently to the God of the Covenant to do His work. Faith believes implicitly in the new heart, with the law written in it, because it believes in the promise, and in the God who gave and fulfils the promise.

It may be well to add here that the same truth holds good of all the promises concerning the new heart—they must be accepted and acted on by faith. When we read of "the love of God shed abroad in the heart by the Holy Spirit," of "Christ dwelling in the heart," of "a clean heart," of "loving each other with a clean heart fervently," of "God establishing our heart unblamable in holiness," we must; with the eye of faith, regard these spiritual realities as actually and in very deed existing within us. In His hidden unseen way God is working them there. Not by sight or feeling, but by faith in the Living God and His Word, we know they are as the power for the dispositions and inclinations of the new heart. In this faith we are to act, knowing that we have the power to love, to obey, to be holy. The New Covenant gives us a God who works all in us; faith in Him gives us the assurance, above and beyond all feeling, that this God is doing His blessed work.

And if the question be asked what we are to think of all there is within us that contradicts this faith, let us remember what Scripture teaches us of it. We sometimes speak of an old and a new heart. Scripture does not do so. It speaks of the old, the stony, heart, being taken away—the heart, with its will, disposition, affections, being made new with a Divine newness. This new heart is placed in the midst of what Scripture calls the flesh, in which there dwelleth no good thing. We shall find it a great advantage to adhere as closely as possible to Scripture language. It will greatly help our faith even to use the very words God by His Holy Spirit has used to teach us. And it will greatly clear our view for knowing what to think of the sin that remains in us if we think of it and deal with it in the light of God's truth. Every evil desire and affection comes from the flesh, man's sinful natural life. It owes its power greatly to our ignorance of its nature, and our trusting to its help and strength to cast out its evil. I have already pointed out how sinful flesh and religious flesh is one, and how all failure in religion is owing to a secret trust in ourselves. As we accept and make use of what God says of the flesh, we shall see in it the source of all evil in us; we shall say of its temptations: "It is no more I, but sin that dwelleth in me"; we shall maintain our integrity as we maintain a good conscience that condemns us for nothing knowingly done against God's will; and we shall be strong in the faith of the Holy Spirit, who dwells in the new heart, so to strengthen that we need not and "shall not fulfil the lusts of the flesh."

I conclude with an extract of an address by Rev. F. Webster, at Keswick last year, in confirmation of what I have just said: "Put ye on the Lord Jesus Christ, and make not provision for the flesh, to fulfil the lusts thereof. 'Make no provision for the flesh.' The flesh is there, you know. To deny or ignore the existence of an enemy is to give him a great chance against you; and the flesh is in the believer to the very end, a force of evil to be reckoned with continually, an evil force inside a man, and yet, thank God, a force which can be so dealt with by the power of God, that it shall have no power to defile the heart or deflect the will. The flesh is in you, but your heart may be kept clean moment by moment in spite of the existence of evil in your fallen nature. Every avenue, every opening that leads into the heart, every thought and desire and purpose and imagination of your being, may be closed against the flesh, so that there shall be no opening to come in and defile the heart or deflect the will from the will of God.

"You say that is a very high standard. But it is the Word of God. There is to be no secret sympathy with sin. Although the flesh is there, you are to make it no excuse for sins. You are not to say, I am naturally irritable, anxious, jealous, and I cannot help letting these things crop up; they come from within. Yes, they come from within, but then there need be no provision, no opening in your heart for these things to enter. Your heart can be barricaded with an impassable barrier against these things. 'No provision for the flesh.' Not merely the front door barred and bolted so that you do not invite them to come in, but the side and back door closed too. You may be so Christ-possessed and Christ-enclosed that you shall positively hate everything that is of the flesh.

"'Make no provision for the flesh.' The only way to do so is to 'put on the Lord Jesus Christ.' I spoke of the heart being so barricaded that there should be no entrance to it, that the flesh should never be able to defile it or deflect the will from the will of God. How can that be done? By putting on the Lord Jesus Christ. It has been such a blessing to me just to learn that one secret, just to learn the positive side of deliverance—putting on the Lord Jesus Christ."

George Muller and his Second Conversion

In the life of George Muller of Bristol there was an epoch, four years after his conversion, to which he ever after looked back, and of which he often spoke, as his entrance into the true Christian life.

In an address given to ministers and workers after his ninetieth birthday, he spoke thus of it himself: "That leads to another thought—the full surrender of the heart to God. I was converted in November 1825, but I only came, into the full surrender of the heart four years later, in July 1829. The love of money was gone, the love of place was gone, the love of position was gone, the love of worldly pleasures and engagements was gone. God, God, God alone became my portion. I found my all in Him; I wanted nothing else. And by the grace of God this has remained, and has made me a happy man, an exceedingly happy man, and it led me to care only about the things of God. I ask, affectionately, my beloved brethren, have you fully surrendered the heart to God, or is there this thing or that thing with which you are taken up irrespective of God? I read a little of the Scriptures before, but preferred other books, but since that time the revelation He has made of Himself has become unspeakably blessed to me, and I can say from my heart, God is an infinitely lovely Being. Oh! be not satisfied until in your inmost soul you can say, God is an infinitely lovely Being!"

The account he gives of this change in his journal is as follows. He speaks of one whom he had heard preach at Teignmouth, where he had gone for the sake of his health. "Though I did not like all he said, yet I saw a gravity and solemnity in him different from the rest. Through the instrumentality of this brother the Lord bestowed a great blessing upon me, for which I shall have cause to thank Him throughout eternity. God then began to show me that the Word of God alone is to be our standard of judgment in spiritual things; that it can only be explained by the Holy Spirit, and that in our day, as well as in former times, He is the Teacher of His people. The office of the Holy Spirit I had not experimentally understood before that time. I had not before seen that the Holy Spirit alone can teach us about our state by nature, show us our need of a Saviour, enable us to believe in Christ, explain to us the Scriptures, help us in preaching, etc.

"It was my beginning to understand this point in particular which had a great effect on me; for the Lord enabled me to put it to the test of experience by laying aside commentaries and almost every other book, and simply reading the Word of God and studying it. The result of this was that the first evening that I shut myself into my room to give myself to prayer and meditation over the Scriptures, I learned more in a few hours than I had done during a period of several months previously. But the particular difference was that I received real strength in my soul in doing so.

"In addition to this, it pleased the Lord to lead me to see a higher standard of devotedness than I had seen before. He led me, in a measure, to see what is my glory in this world, even to be despised, to be poor and mean with Christ . . . I returned to London much better in body. And as to my soul, the change was so great that it was like a second conversion."

In another passage he speaks thus: "I fell into the snare into which so many young believers fall, the reading of religious books is preferred to the Scriptures. Now the scriptural way of reasoning would have been: God Himself has condescended to become an author, and I am ignorant of that precious Book which His Holy Spirit has caused to be written; therefore I ought to read again this Book of books most earnestly, most prayerfully, and with much meditation. Instead of acting thus, and being led by my ignorance of the Word to study it more, my difficulty of understanding it made me careless of reading it, and then, like many believers, I practically preferred for the first four years of my Christian life, the works of uninspired men to the oracles of the Living God. The consequence was that I remained a babe, both in knowledge and grace. In knowledge, I say, for all true knowledge must be derived by the Spirit from the Word. This lack of knowledge most sadly kept me back from walking steadily in the ways of God. For it is the truth makes us free, by delivering us from the slavery of the lusts of the flesh, the lusts of the eyes, and the pride of life. The Word proves it, the experience of the saints proves it, and also my own experience most decidedly proves it. For when it pleased the Lord, in August 1829, to bring me really to the Scriptures, my life and walk became very different.

"If anyone would ask me how he may read the Scriptures most profitably, I would answer him:—

"1. Above all he must seek to have it settled in his own mind that God alone, by the Holy spirit, can teach him, and that, therefore, as God will be inquired for all blessings, it becomes him to seek for God's blessing previous to reading, and also while reading.

"2. He should also have it settled in his mind that though the Holy spirit is the best and sufficient Teacher, yet that He does not always teach immediately when we desire it, and that, therefore, we may have to entreat Him again and again for the explanation of certain passages; but that He will surely teach us at last, if we will seek for light prayerfully, patiently, and for the glory of God."

Just one more passage, from an address given on his ninetieth birthday: "For sixty-nine years and ten months he had been a very happy man. That he attributed to two things. He had maintained a good conscience, not wilfully going on in a course he knew to be contrary to the mind of God; he did not, of course, mean that he was perfect; he was poor, weak, and sinful. Secondly, he attributed it to his love of Holy Scripture. Of late years his practice had been four times every year to read through the Scriptures, with application to his own heart, and with meditation; and that day he was a greater lover of God's Word than he was sixty-six years ago. It was this, and maintaining a good conscience, that had given him all these years peace and joy in the Holy Ghost."

In connection with what has been said about the New Covenant being a ministration of the Spirit this narrative is most instructing. It shows us how George Muller's power lay in God's revealing to him the work of the Holy Spirit. He writes that up to the time of that change he had "not experimentally understood the office of the Holy Spirit." We speak much of George Muller's power in prayer; it is of importance to remember that that power was entirely owing to his love of, and faith in, God's Word. But it is of still more importance to notice that his power to believe God's Word so fully was entirely owing to his having learned to know the Holy Spirit as his Teacher. When the words of God are explained to us, and made living within us by the Holy Spirit, they have a power to awaken faith which they otherwise have not. The Word then brings us into contact with God, comes to us as from God direct, and binds our whole life to Him.

When the Holy Spirit thus feeds us on the Word, our whole life comes under His power, and the fruit is seen, not only in the power of prayer, but as much in the power of obedience. Notice how Mr. Muller tells us this, that the two secrets of his great happiness were, his great love for God's Word, and his ever maintaining a good conscience, not knowingly doing anything against the will of God. In giving himself to the teaching of the Holy Spirit, as he tells us in his birthday address, he made a full surrender of the entire heart to God, to be ruled by the Word. He gave himself to obey that Word in everything, he believed that the Holy Spirit gave the grace to obey, and so he was able to maintain a walk free from knowingly transgressing God's law. This is a point he always insisted on. So he writes, in regard to a life of dependence upon God: "It will not do—it is not possible—to live in sin, and at the same time, by communion with God, to draw down from heaven everything one needs for the life that now is." Again, speaking of the strengthening of faith: "It is of the utmost importance that we seek to maintain an upright heart and a good conscience, and therefore do not knowingly and habitually indulge in those things which are contrary to the mind of God. All my confidence in God, all my leaning upon Him in the hour of trial, will be gone if I have a guilty conscience, and do not seek to put away this guilty conscience, but still continue to do things which are contrary to His mind."

A careful perusal of this testimony will show us how the chief points usually insisted upon in connection with the second blessing are all found here. There is the full surrender of the heart to be taught and led alone by the Spirit of God. There is the higher standard of holiness which is at once set up. There is the tender desire in nothing to offend God, but to have at all times a good conscience, that testifies that we are pleasing to God. And there is the faith that where the Holy Spirit reveals to us in the Word the will of God, He gives the sufficient strength for the doing of it. "The particular difference," he says of reading with faith of the Holy Spirit's teaching, "was that I received real strength in my soul in doing so." No wonder that he said: The change was so great, that it was like a second conversion.

All centres in this, that we believe in the New Covenant and its promises as a ministration of the Spirit. That belief may come to some suddenly, as to George Muller ; or it may dawn upon others by degrees. Let all say to God that they are ready to put their whole heart and life under the rule of the Holy Spirit dwelling in them, teaching them by the Word, and strengthening them by His grace. He enables us to live pleasing to God.

Canon Battersby

I do not know that I can find a better case by which to illustrate the place Christ, the Mediator of the Covenant, takes in leading into its full blessing than that of the founder of the Keswick Convention, the late Canon Battersby.

It was at the Oxford Convention in 1873 that he witnessed to having "received a new and distinct blessing to which he had been a stranger before." For more than twenty-five years he had been most diligent as a minister of the gospel, and, as appears from his journals, most faithful in seeking to maintain a close walk with God. But he was ever disturbed by the consciousness of being overcome by sin. So far back as 1853 he had written, "I feel again how very far I am from enjoying habitually that peace and love and joy which Christ promises. I must confess that I have it not; and that very ungentle and unchristian tempers often strive within me for the mastery." When in 1873 he read what was being published of the Higher Life, the effect was to render him utterly dissatisfied with himself and his state. There were indeed difficulties he could not quite understand in that teaching, but he felt that he must either reach forward to better things, nothing less than redemption from all iniquities, or fall back more and more into worldliness and sin. At Oxford he heard an address on the rest of faith. It opened his eyes to the truth that a believer who really longs for deliverance from sinning must simply take Christ at His word, and reckon, without feeling, on Him to do His work of cleansing and keeping the soul. "I thought of the sufficiency of Jesus, and said, I will rest in Him, and I did rest in Him. I was afraid lest it should be a passing emotion; but I found that a presence of Jesus was graciously manifested to me in a way I knew not before, and that I did abide in Him. I do not want to rest in these emotions, but just to believe, and to cling to Christ as my all." He was a man of very reserved nature, but felt it a duty ere the close of the Conference to confess publicly his past shortcoming, and testify openly to his having entered upon a new and definite experience.

In a paper written not long after this he pointed out what the steps are leading to this experience. First, a clear view of the possibilities of Christian attainment—a life in word and action, habitually governed by the Spirit, in constant communion with God, and continual victory over sin through abiding in Christ. Then, the deliberate purpose of the will for a full renunciation of all the idols of the flesh or spirit, and a will-surrender to Christ. And then this last and important step: We must look up to, and wait upon our ascended Lord for all that we need to enable us to do this.

A careful perusal of this very brief statement will prove how everything centred here in Christ. The surrender for a life of continual communion and victory is to be to Christ. The strength for that life is to be in Him and from Him, by faith in Him. And the power to make the full surrender and rest in Him was to be waited for from Him alone.

In June 1875 the first Keswick Convention was held. In the circular calling it, we read : "Many are everywhere thirsting that they may be brought to enjoy more of the Divine presence in their daily life, and a fuller manifestation of the Holy Spirit's power, whether in subduing the lusts of the flesh, or in enabling them to offer more effective service to God. It is certainly God's will that His children should be satisfied in regard to these longings, and there are those who can testify that He has satisfied them, and does satisfy them with daily fresh manifestations of His grace and power." The results of the very first Convention were most blessed, so that after its close he wrote: "There is a very remarkable resemblance in the testimonies I have since received as to the nature of the blessing obtained, viz., the ability given to make a full surrender to the Lord, and the cousequent experience of an abiding peace, far exceeding anything previously experienced." Through all the chief thought, was Christ, first drawing and enabling the soul to rest in Him, and then meeting it with the fulfilment of its desire, the abiding experience of His power to keep it in victory over sin, and communion with God.

And what was the fruit of this new experience? Eight years later Canon Battersby spoke; "It is now eight years since that I knew this blessing as my own. I cannot say that I have never for a moment ceased to trust the Lord to keep me. But I can say that so long as I have trusted Him, He has kept me; He has been faithful."

Nothing of Myself

One would think that no words could make it plainer than the words of the Covenant state it—that the one difference between Old and New is, that in the latter everything is to be done by God Himself. And yet believers and even teachers do not take it in. And even those who do, find it hard to live it out. Our whole being is so blinded to the true relation to God, His inconceivable Omnipresent Omnipotence working every moment in us is so far beyond the reach of human conception, our little hearts cannot rise to the reality of His Infinite Love making itself one with us, and delighting to dwell in us, and to work all in us that has to be done there—that, when we think we have accepted the truth, we find it is only a thought. We are such strangers to the knowledge of what a *God* really is, as the actual life by which His creatures live. In Him we live and move and have our being. And specially is the knowledge of the Triune God too high for us, in that wonderful, most real, and most practical indwelling, to make which possible the Son became Incarnate, and the Holy Spirit was sent forth into our hearts. Only they who confess their ignorance, and wait very humbly and persistently on our Blessed God to teach us by His Holy Spirit what that all-working indwelling is, can hope to have it revealed to them.

It is not long since I had occasion, in preparing a series of Bible Lessons for our Students Association here, to make a study of the Gospel of St. John, and of the life of our Lord as set forth there. I cannot say how deeply I have been afresh impressed with that which I cannot but regard as the deepest secret of His life on earth, His dependence on the Father. It has come to me like a new revelation. Some twelve times and more He uses the word not and nothing of Himself. Not My will. Not My words. Not My honour. Not Mine own glory. I can do nothing of Myself. I speak not of Myself. I came not of Myself. I do nothing of Myself.

Just think a moment what this means in connection with what He tells us of His life in the Father. "As the Father hath life in Himself, so He hath given to the Son to have life in Himself" (v. 26). "That all men should honour the Son, even as they honour the Father" (v. 23). And yet this Son, who hath life in Himself even as the Father has, immediately adds (v. 30): "I can of mine own self do nothing." We should have thought that with this life in Himself He would have the power of independent action as the Father has. But no. "The Son can do nothing of Himself, but what He seeth the Father do." The chief mark of this Divine life He has in Himself is evidently unceasing dependence, receiving from the Father, by the moment, what He bad to speak or do. Nothing of Myself is manifestly as true of Him as it ever could be of the weakest or most sinful man. The life of the Father dwelling in Christ, and Christ in the Father, meant that just as truly as when He was begotten of the Father, He received Divine life and glory from Him, so the continuation of that life came only by an eternal process of giving and receiving, as absolute as is the eternal generation itself. The more closely we study this trutb, and Christ's life in the light of it, the more we are compelled to say, the deepest root of Christ's relationship to the Father, the true reason why He was so well-pleasing, the secret of His glorifying the Father, was this: He allowed God to do all in Him. He only received and wrought out what God wrought in Him. His whole attitude was that of the open ear, the servant spirit, the childlike dependence that waited for all on God.

The infinite importance of this truth in the Christian life is easily felt. The life Christ lived in the Father is the life He imparts to us. We are to abide in Him and He in us, even as He in the Father and the Father in Him. And if the secret of His abiding in the Father be this unceasing self-abnegation—"I can do nothing of Myself"—this life of most entire and absolute dependence and waiting upon God, must it not far more be the most marked feature of our Christian life, the first and all-pervading disposition we seek to maintain? In a little book of William Law's, that has just been issued, Dying to Self: A Golden Dialogue. by William Law. With Notes. The thought is worked out with exceeding power, and the lesson taught that the only thing man can do for his salvation is to deny and cease from himself, that God may work in him. he specially insists upon this in his so striking repetition of the call, if we would die to self in order to have the birth of Divine love in our souls, to sink down in humility, meekness, patience, and resignation to God. I think that no one who at all enters into this advice, but will feel what new point is given to it by the remembrance of how this entire self-renunciation was not only one of the many virtues in the character of Christ, but, indeed, that first essential one without which God could have wrought nothing in Him, through which God did work all.

Let us make Christ's words our own: "I can do nothing of Myself." Take it as the keynote of a single day. Look up and see the Infinite God waiting to do everything as soon as we are ready to give up all to Him, and receive all from Him. Bow down in lowly worship, and wait for the Holy Spirit to work some measure of the mind of Christ in you. Do not be disconcerted if you do not learn the lesson at once: there is the God of love waiting to do everything in him who is willing to be nothing. At moments the teaching appears dangerous, at other times terribly difficult. The Blessed Son of God teaches it us—this was His whole life: I can do nothing of Myself. He is our life; He will work it in us. And when as the Lamb of God He begets this His disposition in us, we shall be prepared for Him to rise on us and shine in us in His heavenly glory.

"Nothing of Myself"—that word spoken eighteen hundred years ago, coming out of the inmost depths of the heart of the Son of God—is a seed in which the power of the eternal life is hidden. Take it straight from the heart of Christ, and hide it in your heart. Meditate on it till it reveals the beauty of His Divine meekness and humility, and explains how all the power and glory of God could work in Him. Believe in it as containing the very life and disposition which you need, and believe in Christ, whose Spirit dwells in the seed to make it true in you. Begin, in single acts of self-emptying, to offer it to God as the one desire of your heart. Count upon God accepting them, and meeting them with His grace, to make the acts into habits, and the habits into dispositions. And you may depend upon it, there is nothing that will lift you so near to God, nothing that will unite you closer to Christ, nothing that will prepare you for the abiding presence and power of God working in you, as the death to self which is found in the simple word—*nothing of myself*.

This word is one of the keys to the New Covenant Life. As I believe that God is actually to work all in me, I shall see that the one thing that is hindering me is, my doing something of myself. As I am willing to learn from Christ by the Holy Spirit to say truly, Nothing of myself, I shall have the true preparation to receive all God has engaged to work, and the power confidently to expect it. I shall learn that the whole secret of the New Covenant is just one thing: *God works all*! The seal of the Covenant stands sure: "I the Lord have spoken it, *and I will do it*."

The Whole Heart

Let me give the principal passages in which the words "the whole heart," "all the heart," are used. A careful study of them will show how wholehearted love and service is what God has always asked, because He can, in the very nature of things, ask nothing less. The prayerful and believing acceptance of the words will waken the assurance that such wholehearted love and service is exactly the blessing the New Covenant was meant to make possible. That assurance will prepare us for turning to the Omnipotence of God to work in us what may have hitherto appeared beyond our reach.

Hear, first, God's word in Deuteronomy—

iv. 29: "If thou seek the Lord thy God, thou shalt find Him, if thou seek Him with all thy heart and all thy soul."

vi. 4, 5: "Hear, O Israel, the Lord our God is one Lord; and thou shalt love the Lord thy God with all thy heart, and with all thy soul, and with all thy might."

x. 12: "What doth the Lord thy God require of thee but to fear the Lord thy God, to walk in all His ways, and to love Him, and to serve Him with all thy heart and all thy soul."

xi. 13: "Hearken diligently unto My commandments, to love the Lord your God, and to serve Him with all your heart and all your soul."

xiii. 3: "The Lord your God proveth you, whether ye love the Lord your God with all your heart and all your soul."

xxvi. 16 : "Thou shalt therefore keep these statutes and do them with all thy heart and all thy soul."

xxx. 2: "Thou shalt obey His voice with all thine heart and with all soul."

xxx. 6: "The Lord thy God will circumcise thine heart, to love the Lord thy God with all thine heart and with all thy soul" (see also v. 9, 10).

Take these oft-repeated words as the expression of God's will concerning His people, and concerning yourself; ask if you could wish to give God anything less. Take the last-cited verse as the Divine promise of the New Covenant—that He will circumcise, will so cleanse the heart to love Him with a wholehearted love, that obedience is within your reach; and say whether you will not vow afresh to keep this His first and great commandment.

Listen to Joshua (xxii. 5): "Take diligent heed to love the Lord your God, and to walk in all His ways, and to keep His commandments, and to cleave unto Him, and to serve Him, with all your heart and with all your soul."

Listen to Samuel (1 Sam. xii. 20, 24): "Turn not aside from following the Lord, but serve the Lord with all your heart. Only fear the Lord, and serve Him in truth with all your heart."

Hear David repeating God's promise to Solomon (1 Kings ii. 4) "If thy children take heed to their way, to walk before Me in truth with all their heart and all their soul."

Hear God's word concerning David (1 Kings xiv. 8): "My servant David, who followed Me with all his heart, to do that only which was right in Mine eyes."

Hear Solomon in his temple prayer (1 Kings viii. 48): "If they return to Thee with all their heart and all their soul, hear Thou their prayer."

Listen to what is said of Jehu (2 Kings x. 31): "The Lord said unto Jehu, Thou hast done well in executing that which is right in Mine eyes. But Jehu took no heed to walk in the law of the Lord with all his heart."

Of Josiah we read (2 Kings xxiii. 3, 25): "The king and all the men of Judah made a covenant with the Lord, to walk after the Lord, with all their heart and with all their soul, to perform the words of this covenant that were written in this book. There was no king like him, that turned to the Lord with all his heart, and all his soul, and all his might."

The words concerning Asa, in 2 Chron. xv. 12, 15, we had as our text.

Of Jehoshaphat, men said (2 Chron. xxii. 9): "He sought the Lord with all his heart."

And of Hezekiah it is written (2 Chron. xxxi. 21) : "In every work that he began, to seek his God, he did it with all his heart and prospered."

Oh that all would ask God to give them, by the Holy Spirit, a simple vision of Himself!—claiming, giving, accepting, blessing, delighting in, the love and service of the whole heart—the sacrifice of the whole burnt-offering. Surely they would fall down and join the ranks of those who have given it; and refuse to think of anything as religious life, or worship, or service, but that in which their whole heart went out to God. Turn to the Psalms. Hear David (ix. 1, cxi. 1, cxxxviii. 1): "I will praise Thee with my whole heart." And in Psalm cxix., the Psalm of the way of blessedness: "Blessed who seek Him with the whole heart. With my whole heart have I sought Thee. I shall keep Thy law, yea I shall observe it with my whole heart. I entreated Thy favour with my whole heart. I will keep Thy precepts with my whole heart. I cried with my whole heart." Praise and prayer; seeking God and keeping His precepts; all equally with the whole heart.

Shall we not begin asking more earnestly than ever, as often as we see men engaged in their earthly pursuits in search of money, or pleasure, or fame, or power, with their whole heart. Is this the spirit in which Christians consider that God must be served? Is this the spirit in which I serve Him? Is not this the one thing needful in our religion? Lord, reveal unto us Thy will!

Now, just a few words more from the Prophets about the new time, the great change that can come into our lives.

Jer. xxiv. 7 : "I will give them an heart to know Me that I am the Lord; and they shall be My people and I will be their God; for they shall return to Me with their whole heart."

xxix. 13: "Ye shall seek Me, and find Me, when ye shall search for Me with all your heart. And I will be found of you, saith the Lord."

xxxii. 39-41.—Let my reader not be weary of reading carefully these Divine words: they contain the secret, the seed, the living power of a complete transition out of a life in the bondage of half-hearted service, to the glorious liberty of the children of God.—"I will give them one heart, that they may fear Me for ever. And I will make an everlasting covenant with them, that I will not turn away from them to do them good ; but I will put my fear in their heart, that they shall not depart from Me. Yea, I will rejoice over them to do them good, with My whole heart and My whole Soul!"

It is to be all God's doing. And He is to do it with His whole heart and His whole soul. It is the vision of this God with His whole heart loving us, longing and delighting to fulfil His promise, and make us wholly His own, that we need. This vision makes it impossible not to love Him with our whole heart. Lord, open our eyes that we may see!

Joel ii. 12: "Therefore also now, saith the Lord, turn ye even to Me with all your heart."

Zeph. iii. 14: "Shout, O Israel; *be glad and rejoice with all the heart*; The Lord hath taken away thy judgments. *He hath cast out thine enemy; the king of israel, the lord, is in the midst of thee; thou shalt not see evil any more*."

Now one word from our Lord Jesus (Matt. xxii. 37): "Jesus said, Thou shalt love the Lord thy God with all thy heart." This is the first and great commandment. This is the sum of that law He came to fulfil for us and in us, came to enable us to fulfil. "For what the law could not do, in that it was weak through the flesh, God, sending His own Son, condemned sin in the flesh, that the righteousness of the law might be fulfilled in us who walk after the Spirit."

Praise God! this righteousness of the law—loving God with all the heart, for love is the fulfilling of the law—this righteousness of the law is fulfilled in us, who walk after the Spirit. Jesus came to make it possible. He gives His Spirit—the Spirit of life in Christ Jesus—to make it actual. Let us not fear to give ourselves a whole burnt offering, acceptable to God; loving Him with all our heart and mind and strength.

May I ask the reader just once again to peruse Chapter VI., on "The Everlasting Covenant," and Chapter XVIII., on "Entering into the Covenant with the Whole Heart." And say then, if you have never yet entered fully into this covenant of the whole heart, whether you are not ready to do it now. God demands, God works, God is, oh, so infinitely worthy of, the whole heart! Fear not to say He shall have it. You may confidently count upon the blessed Lord Jesus, the Surety of the Covenant, whose it is to make it true in you by His Spirit, to enable you to exercise the faith that knows that God's power will work what He has promised. In His Name say: With my whole heart I do love Thee!

School of Obedience

Table of Contents

Preface

These addresses on Obedience are issued with the very fervent prayer that it may please our gracious Father to use them for the instruction and strengthening of the young men and women, on whose obedience and devotion so much depends for the Church and the world. To all of them who read this I send my loving greeting. The God of all grace bless them abundantly!

It often happens after a Conference, or even after writing a book, that it is as if one only then begins to see the meaning and importance of the truth with which one has been occupied. So I do indeed feel as if I had utterly failed in grasping or expounding the spiritual character, the altogether indispensable necessity, the divine and actual possibility, the inconceivable blessedness of a life of true and entire obedience to our Father in heaven. Let me, therefore, just in a few sentences gather up the main points which have come home to myself with special power, and ask every reader at starting to take note of them as *some of the chief lessons* to be learnt in Christ's school of obedience.

The Father in heaven asks, and requires, and actually expects, that every child of His yield Him whole-hearted and entire obedience, day by day, and all the day.

To enable His child to do this, He has made a most abundant and altogether sufficient provision in the promise of the New Covenant, and in the gift of His Son and Spirit.

This provision can alone, but can most certainly, be enjoyed, and these promises fulfilled, in the soul that gives itself up to a life in the abiding communion with the Three-One God, so that His presence and power work in it all the day.

The very entrance into this life demands the vow of absolute obedience, or the surrender of the whole being, to be, think, speak, do, every moment, nothing but what is according to the will of God, and well-pleasing to Him.

If these things be indeed true, it is not enough to assent to them: we need the Holy Spirit to give us such a vision of their glory and divine power, and the demand they make on our immediate and unconditional submission, that there may be no rest till we accept all that God is willing to do for us.

Let us all pray that God may, by the light of His Spirit, so show His loving and almighty will concerning us, that it may be impossible for us to be disobedient to the heavenly vision.

Andrew Murray.

Wellington, 9th August, 1898.

Obedience: Its place In Holy Scripture

In undertaking the study of a Bible word, or of a truth of the Christian life, it is a great help to take a survey of the place it takes in Scripture. As we see where, and how often, and in what connections it is found, its relative importance may be apprehended as well as its bearing on the whole of revelation. Let me try in this first chapter to prepare the way for the study of what obedience is, by showing you where to go in God's Word to find the mind of God concerning it.

1. Take Scripture as a Whole.

We begin with Paradise. In Gen. 2:16, we read: 'And the Lord God commanded the man, saying.' And later (3:11), 'Hast thou eaten of the tree, whereof I commanded thee that thou shouldest not eat?'

Note how obedience to the command is the one virtue of Paradise, the one condition of man's abiding there, the one thing his Creator asks of him. Nothing is said of faith, or humility, or love: obedience includes all. As supreme as is the claim and authority of God is the demand for obedience as the one thing that is to *decide his destiny.*

In the life of man, to obey is the one thing needful.

Turn now from the beginning to the close of the Bible. In its last chapter you read (Rev. 22:14), 'Blessed are they that do His commandments, that they may have a right to the tree of life.' Or, if we accept the Revised Version, which gives another reading, we have the same thought in chapters 12 and 14, where we read of the seed of the woman (12:17), 'which keep the commandments of God, and hold the testimony of Jesus'; and of the patience of the saints (14:12), 'Here are they that keep the commandments of God, and the faith of Jesus.'

From beginning to end, from Paradise lost to Paradise regained, the law is unchangeable—it is only obedience that gives access to the tree of life and the favor of God.

And if you ask how the change was effected out of the disobedience at the beginning that closed the way to the tree of life, to the obedience at the end that again gained entrance to it, turn to *that which stands midway*

between the beginning and the end—the cross of Christ. Read a passage like Rom. 5:19, 'Through the obedience of the One shall the many be made righteous'; or Phil. 2:8, 'He became obedient unto death, therefore God hath highly exalted Him'; or Heb. 5:8, 9, 'He learned obedience and became the Author of salvation to them that obey Him,' and you see how the whole redemption of Christ consists in restoring obedience to its place. The beauty of His salvation consists in this, that He brings us back to the life of obedience, through which alone the creature can give the Creator the glory due to Him, or receive the glory of which his Creator desires to make him partaker.

Paradise, Calvary, Heaven, all proclaim with one voice:

'Child of God! the first and the last thing thy God asks of thee is simple, universal, unchanging obedience.'

II. Let Us Turn to the Old Testament.

Here let us specially notice how, with any new beginning in the history of God's kingdom, obedience always comes into special prominence.

1. Take Noah, the new father of the human race, and you will find four times written (Gen. 6:22; 7:5, 9, 16),

'According to all that God commanded Noah, so did he.'

It is the man who does what God commands, to whom God can entrust His work, whom God can use to be a savior of men.

2. Think of Abraham, the father of the chosen race. 'By faith Abraham obeyed' (Heb. 11:7).

When he had been forty years in this school of faith-obedience, God came to perfect his faith, and to crown it with His fullest blessing. Nothing could fit him for this but a crowning act of obedience. When he had bound his son on the altar, God came and said (Gen. 22:12, 18),

'By Myself have I sworn, in blessing I will bless thee, and in multiplying I will multiply thee; and in thy seed shall all nations be blessed, because thou hast obeyed My voice.'

And to Isaac He spake (26:3, 5), 'I will perform the oath which I sware to Abraham, because that Abraham obeyed my voice.'

Oh, when shall we learn how unspeakably pleasing obedience is in God's sight, and how unspeakable is the reward He bestows upon it! The way to be a blessing to the world is to be men of obedience; known by God and the world by this *one mark*

— a will utterly given up to God's will. Let all who profess to walk in Abraham's footsteps walk thus.

3. Go on to Moses. At Sinai, God gave him the message to the people (Ex. 19:4), 'If you will obey My voice indeed, ye shall be a peculiar treasure to Me above all people.'

In the very nature of things it cannot be otherwise. God's holy will is His glory and perfection; it is only by an entrance into His will, by obedience, that it is possible to be His people.

4. Take the building of the sanctuary in which God was to dwell. In the last three chapters of Exodus you have the expression nineteen times, 'According to all the Lord commanded Moses, so did he,' And then, 'The glory of the Lord filled the tabernacle.' Just so again in Lev. 8 and 9, you have, with reference to the consecration of the priests and the tabernacle, the same expression twelve times. And then, 'The glory of the Lord appeared before all the people, and fire came out from before the Lord, and consumed the burnt-offering.'

Words cannot make it plainer, that it is amid what the obedience of His people has wrought that God delights to dwell, that it is the obedient He crowns with His favor and presence.

5. After the forty years wandering in the wilderness, and its terrible revelation of the fruit of disobedience, there was again a new beginning when the people were about to enter Canaan. Read Deuteronomy, with all Moses spoke in sight of the land, and you will find there is no book of the Bible which uses the word 'obey' so frequently, or speaks so much of the blessing obedience will assuredly bring. The whole is summed up in the words (11:27),

'I set before you a blessing if ye obey, a curse if ye will not obey.'

Yes, 'a Blessing if ye Obey'! that is the key-note of the blessed life. Canaan, just like Paradise and Heaven, can be the place of blessing as it is the place of obedience. Would God we might take it in! Do beware only of praying only for a blessing. Let us care for the obedience, God will care for the blessing. Let my one thought as a Christian be, how I can obey and please my God perfectly.

6. The next new beginning we have is in the appointment of kings in Israel. In the story of Saul we have the most solemn warning as to the need of exact and entire obedience in a man whom God is to trust as ruler of His people. Samuel had commanded Saul (1 Sam. 10:8) to wait seven days for him to

come and sacrifice, and to show him what to do. When Samuel delayed (13:8-14) Saul took it upon himself to sacrifice.

When Samuel came he said: 'Thou hast not kept the commandment of the Lord thy God, which He commanded thee; thy kingdom shall not continue, because thou hast not kept that which the Lord commanded thee.'

God will not honor the man who is not obedient.

Saul has a second opportunity given him of showing what is in his heart. He is sent to execute God's judgment against Amelek. He obeys. He gathers an army of two hundred thousand men, undertakes the journey into the wilderness, and destroys Amelek. But while God had commanded him 'utterly to destroy all; and not to spare,' he spared the best of the cattle and Agag.

God speaks to Samuel, 'It repenteth Me that I have set up Saul to be king, for he hath not performed My commandment.'

When Samuel comes, Saul twice over says, 'I have performed the commandment of the Lord;' 'I have obeyed the voice of the Lord.'

And so he had, as many would think, But his obedience had not been entire. God claims exact, full obedience. God had said, 'Utterly destroy all! spare not!' This he had not done. He had spared the best sheep for a sacrifice unto the Lord. And Samuel said.

'To obey is better than any sacrifice. Because thou hast rejected the word of the Lord, the Lord hath rejected thee.'

Sad type of so much obedience, which in part performs God's commandment, and yet is not the obedience God asks! God says of all sin and all disobedience: 'Utterly destroy all! spare not!' May God reveal to us whether we are indeed going all lengths with Him, seeking utterly to destroy all and spare nothing that is not in perfect harmony with His will. It is only a whole-hearted obedience, down to the minutest details, that can satisfy God. Let nothing less satisfy you; lest while we say, 'I have obeyed,' God says, 'Thou hast rejected the word of the Lord.'

7. Just one word more from the Old Testament. Next to Deuteronomy Jeremiah is the book most full of the word 'obey,' though alas! mostly in connection with the complaint that the people had not obeyed. God sums up all His dealings with the fathers in the one word,

'I spake not with them concerning sacrifices, but this thing I commanded them, Obey My voice and I will be your God.'

Would God that we could learn that all that God speaks of sacrifices, even of the sacrifice of His beloved Son, is subordinate to the one thing—to have His creature restored to full obedience. Into all the inconceivable meaning of the word, 'I will be your God,' there is no gateway but this, 'Obey My voice.'

III. We Come to the New Testament

1. Here we think at once of our blessed Lord, and the prominence He gives to obedience as the one thing for which He was come into the world. He who entered it with His 'Lo, I come to do Thy will, O God,' ever confessed to men, 'I seek not My own will, but the will of Him that sent Me.'

Of all He did and of all He suffered, even to the death, He said, 'This commandment have I received of My Father.'

If we turn to His teaching, we find everywhere, that the obedience He rendered is what He claims from everyone who would be His disciple.

During His whole ministry, from beginning to end, obedience is *the very essence of salvation.*

In the Sermon on the Mount He began with it: No one could enter the kingdom, 'but he that doeth the will of My Father which is in heaven.' And in the farewell discourse, how wonderfully He reveals the spiritual character of true obedience as it is born of love and inspired by it, and as it also opens the way into the love of God. Do take into your heart the wonderful words, (John 14:15, 16, 21, 23), 'If ye love Me, ye will keep my commandments. And the Father will send forth the Spirit. He hath My commandments and keepeth them, he it is that loveth Me: and he shall be loved of My Father, and I will love him, and will manifest Myself unto him. If a man love Me, he will keep My words: and My Father will love him, and We will come unto him, and make Our abode with him.'

No words could express more simply or more powerfully the inconceivably glorious place Christ gives to obedience, with its twofold possibility, (1) as only possible to a loving heart, (2) as making possible all that God has to give of His Holy Spirit, of His wonderful love, of His indwelling in Christ Jesus. I know of no passage in Scripture that gives a higher revelation of the spiritual life, or the power of loving obedience as its one condition. Let us pray God very earnestly that by His Holy Spirit its light may transfigure our daily obedience with its heavenly glory.

See how all this is confirmed in the next chapter. How well we know the parable of the vine! How often and how earnestly we have asked how to be able to abide continually in Christ We have thought of more study of the Word, more faith, more prayer, more communion with God, and we have overlooked the simple truth that Jesus teaches so clearly, 'If ye keep My commandments, ye shall abide in My love,' with its divine sanction, 'Even as I kept My Father's commandments, and abide in His love.'

For Him as for us, the only way under heaven to abide in divine love is to keep the commandments. Do let me ask, have you known it, have you heard it preached, have you believed it and proved it true in your experience: obedience on earth is the key to a place in God's love in heaven? Unless there be some correspondence between God's whole-hearted love in heaven, and our whole-hearted, loving obedience on earth, Christ cannot manifest Himself to us, God cannot abide in us, we cannot abide in His love.

2. If we go on from our Lord Jesus to His apostles, we find in the Acts two words of Peter's which show how our Lord's teaching had entered into him. In the one, 'God hath given His Holy Spirit to them that obey Him,' —he proves how he knew what had been the preparation for Pentecost, the surrender to Christ. In the other, 'We must obey God rather than man' —we have the man-ward side: obedience is to be unto death; nothing on earth dare or can hinder it in the man who has given himself to God.

3. In Paul's Epistle to the Romans, we have, in the opening and closing verses the expression, 'the obedience of faith among all nations' (1:5; 16:26), as that for which he was made an apostle. He speaks of what God had wrought 'to make the Gentiles obedient.' He teaches that, as the obedience of Christ makes us righteous, we become the servants of obedience unto righteousness. As disobedience in Adam and in us was the one thing that wrought death, so obedience, in Christ and in us, is the one thing that the gospel makes known as the way of restoration to God and His favor.

4. We all know how James warns us not to be hearers of the Word only but doers, and expounds how Abraham was justified, and his faith perfected, by his works.

5. In Peter's First Epistle we have only to look at the first chapter, to see the place obedience has in his system. In ver. 2 he speaks to the 'Elect, in sanctification of the Spirit, unto obedience and blood-sprinkling of Jesus Christ,' and so points us to obedience as the eternal purpose of the Father, as the great object of the work of the Spirit, and a chief part of the salvation of Christ. In ver. 13 he writes, 'As children of obedience,' born of it, marked by it, subject to it, 'be ye holy in all manner of conversation.' Obedience is *the very starting point of true holiness.*

In ver. 22 we read, 'Seeing ye have purified your souls in your obedience to the truth,' —the whole acceptance of the truth of God was not merely a matter of intellectual assent or strong emotion: it was a subjection of the life to the dominion of the truth of God: the Christian life was in the first place obedience.

6. Of John we know how strong his statements are. 'He that saith, I know Him, and keepeth not His Commandments, is a liar.' Obedience is *the one certificate of Christian character.*

'Let us love in deed and truth; hereby we shall assure our hearts before Him. And whatsoever we ask we receive of Him, because we keep His commandments, and do the things that are pleasing in His sight.' Obedience is the secret of good conscience, and of the confidence that God heareth us. 'This is the love of God, that we keep His Commandments.' The obedience that keeps His commandments: this is the garment in which the hidden, invisible love reveals itself, and whereby it is known.

Such is the place obedience has in Holy Scripture, in the mind of God, in the hearts of His servants. We may well ask, Does it take that place in my heart and life? Have we indeed given obedience that supreme place of authority over us that God means it to have, as the inspiration of every action, and of every approach to Him? If we yield ourselves to the searching of God's Spirit, we may find that we never gave it its true proportion in our scheme of life, and that this lack is the cause of all our failure in prayer and in work. We may see that the deeper blessings of God's grace, and the full enjoyment of God's love and nearness, have been beyond our reach, simply because obedience was never made what God would have it be—the starting-point and the goal of our Christian life.

Let this, our first study, waken in us an earnest desire to know God's will fully concerning this truth. Let us unite in praying that the Holy Spirit may show us how defective the Christian's life is, where obedience does not rule all; how that life can be exchanged for one of full surrender to absolute obedience; and how sure it is that God in Christ will enable us to live it out.

The Obedience of Christ.

'Through the obedience of the One shall all the many be made righteous.... Know ye not that ye are servants of obedience unto righteousness?' —Rom. 5:19; 6:16.

'Through the obedience of the One shall the many be made righteous.' These words tell us what we owe to Christ. As in Adam we were made sinners, in Christ we are made righteous.

The words tell us, too, to what in Christ it is we owe our righteousness. As Adam's disobedience made us sinners, the obedience of Christ makes us righteous. To the obedience of Christ we owe everything.

Among the treasures of our inheritance in Christ this is one of the richest. How many have never studied it, so as to love it and delight in it, and get the full blessing of it! May God, by His Holy Spirit, reveal its glory, and make us partakers of its power.

You are familiar with the blessed truth of justification by faith. In the section of the Epistle to the Romans preceding our passage (3:21–5:11) Paul had taught what its ever-blessed foundation was—the atonement of the blood of Christ; what its way and condition—faith in the free grace of a God who justifies the ungodly; and what its blessed fruits—the bestowment of the righteousness of Christ, with an immediate access into the favor of God, and the hope of glory. In our passage he now proceeds to unfold the deeper truth of the union with Christ by faith, in which justification has its root, and which makes it possible and right for God to accept us for His sake. Paul goes back to Adam and our union with him, with all the consequences that flowed from that union, to prove how reasonable, how perfectly natural (in the higher sense of the word) it is that those who receive Christ by faith, and are so united with Him, become partakers of His righteousness and His life. It is in this argument that he specially emphasizes the contrast between the disobedience of Adam, with the condemnation and death it wrought, and the obedience of Christ, with the righteousness and life it brings. As we study the place the obedience of Christ takes in His work for our salvation, and see in it the very root of our redemption, we shall know what place to give it in our heart and life.

'Through the one man's disobedience many were made sinners.' How was this?

There was a twofold connection between Adam and his descendants—the judicial and the vital.

Judicial and Vital Connection.

Through the judicial, the whole race, though yet unborn, came at once under the sentence of death. 'Death reigned from Adam to Moses, even over them' —such as little children— 'who had not sinned after the likeness of Adam's transgression.'

This judicial relation was rooted in the vital connection. The sentence could not have come upon them, if they had not been in Adam. And the vital again became the manifestation of the judicial; each child of Adam enters life under the power of sin and death. 'Through the disobedience of the one, the many were constituted sinners,' both by position subject to the curse of sin and by nature subject to its power.

'Adam is the figure of Him who was to come,' and who is called the Second Adam, the Second Father of the race. Adam's disobedience in its effects is the exact similitude of what the obedience of Christ becomes to us. 'When a sinner believes in Christ, he is united to Him, and is at once, by a judicial sentence, pronounced and accepted as righteous in God's sight. The judicial relationship is rooted in the vital. He has Christ's righteousness only by having Christ Himself, and being in Him. Before he knows aught of what it is to be in Christ, he can know himself acquitted and accepted. But he is then led on to know the vital connection, and to understand that as real and complete as was his participation in Adam's disobedience with the death as well as the sinful nature that followed on it, is his participation in Christ's obedience, with both the righteousness and the obedient life and nature that come from it.

Let us see and understand this:

Through Adam's disobedience we are made sinners. The one thing God asked of Adam in Paradise was obedience. The one thing by which a creature can glorify God, or enjoy His favor and blessing, is obedience. The one cause of the power sin has got in the world, and the ruin it has wrought, is disobedience. The whole curse of sin on us is owing to disobedience imputed to us. The whole power of sin working in us, is nothing but this—that as we receive Adam's nature, we inherit his disobedience—we are born 'the children of disobedience.'

It is evident that *the one work a Christ was needed for* was to remove this disobedience—its curse, its dominion, its evil nature and workings. Disobedience was the root of all sin and misery. The first object of His salvation was to cut away the evil root, and restore man to his original destiny—a life in obedience to his God.

How did Christ do this?

First of all, by coming as the Second Adam, to undo what the first had done. Sin had made us believe that it was a humiliation always to be seeking to know and do God's will. Christ came to show us the nobility, the blessedness, the heavenliness of obedience. When God gave us the robe of creaturehood to wear, we knew not that its beauty, its unspotted purity, was obedience to God. Christ came and put on that robe that He might show us how to wear it, and how with it we could enter into the presence and glory of God. Christ came to overcome, and so bear away our disobedience, and to replace it by His own obedience on us and in us. As universal, as mighty, as all pervading as was the disobedience of Adam, yea, far more so, was to be the power of the obedience of Christ.

The object of Christ's life of obedience was threefold: (1) As an Example, to show us what true obedience was. (2) As our Surety, by His obedience to fulfill all righteousness for us. (3) As our Head, to prepare a new and obedient nature to impart to us.

So He died, too, to show us that His obedience means a readiness to obey to the uttermost, to die for God; that it means the vicarious endurance and atonement of the guilt of our disobedience; that it means a death to sin as an entrance to the life of God for Him and for us.

The disobedience of Adam, in all its possible bearings, was to be put away and replaced by the obedience of Christ. Judicially, by that obedience we are made righteous. Just as we were made sinners by Adam's disobedience, we are at once and completely justified and delivered from the power of sin and death: we stand before God as righteous men. Vitally—for the judicial and the vital are as inseparable as in the case of Adam—we are made one plant with Christ in His death and resurrection, so that we are as truly dead to sin and alive to God, as He is. And the life we receive in Him is no other than a life of obedience.

Let every one of us who would know what obedience is, consider well: It is the obedience of Christ that is the secret of the righteousness and salvation I find in Him. The obedience is the very essence of that righteousness:

obedience is salvation. His obedience, first of all to be accepted, and trusted to, and rejoiced in, as covering and swallowing, up and making an end of my disobedience, is the one unchanging, never-to-be-forsaken ground of my acceptance. And then, His obedience—just as Adam's disobedience was the power that ruled my life, the power of death in me—becomes the life-power of the new nature in me. Then I understand why Paul in this passage so closely links the righteousness and the life. 'If by the trespass of one, death reigned through the one, much more shall they who receive the abundance of grace and the gift of righteousness reign in life through One,' even here on earth. 'The gift came unto all men unto justification of life.'

The more carefully we trace the parallel between the first and Second Adam, and see how in the former the death and disobedience reigned in his seed equally with himself, and how both were equally transmitted, through union with him, the more will the conviction be forced upon us that the obedience of Christ is equally to be ours, not only by imputation, but by personal possession. It is so inseparable from Him that to receive Him and His life is to receive His obedience. When we receive the righteousness which God offers us so freely, it at once points us to the obedience out of which it was born, with which it is inseparably one, in which alone it can live and flourish.

See how this connection comes out in the next chapter. After having spoken of our life—union to Christ, Paul, for the first time in the epistle (6:12), gives an injunction, 'Let not sin reign;... present yourselves unto God'; and then immediately proceeds to teach how this means nothing but obedience: 'Know ye not, that ye are servants of sin unto death, or of obedience unto righteousness?' Your relation to obedience is a practical one; you have been delivered from disobedience (Adam's and your own), and now are become servants of obedience—and that 'unto righteousness.' Christ's obedience was unto righteousness—the righteousness which is God's gift to you. Your subjection to obedience is the one way in which your relation to God and to righteousness can be maintained. Christ's obedience unto righteousness is the only beginning of life for you; your obedience unto righteousness, its only continuance. There is but one law for the head and the members. As surely as it was with Adam and his seed, disobedience and death, it is with Christ and his seed, obedience and life. The one bond of union, the one mark of likeness, between Adam and his seed was disobedience. The one bond of union between Christ and His seed, the one mark of resemblance, is obedience.

It was obedience made Christ the object of the Father's love (John 10:17, 18) and our Redeemer; it is Obedience Alone can lead us in the way to dwell in that love (John 14:21, 23) and enjoy that redemption.

'Through the obedience of the One shall the many be made righteous.' Everything depends upon our knowledge of and participation in the obedience, as the gateway and path to the full enjoyment of the righteousness. At conversion the righteousness is given to faith, once for all, completely and forever, with but little or no knowledge of the obedience. But as the righteousness is indeed believed in and submitted to, and its full dominion over us, as 'servants of righteousness,' sought after, it will open to us its blessed nature, as born out of obedience, and therefore ever leading us back to its divine origin. The truer our hold of the righteousness of Christ, in the power of the Spirit, the more intense will be our desire to share in the obedience out of which it sprang. In this light let us *study the obedience of Christ*, that like Him we may live as servants of obedience unto righteousness.

1. In Christ this obedience was a life principle.

Obedience with Him did not mean a single act of obedience now and then, not even a series of acts, but the spirit of His whole life. 'I came, not to do My own will.' 'Lo, I come, to do Thy will, O God.' He had come into the world for one purpose. He only lived to carry out God's will. The one supreme, all-controlling power of His life was obedience.

He is willing to make it so in us. This was what He promised when He said, 'Whosoever shall do the will of My Father which is in heaven, the same is My brother and sister and mother.'

The link in a family is a common life shared by all and a family likeness. The bond between Christ and us is that He and we together do the will of God.

2. In Christ this obedience was a joy. 'I delight to do Thy will, O God.' 'My meat is to do the will of Him that sent Me.'

Our food is refreshment and invigoration. The healthy man eats his bread with gladness. But food is more than enjoyment—it is the one necessary of life. And so, doing the will of God was the food that Christ hungered after and without which He could not live, the one thing that satisfied His hunger, the one thing that refreshed and strengthened Him and made Him glad.

It was something of this David meant when he spoke of God's words being 'sweeter than honey and the honeycomb.' As this is understood and accepted, obedience will become more natural to us and necessary to us, and more refreshing than our daily food.

3. In Christ this obedience led to a waiting on God's will.

God did not reveal all His will to Christ at once, but day by day, according to the circumstances of the hour. In His life of obedience there was growth and progress; the most difficult lesson came the last. Each act of obedience fitted Him for the new discovery of the Father's further command. He spake, 'Mine ears hast Thou opened; I delight to do Thy will, O God.'

It is as obedience becomes the passion of our life that the ears will be opened by God's Spirit to wait for His teaching, and we be content with nothing less than a divine guidance into the divine will for us.

4. In Christ this obedience was unto death.

When He spake, 'I came not to do My own will, but the will of Him that sent Me,' He was ready to go all lengths in denying His own will and doing the Father's. He meant it. 'In nothing My will; at all costs God's will.'

This is the obedience to which He invites and for which He empowers us. This whole-hearted surrender to obedience in everything is the only true obedience, is the only power that will avail to carry us through. Would God that Christians could understand that nothing less than this is what brings the soul gladness and strength!

As long as there is a doubt about universal obedience, and with that a lurking sense of the possibility of failure, we lose the confidence that secures the victory. But when once we set God before us, as really asking full obedience, and engaging to work it, and see that we dare offer Him nothing less, we give up ourselves to the working of the divine power, which by the Holy Ghost can master our whole life.

5. In Christ this obedience sprang from the deepest humility. 'Have this mind in you, which was also in Christ Jesus, who emptied Himself—who took the form of a servant—who humbled Himself, becoming obedient to death.'

It is the man who is willing for entire, self-emptying, is willing to be and live as the servant, 'a servant of obedience,' is willing to be humbled very low before God and man, to whom the obedience of Jesus will unfold its heavenly beauty and its constraining power. There may be a strong will, that secretly trusts in self, that strives for the obedience, and fails. It is as we sink low before God in humility, meekness, patience, and entire resignation to His will, and are willing to bow in an absolute helplessness and dependence on Him, as we turn away wholly from self, that it will be revealed to us how it is the one only duty and blessing of a creature to obey this glorious God!

6. In Christ this obedience was of faith—in entire dependence upon God's strength. 'I can do nothing of Myself.' 'The Father that dwelleth in Me doeth the works.'

The Son's unreserved surrender to the Father's will was met by the Father's unceasing and undeserved bestowment of His power working in Him.

Even so it will be with us. If we learn that our giving up our will to God is ever the measure of His giving His power in us, we shall see that a surrender to full obedience is nothing but a full faith that God will work all in us.

God's promises of the New Covenant all rest on this: 'The Lord Thy God will circumcise thine heart to love the Lord thy God with all thine heart, and thou shall obey the Lord thy God.' 'I will put My Spirit within you, and cause you to walk in My statutes, and ye shall keep My judgments.'

Let us, like the Son, believe that God works all in us, and we shall have the courage to yield ourselves to an unreserved obedience—an obedience unto death. That yielding ourselves up to God will become the entrance into the blessed experience of conformity to the Son of God in His doing the Father's will, because He counted on the Father's power. Let us give our all to God. He will work His all in us.

Know ye not that ye, made righteous by the obedience of One, are like Him and in Him servants of obedience unto righteousness? It is in the obedience of the One the obedience of the many has its root, its life, its security. Let us turn and gaze upon, and study, and believe in Christ, as the obedient One, as never before. Let this be the Christ we receive and love, and seek to be made conformable to. As His righteousness is our one hope, let His obedience be our one desire. Let our faith in Him prove its sincerity and its confidence in God's supernatural power working in us by accepting Christ, the obedient One, as in very deed our life, as the Christ who dwells in us.

The Secret of True Obedience.

'He learned obedience.'—Heb. 5:8.

The secret of true obedience—let me say at once what I believe it to be—is the clear and close personal relationship to God. All our attempts after full obedience will be failures until we get access to His abiding fellowship. It is God's holy presence, consciously abiding with us, that keeps us from disobeying Him.

Defective obedience is always the result of a defective life. To rouse and spur on that defective life by arguments and motives has its use, but their chief blessing must be that they make us feel the need of a different life, a life so entirely under the power of God that obedience will be its natural outcome. The defective life, the life of broken and irregular fellowship with God, must be healed, and make way for a full and healthy life; then full obedience will become possible. The secret of a true obedience is the return to close and continual fellowship with God.

'He learned obedience' (Heb. 5:8). And why was this needful? And what is the blessing He brings us? Listen, 'He learned obedience by the things which He suffered, and became the author of eternal salvation to all them that obey Him.'

Suffering is unnatural to us, and therefore calls for the surrender of our will.

Christ needed suffering that in it He might learn to obey and give up His will to the Father at any cost. He needed to learn obedience that as our great High Priest He might be made perfect. He learned obedience, He became obedient unto death, that He might become the author of our salvation. He became the author of salvation through obedience, that He might save those 'who obey Him.'

As obedience was with Him absolutely necessary to procure, it is with us absolutely necessary to inherit, salvation. The very essence of salvation is—obedience to God. Christ as the obedient One saves us as His obedient ones. Whether in His suffering on earth, or in His glory in heaven, whether in Himself or in us, obedience is what the heart of Christ is set upon.

On earth Christ was a learner in the school of obedience; in heaven He teaches it to His disciples here on earth. In a world where disobedience reigns unto death, the restoration of obedience is in Christ's hands. As in His own life, so in us, He has undertaken to maintain it. He teaches and works it in us.

Let us try and think what and how He teaches: it may be we shall see how little we have given ourselves to be pupils in this school, where alone obedience is to be learnt. When we think of an ordinary school, the principal things we ask often are,— (1) the teacher, (2) the class-books, (3) the pupils. Let us see what each of these is in Christ's school of obedience.

I. The Teacher

'He learned obedience.' And now that He teaches it, He does so first and most by unfolding the secret of His own obedience to the Father.

I have said that the power of true obedience is to be found in the clear personal relationship to God. It was so with our Lord Jesus. Of all His teaching He said, 'I have not spoken of Myself, but the Father which sent Me gave Me a commandment, what I should say and what I should speak. And I know that His commandment is life everlasting; whatever I speak therefore, even as the Father said unto Me, so I speak.'

This does not mean that Christ received God's commandment in eternity as part of the Father's commission to Him on entering the world. No. Day by day, each moment as He taught and worked, He lived, as man, in continual communication with the Father, and received the Father's instructions just as He needed them. Does He not say, 'The Son can do nothing of Himself but what He seeth the Father do; for the Father showeth the Son all things that Himself doeth; and He will show Him greater things,' 'As I hear, I judge,' 'I am not alone, but I and the Father that sent Me,' 'The words that I speak, I speak not of Myself, but the Father that dwelleth in Me'? It is everywhere a dependence upon a present fellowship and operation of God, a hearing and a seeing of what God speaks and does and shows.

Our Lord ever spoke of His relation to the Father as the type and the promise of our relation to Him, and to the Father through Him. With us as with Him, the life of continual obedience is impossible without continual fellowship and continual teaching. It is only when God comes into our lives, in a degree and a power which many never consider possible, when His presence as the Eternal and Ever-present One is believed and received, even as the Son believed and received it, that there can be any hope of a life in which every thought is brought into captivity to the obedience of Christ.

The imperative need of the continual receiving our orders and instructions from God Himself is what is implied in the words: '*obey my voice, and I will be your god.*'

The expression 'obeying the commandments' is very seldom used in Scripture; it is almost always obeying Me, or obeying or hearkening to My voice. With the commander of an army, the teacher of a school, the father of a family, it is not the code of laws, however clear and good, with its rewards or threats, that secures true obedience; it is *the personal living influence*, wakening love and enthusiasm. It is the joy of ever hearing the Father's voice that will give the joy and the strength of true obedience. It is the voice gives power to obey the word; the word without the living voice does not avail.

How clearly this is illustrated by the contrast of what we see in Israel. The people had heard the voice of God on Sinai, and were afraid. They asked Moses that God might no more speak to them. Let Moses receive the word of God and bring it to them. They only thought of the commands; they knew not that the only power to obey is in the presence of God and His voice speaking to us. And so with only Moses to speak to them, and the tables of stone, their whole history is one of disobedience, because they were afraid of direct contact with God.

It is even so still. Many, many Christians find it so much easier to take their teaching from godly men than to wait upon God to receive it from Himself. Their faith stands in the wisdom of men, and not in the power of God.

Do let us learn the great lesson our Lord, 'who learned obedience' by every moment waiting to see and hear the Father, has to teach us. It is only when, like Him, with Him, in and through Him, we ever walk with God, and hear His voice, that we can possibly attempt to offer God the obedience He asks and promises to work.

Out of the depths of His own life and experience, Christ can give and teach us this. Pray earnestly that God may show you the folly of attempting to obey without the same strength Christ needed, may make you willing to give up everything for the Christlike joy of the Father's presence all the day.

II. The Text-Book.

Christ's direct communication with the Father did not render Him independent of Holy Scripture.

In the divine school of obedience there is but one text-book, whether for the Elder Brother or the younger children. In His learning obedience He used the same text-book as we have. Not only when He had to teach or to convince others did He appeal to the Word—He needed it and He used it for His own spiritual life and guidance.

From the commencement of His public life to its close He lived by the Word of God. 'It is written' was the sword of the Spirit with which He conquered Satan. 'The Spirit of the Lord God is upon Me': this word of Scripture was the consciousness with which He opened His preaching of the gospel. 'That the Scripture might be fulfilled' was the light in which He accepted all suffering, and even gave Himself to the death. After the resurrection He expounded to the disciples 'in all the Scriptures the things concerning Himself.'

In Scripture He had found God's plan and path for Him marked out. He gave Himself to fulfill it. It was in and with the use of God's Word that He received the Father's continual direct teaching.

In God's school of obedience the Bible is the only text-book. That shows us the disposition in which we are to come to the Bible—with the simple desire in it to find what is written concerning us as to God's will, and to do it.

Scripture was not written to increase our knowledge but to guide our conduct; 'that the man of God may be perfect, thoroughly furnished unto all good works.' 'If any man will do, he shall know.' Learn from Christ to consider all there is in Scripture of the revelation of God, and His love, and His counsel, as simply auxiliary to God's great end: that the man of God may be fitted to do His will, as it is done in heaven; that man may be restored to that perfect obedience on which God's heart is set, and which alone is blessedness.

In God's school of obedience God's Word is the only text-book. To apply that Word in His own life and conduct, to know when each different portion was to be taken up and carried out, Christ needed and received a divine teaching. It is He who speaks in Isaiah, 'The Lord God wakeneth morning by morning, He wakeneth Mine ear to hear as the learned; the Lord God hath opened My ear.'

Even so does He who thus learned obedience teach it us, by giving us the Holy Spirit in our heart as the divine Interpreter of the Word. This is the great work of the indwelling Holy Spirit—to draw the Word we read and think upon into our heart, and make it quick and powerful there, so that God's living Word may work effectually in our will, our love, our whole being.

It is because this is not understood that the Word has no power to work obedience.

Let me try and speak very plainly about this. We rejoice in increased attention given to Bible study, and in testimonies as to the interest awakened and benefit received. But let us not deceive ourselves. We may delight in studying the Bible; we may admire and be charmed with the views we get of God's truth; the thoughts suggested may make a deep impression and waken the most pleasing religious emotions; and yet the practical influence in making us holy or humble, loving, patient, ready either for service or suffering, be very small. The one reason for this is that we do not receive the Word, as it is in very deed, as the Word of a living God, who must Himself speak to us, and into us, if it is to exert its divine power.

The letter of the Word, however we study and delight in it, has no saving or sanctifying power. Human wisdom and human will, however strenuous their effort, cannot give, cannot command that power. The Holy Spirit is the mighty power of God: it is only as the Holy Spirit teaches you, only as the gospel is preached to you by man or by book, 'with the Holy Ghost sent down from heaven,' that it will really give you, with every command, the strength to obey, and work in you the very thing commanded.

With man, knowing and willing, knowing and doing, even willing and performing, are, for lack of power, often separate, and even at variance. Never in the Holy Spirit. He is at once the light and the might of God. All He is and does and gives has in it equally the truth and the power of God. When He shows you God's command, He always shows it you as a possible and a certain thing, a divine life and gift prepared for you, which He who shows is able to impart.

Beloved Bible students! do learn to believe that it is only when Christ, through the Holy Spirit, teaches you to understand and take the Word into your heart, that He can really teach you to obey as He did. Do believe, every time you open your Bible, that just as sure as you listen to the divine, Spirit-breathed Word, so surely will our Father, in answer to the prayer of faith and docile waiting, give the Holy Spirit's living operation in your heart. Let all your Bible study be a thing of faith. Do not only try and believe the truths or promises you read. This may be in your own power. Before that, believe in the Holy Spirit, in His being in you, in God's working in you through Him. Take the Word into your heart, in the quiet faith that He will enable you to love it, and yield to it, and keep it; and our blessed Lord Jesus will make the book to you what it was to Him when He spoke of 'the things which are written concerning Me.' All Scripture will become the simple revelation of what God is going to do for you, and in you, and through you.

III. The Pupil.

We have seen how our Lord teaches us obedience by unfolding the secret of His learning it, in unceasing dependence on the Father. We have seen how He teaches us to use the Sacred Book as He used it, as a divine revelation of what God has ordained for us, with the Holy Spirit to expound and enforce. If we now consider the place the believer takes in the school of obedience as a pupil, we shall better understand what Christ the Son requires to do His work in us effectually.

In a faithful student there are several things that go to make up his feelings towards a trusted teacher. He submits himself entirely to his leading. He reposes perfect trust in him. He gives him just as much time and attention as he asks.

When we see and consent that Jesus Christ has a right to all this, we may hope to experience how wonderfully He can teach us an obedience like His own.

1. The true pupil, say of some great musician or painter, yields his master a whole-hearted and unhesitating submission.

In practicing his scales or mixing the colors, in the slow and patient study of the elements of his art, he knows that it is wisdom simply and fully to obey.

It is this whole-hearted surrender to His guidance, this implicit submission to His authority, Christ asks. We come to Him asking Him to teach us the lost art of obeying God as He did. He asks us if we are ready to pay the price. It is entirely and utterly to deny self! It is to give up our will and our life to the death! It is to be ready to do whatever He saith!

The only way of learning to do a thing is to do it. The only way of learning obedience from Christ is to give up your will to Him, and to make the doing of His will the one desire and delight of your heart.

Unless you take the vow of absolute obedience as you enter this class of Christ's school, it will be impossible for you to make any progress.

2. The true scholar of a great master finds it easy to render him this implicit obedience, simply because he trusts him.

He gladly sacrifices his own wisdom and will to be guided by a higher.

We need this confidence in our Lord Jesus. He came from heaven to learn obedience, that He might be able to teach it well. His obedience is the treasury out of which, not only the debt of our past disobedience is paid, but out of which the grace for our present obedience is supplied. In His divine love and perfect human sympathy, in His divine power over our hearts and lives, He invites, He deserves, He wins our trust. It is by the power of a personal admiration and attachment to Himself, it is by the power of His divine love, in every deed shed into our heart by the Holy Spirit and wakening within us a responsive love, that He wakens our confidence, and communicates to us the true secret of success in His school. As absolutely as we have trusted Him as a Savior to atone for our disobedience, so let us trust him as a Teacher to lead us out of it. Christ is our Prophet or Teacher. A heart that enthusiastically believes in His power and success as a Teacher, will, in the joy of that faith, find it possible and easy to obey. It is the presence of Christ with us all the day that will be the secret of true obedience.

3. A scholar gives his master just as much of his attendance and attention as he asks. The master fixes how much time must be devoted to personal intercourse and instruction.

Obedience to God is such a heavenly art, our nature is so utterly strange to it, the path in which the Son Himself learned it was so slow and long, that we must not wonder if it does not come at once. Nor must we wonder if it needs more time at the Masterfeet in meditation, and prayer, and waiting, in dependence and self-sacrifice, than the most are ready to give. But let us give it.

In Christ Jesus heavenly obedience has become human again, obedience has become our birth-right and our life-breath: let us cling to Him, let us believe and claim His abiding presence. With Jesus Christ who learned obedience as our Savior, with Jesus Christ who teaches obedience as our Master, we can live lives of obedience. His obedience—we cannot study the lesson too earnestly—His obedience is our salvation; in Him, the living Christ, we find it and partake of it moment by moment.

Let us beseech God to show us how Christ and His obedience are actually to be our life every moment: that will then make us pupils who give Him all our heart and all our time. And He will teach us to keep His commandments and abide in His love, even as He kept His Father's commandments and abides in His love.

The Morning Watch in the Life of Obedience.

'If the first fruit is holy, so is the lump; and if the root is holy, so are the branches.' —*Rom. 11:16.*

How wonderful and blessed is the divine appointment of the first day of the week as a holy day of rest. Not, (as some think), that we might have at least one day of rest and spiritual refreshment amid the weariness of life, but that that one holy day, at the opening of the week, might sanctify the whole, might help and fit us to carry God's holy presence into all the week and its work. With the first-fruit holy, the whole lump is holy; with the root holy, all the branches are holy too.

How gracious, too, the provision suggested by so many types and examples of the Old Testament, by which a morning hour at the opening of the day can enable us to secure a blessing for all its work, and give us the assurance of *power for victory* over every temptation. How unspeakably gracious, that in the morning hour the bond that unites us with God can be so firmly tied that during hours when we have to move amid the rush of men or duties, and can scarce think of God, the soul can be kept safe and pure; that the soul can so give itself away, in the time of secret worship, into His keeping, that temptation shall only help us to unite it closer with Him. What cause for praise and joy, that the morning watch can so each day renew and strengthen the surrender to Jesus and the faith in Him, that the life of obedience can not only be maintained in fresh vigor, but can indeed go on from strength to strength.

I would fain point out how intimate and vital the connection between obedience and the morning watch is. The desire for a life of entire obedience will give new meaning and value to the morning watch, even as this again can alone give the strength and courage needed for the former.

I. The Motive Principle.

Think first of the motive principle that will make us love and faithfully keep the morning watch.

If we take it upon us simply as a duty, and a necessary part of our religious life, it will very soon become a burden. Or, if the chief thought be our own happiness and safety, that will not supply the power to make it truly attractive. There is only one thing will suffice—the desire for fellowship with God.

It is for that we were created in God's likeness. It is that in which we hope to spend eternity. It is that alone can fit us for a true and blessed life, either here, or hereafter. To have more of God, to know Him better, to receive from Him the communication of His love and strength, to have our life filled with His,—it is for this He invites us to enter the inner chamber and shut the door.

It is in the closet, in the morning watch, that our spiritual life is both tested and strengthened. There is the battlefield where it is to be decided every day whether God is to have all, whether our life is to be absolute obedience. If we truly conquer there, getting rid of ourselves into the hands of our Almighty Lord, the victory during the day is sure. It is there, in the inner chamber, proof is to be given whether we really delight in God, and make it our aim to love Him with our whole heart.

Let this, then, be our first lesson: the presence of God is the chief thing, in our devotions. To meet God, to give ourselves into His holy will, to know that we are pleasing to Him, to have Him give us our orders, and lay His hand upon us, and bless us, and say to us, 'Go in this thy strength' —it is when the soul learns that this is what is to be found in the morning watch, day by day, that we shall learn to long for it and delight in it.

II. Reading the Bible.

Let us next speak of the reading of God's Word, as part of what occupies us there. With regard to this I have more than one thing I wish to say.

1. One is that unless we beware, the Word, which is meant to point us away to God, may actually intervene and hide Him from us.

The mind may be occupied and interested and delighted at what it finds, and yet, because this is more head knowledge than anything else, it may bring little good to us. If it does not lead us to wait on God, to glorify Him, to receive His grace and power for sweetening and sanctifying our lives, it becomes a hindrance instead of a help.

2. Another lesson that cannot be repeated too often, or pressed too urgently, is that it is only by the teaching of the Holy Ghost that we can get at the real meaning of what God means by His Word, and that the Word will really reach into our inner life, and work in us.

The Father in heaven, who gave us His Word from heaven, with its divine mysteries and message, has given us His Holy Spirit in us, to explain and internally appropriate that Word. The Father wants us each time to ask that He teach us by His Spirit. He wants us to bow in a meek, teachable frame of mind, and believe that the Spirit will, in the hidden depth of our heart, make His Word live and work. He wants us to remember that the Spirit is given us that we should be led by Him, should walk after Him, should have our whole life under His rule, and that therefore He cannot teach us in the morning unless we honestly give up ourselves to His leading. But if we do this and patiently wait on Him, not to get new thoughts but to get the power of the Word in our heart, we can count upon His teaching.

Let your closet be the classroom, let your morning watch be the study hour, in which your relation of entire dependence on, and submission to, the Holy Spirit's teaching is proved to God.

3. A third remark I want to make, in confirmation of what was said above, is this: ever study in God's Word in the spirit of an unreserved surrender to obey.

You know how often Christ, and His apostles in their Epistles, speak of hearing and not doing. If you accustom yourself to study the Bible without an earnest and very definite purpose to obey, you are getting hardened in disobedience.

Never read God's will concerning you without honestly giving up yourself to do it at once, and asking grace to do so. God has given us His Word, to tell us what He wants us to do and what grace He has provided to enable us to do it: how sad to think it a pious thing just to read that Word without any earnest effort to obey it! May God keep us from this terrible sin!

Let us make it a sacred habit to say to God, 'Lord, whatever I know to be Thy will, I will at once obey.' Ever read with a heart yielded up in willing obedience.

4. One more remark. I have here spoken of such commands as we already know, and as are easily understood. But, remember, there are a great many commands to which your attention may never have been directed, or others of which the application is so wide and unceasing that you have not taken it in. Read God's Word with a deep desire to know all His will. If there are things which appear difficult, commands which look too high, or for which

you need a divine guidance to tell you how to carry them out,—and there are many such,—let them drive you to seek a divine teaching. It is not the text that is easiest and most encouraging that brings most blessing, but the text, whether easy or difficult, which throws you most upon God. God would have you 'filled with the knowledge of His will in all wisdom and spiritual understanding'; it is in the closet this wonderful work is to be done. Do remember, it is only when you know that God is telling you to do a thing that you feel sure He gives the strength to do it. It is only as we are willing to know all God's will that, He will from time to time reveal more of it to us, and that we, will be able to do it all.

What a power the morning watch may be in the life of one who makes a determined resolve to meet God there; to renew the surrender to absolute obedience; humbly and patiently to wait on the Holy Spirit to be taught all God's will; and to receive the assurance that every promise given him in the Word will infallibly be made true! He that thus prays for himself, will become a true intercessor for others.

III. Prayer.

It is in the light of these thoughts I want now to say a few words on what prayer is to be in the morning watch.

1. First of all, see that you secure the presence of God.

Do not be content with anything less than seeing the face of God, having the assurance that He is looking on you in love, and listening and working in you.

If our daily life is to be full of God, how much more the morning hour, where the life of the day alone can have God's seal stamped upon it. In our religion we want nothing so much as *more of God*—His love, His will, His holiness, His Spirit living in us, His power working in us for men. Under heaven there is no way of getting this but by close personal communion. And there is no time so good for securing and practicing it, as the morning watch.

The superficiality and feebleness of our religion and religious work all come from having so little real contact with God. If it be true that God alone is the fountain of all love and good and happiness, and that to have as much as possible of His presence and His fellowship, of His will and His service, is our truest and highest happiness, surely then to meet Himself alone in the morning watch ought to be *our first care.*

To have had God appear to them, and speak to them, was with all the Old Testament saints the secret of their obedience and their strength. Do give

God time in secret so to reveal Himself, that your soul may call the name of the place Peniel,—'for I have seen Him face to face.'

2. My next thought is: let the renewal of your surrender to absolute obedience for that day be a chief part of your morning sacrifice.

Let any confession of sin be very definite—a plucking out and cutting off of everything that has been grieving to God. Let any prayer for grace for a holy walk be as definite—an asking and accepting in faith of the very grace and strength you are specially in need of. Let your outlook on the day you are entering on be a very determined resolve that obedience to God shall be *its controlling principle.*

Do understand that there is no surer way, rather, that there is no other possible way, of getting into God's love and blessing in prayer, than by getting into His will. In prayer, give up yourself most absolutely to the blessed will of God: this will avail more than much asking. Beseech God to show you this great mercy, that He allows you, that He will enable you, to enter into His will, and abide there—that will make the knowing and doing His will in your life a blessed certainty. Let your prayer indeed be a 'morning sacrifice,' a placing yourself as a whole burnt-offering on the altar of the Lord.

The measure of surrender to full obedience will be the measure of confidence toward God.

3. Then remember that true prayer and fellowship with God cannot be all from one side.

We need to be still, to wait and hear what response God gives. This is the office of the Holy Spirit, to be the voice of God to us. In the hidden depths of the heart, He can give a secret but most certain assurance that we are heard, that we are well-pleasing, that the Father engages to do for us what we have asked. What we need, to hear the Voice, to receive this assurance, is the quiet stillness that waits on God, the quiet faith that trusts in God, the quiet heart that bows in nothingness and humility before God, and allows Him to be all in all.

It is when God is waited on to take His part in our prayer that the confidence will come to us that we receive what we ask, that our surrender of ourselves in the sacrifice of obedience is accepted, and that therefore we can count upon the Holy Spirit to guide us into all the will of God, as He means us to know and do it.

What glory would come to us in the morning watch, and through it into our daily life, if it were thus made an hour spent with the Triune God, for the Father, through the Son and the Spirit, to take conscious possession of us for the day. How little need there then would be to urge and plead with God's children to watch the morning watch!

4. And now comes the last and the best of all. Let your prayer be intercessional, on behalf of others.

In the obedience of our Lord Jesus, as in all His fellowship with the Father, the essential element was—it was all for others. This Spirit flows through every member of the body; the more we know it, and yield to it, the more will our life be what God would make it. The highest form of prayer is intercession. The chief object for which God chose Abraham and Israel and us was to make us a blessing to the world. We are a royal priesthood—a priestly people. As long as prayer is only a means of personal improvement and happiness, we cannot know its full power. Let intercession be a real longing for the souls of those around us, a real bearing of the burden of their sin and need, a real pleading for the extension of God's kingdom, real labor in prayer for definite purposes to be realized—let such intercession be what the morning watch is consecrated to, and see what new interest and attraction it will have.

Intercession! Oh to realize what it means! To take the name, and the righteousness, and the worthiness of Christ, to put them on, and in them to appear before God! 'In Christ's stead,' now that He is no longer in the world, to beseech God, by name, for the individual men and needs, where His grace can do its work! In the faith of our own acceptance, and of the anointing with the Spirit to fit us for the work, to know that our prayer can avail to 'save a soul from death,' can bring down and dispense the blessing of heaven upon earth! To think that in the hour of the morning watch this work can be renewed and carried on day by day, each inner chamber maintaining its own separate communication with heaven, and helping together in bringing down its share of the blessing.

It is in intercession, more than in the zeal that works in its own strength with little prayer, that the highest type of piety, the true Christlikeness is cultivated. It is in intercession that a believer rises to his true nobility in the power of imparting life and blessing. It is to intercession we must look for any large increase of the power of God in the Church and its work for men.

One word in conclusion. Turn back and think now again about *the intimate and vital connection* between obedience and the morning watch.

Without obedience there cannot be the spiritual power to enter into the knowledge of God's Word and will. Without obedience there cannot be the confidence, the boldness, the liberty that knows that it is heard. Obedience is fellowship with God in His will; without it there is not the capacity for seeing and claiming and holding the blessings He has for us.

And so, on the other side, without very definite living communion with God in the morning watch, the life of obedience cannot possibly be maintained. It is there that the vow of obedience can every morning be renewed in power and confirmed from above. It is there that the presence and fellowship can be secured which make obedience possible. It is there that in the obedience of the One, and in the union with Himself, the strength is received for all that God can ask. It is there that the spiritual understanding of God's will is received, which leads to walk worthy of the Lord to all well-pleasing.

God has called His children to live a wonderful, heavenly, altogether supernatural life. Let the morning watch each day be to you as *the open gate of heaven*, through which its light and power streams in on your waiting heart, and from which you go out to walk with God all the day

The Entrance to the Life of Full Obedience

'Obedient unto death.' —Phil. 2:8.

After all that has been said on the life of obedience, I purpose speaking in this address of the entrance on that life.

You might think it a mistake to take this text, in which you have obedience in its very highest perfection, as our subject in speaking of the entrance on the course. But it is no mistake. The secret of success in a race is to have the goal clearly defined, and aimed at from the very outset.

'He became obedient unto death.' There is no other Christ for any of us, no other obedience that pleases God, no other example for us to copy, no other Teacher from whom to learn to obey. Christians suffer inconceivably because they do not at once and heartily accept this as the only obedience they are to aim at. The youngest Christian will find it a strength in the school of Christ to make nothing less from the commencement his prayer and his vow: Obedient unto Death. It is at once the beauty and the glory of Christ. A share in it is the highest blessing He has to give. The desire for and the surrender to it is possible to the youngest believer.

If you want to be reminded of what it means, think of the story in ancient history. A proud king, with a great army following him, demands the submission of the king of a small but brave nation. When the ambassadors have delivered their message, he calls one of his soldiers to stab himself. At once he does it. A second is called; he too obeys at once. A third is summoned; he too is obedient to death.

'Go and tell your master that I have three thousand such men; let him come.'

The king dared count upon men who held their life not dear to them when the king's word called for it.

It is such obedience God wants. It is such obedience Christ gave. It is such obedience He teaches. Be it such obedience and nothing less we seek to learn. From the very outset of the Christian life let this be our aim, that we may avoid the fatal mistake of calling Christ Master and yet not doing what He says.

Let all who by these addresses have in any degree been convicted of the sin of disobedience, listen as we study from God's Word the way to escape from that and gain access to the life Christ can give—the entrance to the life of full obedience.

I. The Confession and Cleansing of the Disobedience

It is easy to see that this must be the first step. In Jeremiah, the prophet who more than any other speaks of the disobedience of God's people, God says,

'Return, thou backsliding Israel, saith the Lord; for I am merciful. Only acknowledge thine iniquity that you have not obeyed My voice, saith the Lord God. Turn, O backsliding children, saith the Lord.'

As little as there can be pardon at conversion without confession can there be, after conversion, deliverance from the overcoming power of sin and the disobedience it brings, without a new and deeper conviction and confession.

The thought of our disobedience must not be a vague generality. The special things in which we actually disobey must be definitely found out, and in confession given up and placed in the hands of Christ, and by Him cleansed away. Then only can there be the hope of entering into the way of true obedience.

Let us search our life by the light of the teaching of our Lord.

1. Christ appealed to the law.

He was not come to destroy the law, but to secure its fulfillment. To the young ruler, He said, 'Thou knowest the commandments.' Let the law be our first test.

Let us take a single sin—such as that of lying. I had a note from a young lady once saying that she wished to obey fully, and that she felt urged to confess an untruth she had told me. It was not a matter of importance, and yet she rightly judged that the confession would help her to cast it from her.

How much there is in ordinary society, how much in school life, too, that will not stand the test of strict truthfulness!

And so, there are other commandments, up to the very last, with its condemnation of all coveting and lusting after what is not ours, in which too frequently the Christian gives way to disobedience.

All this must come to a complete end. We must confess it, and in God's strength put it away forever, if there is to be any thought of our entering a life of full obedience.

2. Christ revealed the new law of love.

To be merciful as the Father in heaven, to forgive just as He does, to love enemies and to do good to them that hate us, and to live lives of self-sacrifice and beneficence,—this was the religion Jesus taught on earth.

Let us look upon an unforgiving spirit when we are provoked or ill-used, upon unloving thoughts and sharp or unkind words, upon the neglect of the call to show mercy and do good and bless, all as so much disobedience, which must be felt and mourned over and plucked out like a right eye, ere the power of a full obedience can be ours.

3. Christ spoke much of self-denial.

Self is the root of all lack of love and obedience. Our Lord called His disciple to deny himself and to take up his cross; to forsake all, to hate and lose his own life, to humble himself and become the servant of all. He did so, because self, self-will, self-pleasing, self-seeking, is simply the source of all sin.

When we indulge the flesh in such a simple thing as eating and drinking; when we gratify self by seeking or accepting or rejoicing in what indulges our pride; when self-will is allowed to assert itself, and we make provision for the fulfillment of its desire, we are guilty of disobedience to His command. This gradually clouds the soul and makes the full enjoyment of His light and peace an impossibility,

4. Christ claimed for God the love of the heart.

For Himself He equally claimed the sacrifice of all to come and follow Him. The Christian who has not definitely at heart made this his aim, who has not determined to seek for grace so to live, is guilty of disobedience. There may be much in his religion that appears good and earnest, but he cannot possibly have the joyful consciousness of knowing that he is doing the will of his Lord, and keeping His commandments.

When the call is heard to come and now begin anew a true life of obedience, there are many who feel the desire to do so, and try quietly to slip into it. They think that by more prayer and Bible study they will grow into it—it will gradually come. They are greatly mistaken. The word God uses in Jeremiah might teach them their mistake:

'Turn, ye backsliding children, turn to Me.'

A soul that is in full earnest and has taken the vow of full obedience may grow out of a feeble obedience into a fuller one. But there is no growing out of disobedience into obedience. A turning back, a turning away, a decision, a crisis, is needed. And that only comes by the very definite insight into what has been wrong, and its confession with shame and penitence. Then alone will the soul seek for that divine and mighty cleansing from all its filthiness which prepares for the consciousness of the gift of the new heart, and God's Spirit in it causing us to walk in His statutes.

If you would hope to lead a different life, to become a man or a woman of a Christlike obedience unto death, do begin by beseeching God for the Holy Spirit of conviction, to show you all your disobedience and to lead you in humble confession to the cleansing God has provided. Rest not till you have received it.

II. Faith That Obedience Is Possible.

This is the second step. To take that step we must try and understand clearly what obedience is.

1. To this end we must attend carefully to the difference between voluntary and involuntary sin. It is with the former alone that obedience deals.

We know that the new heart which God gives His child is placed in the midst of the flesh with its sinfulness. Out of this there often arises, even in one who is walking in true obedience, evil suggestions of pride, unlovingness, impurity, over which he has no direct control. They are in their nature utterly sinful and vile; but they are not imputed to a man as acts of transgression. They are not acts of disobedience, which he can break off and cast out, as he can the disobedience of which we have spoken. The deliverance from them comes in another way, not through the will of the regenerate man, by which obedience always comes, but through the cleansing power of the blood and the indwelling Christ. As the sinful nature rises, all he can do is to abhor it and trust in the blood that at once cleanses him and keeps him clean.

It is of great consequence to note the distinction. It keeps the Christian from thinking obedience impossible. It encourages him to seek and offer his obedience in the sphere where it can avail. And it is just in proportion as in its own sphere the power of the will for obedience is maintained, that the power of the Spirit can be trusted and obtained to do the cleansing work in what is beyond the reach of the will.

2. When this difficulty has been removed, there is often a second one arises, to make us doubt whether obedience be indeed possible.

Men connect it with the idea of absolute perfection. They put together all the commands of the Bible; they think of all the graces these commands point to, in their highest possible measure; and they think of a man with all those graces, every moment in their full perfection, as an obedient man. How different is the demand of the Father in heaven! He takes account of the different powers and attainments of each child of His. He asks of him only the obedience of each day, or rather, each hour at a time. He sees whether I have indeed chosen and given myself up to the whole-hearted performance of every known command. He sees whether I am really longing and learning to know and do all His will. And when His child does this, in simple faith and love, the obedience is acceptable. The Spirit gives us the sweet assurance that we are well-pleasing to Him, and enables us to 'have confidence before God, because we know that we keep His commandments, and do the things that are pleasing in His sight.'

This obedience is indeed an attainable degree of grace. The faith that it is, is indispensable to the obedient walk.

You ask for the ground of that faith in God's Word? You find it in God's New Covenant promise,

'I will write My law in their heart. I will put My fear in their heart, and they shall not depart from Me.'

The great defect of the Old Covenant was that it demanded, but did not provide, the power for obedience. This the New Covenant did. The heart means the love, the life. The law put into, written into the heart, means that it has taken possession of the inmost life and love of the renewed man. The new heart delights in the law of God, it is willing and able to obey it.

You doubt this; your experience does not confirm it. No wonder! A promise of God is a thing of faith; you do not believe it, and so cannot experience it.

You know what invisible writing fluid is. You, write with it on paper, and nothing can be seen by a man who is not in the secret. Tell him of it, and by faith he knows it. Hold it up to the sun, or put some chemical on it, and out comes the secret writing. So God's law is written in your heart. If you believe this firmly, and come and say to God that His law is there in your inmost part, and hold up that heart to the light and heat of the Holy Spirit, you will find it true. The law written in the heart will mean to you the fervent love of God's commands, with the power to obey them.22[In a volume being published about the same time, The Two Covenants and the Second Blessing, I have tried to show how plain, how certain, how all sufficient the provision is that has been made in the New Covenant, the Covenant of Grace, for securing our obedience.]

A story is told of one of Napoleon's soldiers. The doctor was seeking to extract a bullet that had lodged in the region of the heart, when the soldier cried,

'Cut deeper, you will find Napoleon graven there.'

Christian! do believe that the law lives in your inmost being! Speak in faith the words of David and of Christ,

'I delight to do Thy will O God! Yea, Thy law is written on my heart.'

The faith of this will assure you that obedience is possible. Such faith will help you into the life of true obedience.

III. The Step out of Disobedience to Obedience Is by Surrender to Christ.

'Turn to Me, ye backsliding children, and I will heal your backsliding,' God said to Israel.

They were His people, but had turned from Him; the return must be immediate and entire. To turn our back upon the divided life of disobedience, and in the faith of God's grace to say 'I will obey,' may be the work of a moment.

The power for it, to take the vow and to maintain it, comes from the living Christ, 'We have said before, the power of obedience lies in the mighty influence of a living personal Presence. As long as we took our knowledge of God's will from a book or from men, we could not but fail. If we take Jesus, in His unchanging nearness, as at once our Lord and our Strength, we can obey. The voice that commands is the voice that inspires. The eye that guides is the eye that encourages. Christ becomes all in all to us; the Master who commands the Example who teaches, the Helper who strengthens. Turn from your life of disobedience to Christ; give up yourself to Him in surrender and faith.

In surrender. Let Him have all. Give up your life to be as full of Him, of His presence, His will, His service, as He can make it. Give up yourself to Him, not to be saved from disobedience, that now you may be happy and live your own life without sinning and trouble. No; but that He may have you wholly for Himself, as a vessel, as a channel, which He can fill with Himself, with His life and love for men, and me in His blessed service.

In faith too. In a new faith. When a soul sees this new thing in Christ, the power for continual obedience, it needs a new faith to take in the special blessing of His great redemption. The faith that only understood 'He became obedient unto death' of His atonement, as a motive to love and obedience, now learns to take the word as Scripture speaks it, 'Have this mind in you, which was also in Christ Jesus, who humbled Himself, becoming obedient even unto death.' It believes that Christ has put His own mind and Spirit into us, and in the faith of that, prepares to live and act it out.

God sent Christ into the world to restore obedience to its place in our heart and life, to restore man to His place in the obedience to God. Christ came, and becoming obedient unto death proved what the only true obedience is. He wrought it out, and perfected it in Himself, as a life that He won through death, and now communicates to us. The Christ who loves us, who leads and teaches and strengthens us, who lives in us, is the Christ who was obedient unto death. 'Obedient unto death' is the very essence of the life He imparts. Shall we not accept it and trust Him to manifest it in us?

Would you enter into the blessed life of obedience? See here the open gate—Christ says, 'I am the door.' See here the new and living way—Christ says, 'I am the way.'

We begin to see it; all our disobedience was owing to our not knowing Christ aright. We see it; obedience is only possible in a life of unceasing fellowship with Himself. The inspiration of His voice, the light of His eyes, the grasp of His hand make it possible, make it certain.

Come and let us bow down, and yield ourselves to this Christ. Obedient unto death, in the faith that He makes us partakers with Himself of all He is and has.

The Obedience of Faith

'By faith Abraham obeyed.' —*Heb. 11:8.*

'By faith Abraham, when he was called to go out into a place which he should after receive as an inheritance, obeyed; and he went out, not knowing whither he went.' He believed that there was a land of Canaan, of which God had spoken. He believed in it as a 'land of promise,' secured to him as an inheritance. He believed that God would bring him there, would show it him, and give it him. In that faith he dared go out, not knowing whither he went. In the blessed ignorance of faith he trusted God, and obeyed, and received the inheritance.

The land of promise that has been set before us is the blessed life of obedience. We have heard God's call to go out and dwell there—about that there can be no mistake. We have heard the promise of Christ to bring us there, and to give us possession of the land—that, too, is clear and sure. We have surrendered ourselves to our Lord, and asked of our Father to make all this true in us. Our desire now is that all our life and work in it may be lifted up to the level of a holy and joyful obedience: and that through us God may make obedience the key-note of the Christian life we aim at promoting in others. Our aim is high: we can only reach it by a new inflow of the power that comes from above. It is only by a faith that gets a new vision and hold of the powers of the heavenly world, secured to us in Christ, that we can obey and obtain the promise.

As we think of all this, of cultivating in ourselves and others the conviction that we only live to please Him to serve His purposes, some are ready to say:

'This is not a land of promise we are called to enter, but a life of burden and difficulty and certain failure.'

Do not say so, my brother! God calls you indeed to a land of promise. Come and prove what He can work in you. Come and experience what the nobility is of a Christlike obedience unto death. Come and see what blessing God will give to him who, with Christ, gives himself the uttermost unto the ever-blessed and most holy will of God. Only believe in the glory of this good land of whole-hearted obedience: in God, in who calls you to it; in Christ, who will bring you in; in the Holy Spirit, who dwells and works all there. He that believeth entereth in.

I wish, then, to speak of the obedience of faith, and of faith as the sufficient power for all obedience. I give you these five simple words as expressive of the disposition of a believing heart entering on that life in the good land:—I see it, I desire it, I expect it, I accept it, I trust Christ for it.

I. Faith Sees It.

We have been trying to show you the map of the land, and to indicate the most important places in that land—the points at which God meets and blesses the soul. What we need now is in faith quietly and definitely to settle the question:

Is there really such a land of promise, in which continuous obedience is certainly, is divinely possible?

As long as there is any doubt on this point, it is out of the question to go up and possess the land.

Just think of Abraham's faith. It rested in God, in His omnipotence and His faithfulness. We have put before you the promises of God. Hear another of them: 'I will give you a new heart. and I will put My Spirit within you, and I will cause you to walk in my judgments, and ye shall keep them.' Here is God's covenant engagement. He adds, 'I the Lord have spoken, and I will do it.' He undertakes to cause and enable you to obey. In Christ and the Holy Spirit He has made the most wonderful provision for fulfilling His engagement.

Just do what Abraham did—fix your heart upon God. 'He was strong in faith, giving glory to God, being fully persuaded that what He had promised He was able to perform.' God's omnipotence was Abraham's stay. Let it be yours. Look out on all the promises God's Word gives of a clean heart, a heart established blameless in holiness, of a life in righteousness and holiness, of a walk in all the commandments of the Lord unblameable and well-pleasing to Him, of God's working in us to will and to do, of His working in us that which is well-pleasing in His sight, in the simple faith: God says this; His power can do it. Let the assurance that a life of full obedience is possible, possess you. Faith can see the invisible and the impossible. Gaze on the vision until your heart says:

'It must be true. It is true. There is a life promised I have never yet known.'

II. Faith Desires It.

When I read the gospel story and see how ready the sick and the blind and the needy were to believe Christ's word, I often ask myself what it was that made them so much more ready to believe than we are. The answer I get in the Word is this, that one great difference lies in the honesty and intensity of the desire. They did indeed desire deliverance with their whole heart. There was no need of pleading with them to make them willing to take His blessing.

Alas, that it should be so different with us! All indeed wish, in a sort of way, to be better than they are. But how few there are who really 'hunger and thirst after righteousness'; how few who intensely long and cry after a life of close obedience, and the continual consciousness of being pleasing to God.

There can be no strong faith without strong desire. Desire is the great motive-power in the universe. It was God's desire to save us moved HIM to send His Son. It is desire that moves one to study and work and suffer. It is alone the desire for salvation that brings a sinner to Christ. It is the desire for God, and the closest possible fellowship with Him, the desire to be just what He would have us be, and to have as much of His will as possible, that will make the promised land attractive to us. It is this will make us forsake everything to get our full share in the obedience of Christ.

And how can the desire be awakened?

Shame on us, that we need to ask the question; that the most desirable of all things, likeness to God in the union with His will and doing it, has so little attraction for us! Let us take it as a sign of our blindness and dullness, and beseech God to give us by His Spirit 'enlightened eyes of the heart,' that we may see and know 'the riches of the glory of our inheritance' waiting upon the life of true obedience. Let us turn and gaze, in this light of God's Spirit, and gaze again on the life as possible, as certain, as divinely secured and divinely blessed, until our faith begins to burn with desire, and to say:

'I do long to have it. With my whole heart will I seek it.'

III. Faith Expects It.

The difference between desire and expectation is great. There is often a strong desire after salvation in a soul who has little hope of really obtaining it. It is a great step in advance when desire passes into expectation, and the soul begins to savor spiritual blessing:

'I am sure it is for me, and, though I do not see how, I confidently expect to obtain it.'

The life of obedience is no longer an unattainable ideal held out by God, to make us strive at least to get a little nearer it, but is become a reality, meant for the life in flesh and blood here on earth. Expect it, as most certainly meant for you. Expect God to make it true.

There is much indeed to hinder this expectation. Your past failure; your unfavorable temperament or circumstances; your feeble faith; your difficulty as to what such a devotion, obedient unto death, may demand; your conscious lack of power for it; —all this makes you say:

'It may be for others; it is not for me, I fear.'

I beseech you, speak not thus. You are leaving God out of account. Expect to get it. Look up to His power and His love, and do begin to say,

'It is for me.'

Take courage from the lives of God's saints who have gone before you. Santa Teresa writes that after her conversion she spent more than eighteen years of her life in that miserable attempt to reconcile God and her life of sin. But at last she was able to write,

'I have made a vow never to offend God in the very least matter. I have vowed that I would rather die a thousand deaths than do anything of that kind, knowing I was doing it—this was obedience unto death. I am resolved never to leave anything whatever undone that I consider still to be more perfect, and more for the honor of my Lord.'33 [She says further: 'We are so long and so slow in giving up our hearts to Thee. And then Thou wilt not permit our possession of Thee without our paying well for so precious a possession. There is nothing in all the world wherewith to buy the shedding abroad of Thy love in our hearts, but our heart's love. God never withholds Himself from them who pay this price and persevere in seeking Him. He will, little by little, and now and then, strengthen and restore that soul, until it is at last victorious.']

Gerhard Tersteegen had from his youth sought and served the Lord. After a time the sense of God's grace was withdrawn from him, and for five long years he was as one far away on the great sea, where neither sun nor stars appear. 'But my hope was in Jesus.' All at once a light broke on him that never went out, and he wrote, with blood drawn from his veins, that letter to the Lord Jesus in which he said:

'From this evening to all eternity, Thy will, not mine be done. Command and rule and reign in me. I yield up myself without reserve, and I promise, with Thy help and power, rather to give up the last drop of my blood than knowingly or willingly be untrue or disobedient to Thee.'

That was his obedience unto death.

Set your heart upon it, and expect it. The same God lives still. Set your hope on Him; He will do it.

IV. Faith Accepts It.

To accept is more than to expect. Many wait and hope and never possess because they do not accept.

To all who have not accepted, and feel as if they were not ready to accept, we say, Expect. If the expectation be from the heart, and be set indeed upon God Himself, it will lead the soul to accept.

To all who say they do expect, we urgently say, Accept. Faith has the wondrous God-given power of saying,

'I accept, I take, I have.'

It is for the lack of this definite faith, that claims and appropriates the spiritual blessing we desire, that so many prayers appear to be fruitless. For such an act of faith all are not ready. Where there is no true conviction of the sin of disobedience, and alas! no true sorrow for it; where there is no strong longing or purpose really in everything to obey God; where there is no deep interest in the message of Holy Scripture, that God wants to 'perfect us to do His will,' by Himself 'working in us that which is pleasing in His sight,' there is not the spiritual capacity to accept the blessing. The Christian is content to be a babe. He wants only to suck the milk of consolation. He is not able to bear the strong meat of which Jesus ate, 'doing, the will of His Father.'

And yet we come to all with the entreaty, Accept it, the grace for this wondrous new life of obedience; accept it now. Without this your act of consecration will come to little. Without this your purpose to try and be more obedient must fail. Has not God shown you that there is an entirely new position for you to take—a possible position of simple childlike obedience, day by day, to every command His voice speaks to you through the Spirit: a possible position of simple childlike dependence on and experience of His all-sufficient grace, day by day, for every command He gives?

I pray you, even now, take that position, make that surrender, take that grace. Accept and enter on the true life of faith, and the unceasing obedience of faith. As unlimited and as sure as God's promise and power are, may your faith be. As unlimited as your faith is, will your simple childlike obedience be. Oh! ask God for His aid, and accept all He has offered you.

V. Faith Trusts Christ for All.

'All the promises of God are in Christ Jesus, and in Him, Amen, unto the glory of God by us.' It is possible that as we have spoken of the life of obedience, there have been questions and difficulties rising to which you cannot at once give answer. You may feel as if you cannot take it all in at once, or reconcile it with all the old habits of thought and speech and action. You fear you will not be able at once to bring all into subjection to this supreme all-controlling principle,

'Do everything as the will of God: do all as obedience to Him.'

To all these questions there is one answer; one deliverance from all these fears; Jesus Christ, the living Savior, knows all, and asks you to trust yourself to Him for the wisdom and the power to walk ever in the obedience of faith.

We have seen more than once how His whole redemption, as He effected it, is nothing but obedience. As He communicates it, it is still the same. He gives us the spirit of obedience as the spirit of our life. This spirit comes to us each moment through Him. He Himself keeps charge of our obedience. There is none under heaven but what He has and gives and works. He offers Himself to us as surety for its maintenance, and asks us to trust Him for it. It is in Jesus Himself all our fears are removed, all our needs supplied, all our desires met. As He the righteous One is your righteousness, He the obedient One is your obedience.

Will you not trust Him for it? What faith sees and desires and expects and accepts, surely it dare trust Christ to give and to work.

Will you not to-day take the opportunity of giving glory to God and His Son, by trusting Jesus now to lead you into the promised land: Look up to your glorified Lord in heaven, and in His strength renew, with new meaning, your vow of allegiance, your vow never to do anything knowingly or willingly that would offend Him. Trust Him for the faith to make the vow, for the heart to keep it, for the strength to carry it out. Trust Him , the loving One, by His living presence, to secure both your faith and obedience. Trust Him, and venture to join in an act of consecration, in the assurance that He undertakes to be its Yea and Amen, to the glory of God by us.

The School of Obedience

'Gather up the fragments that remain, that nothing be lost.' —*John* 6:12.

In this closing chapter I wish to gather up some points not yet touched upon, or not expressed with sufficient clearness, in the hope that they may help some one who has indeed enrolled himself in Christ's school of obedience.

I. On Learning Obedience.

First, let me warn against a misunderstanding of the expression— 'learning obedience.'

We are apt to think that absolute obedience as a principle—obedience unto death—is a thing that can only be gradually learned in Christ's school. This is a great and most hurtful mistake. What we have to learn, and do learn gradually, is the practice of obedience, in new and more difficult commands. But as to the principle, Christ wants us from the very entrance into His school to make the vow of entire obedience.

A little child of five can be implicitly obedient as a youth of eighteen. The difference between the two lies not in the principle, but in the nature of the work demanded. .

Though externally Christ's obedience unto death came at the end of His life, the spirit of His obedience was the same from the beginning. Whole-hearted obedience is not the end, but the beginning of our school life. The end is fitness for God's service, when obedience has placed us fully at God's disposal. A heart yielded to God in unreserved obedience is the one condition of progress in Christ's school, and of growth in the spiritual knowledge of God's will.

Young Christian! do get this matter settled at once. Remember God's rule: all for all. Give Him all: He will give you all. Consecration avails nothing unless it means presenting yourself as a living sacrifice to do nothing but the will of God. The vow of entire obedience is the entrance fee for him who would be enrolled by no assistant teacher, but by Christ Himself, in the school of obedience.

II. Of Learning to Know God's Will.

This unreserved surrender to obey, as it is the first condition of entering Christ's school, is the only fitness for receiving instruction as to the will of God for us.

There is a general will of God for all His children, which we can, in some measure, learn out of the Bible. But there is a special individual application of these commands—God's will concerning each of us personally, which only the Holy Spirit can teach. And He will not teach it, except to those who have taken the vow of obedience.

This is the reason why there are so many unanswered prayers for God to make known His will. Jesus said, 'If any man wills to do His Will, he shall know of the teaching, whether it be of God.' If a man's will is really set on doing God's will, that is, if his heart is given up to do, and he as a consequence does it as far as he knows it, he shall know what God has further to teach him.

It is simply what is true of every scholar with the art he studies, of every apprentice with his trade, of every man in business doing is the one condition of truly knowing. And so obedience, the doing of God's will as far as we know, and the will and the vow to do it all as He reveals it, is the spiritual organ, the capacity for receiving the true knowledge of what is God's will for each of us.

In connection with this let me press upon you three things.

1. Seek to have a deep sense of your very great ignorance of God's will, and of your impotence by any effort to know it aright.

The consciousness of ignorance lies at the root of true teachableness. 'The meek will He guide in the way' —those who humbly confess their need of teaching. Head-knowledge only gives human thoughts without power. God by His Spirit gives a living knowledge that enters the love of the heart, and works effectually.

2. Cultivate a strong faith that God will make you know wisdom in the hidden part, in the heart.

You may have known so little of this in your Christian life hitherto that the thought appears strange. Learn that God's working, the place where He gives His life and light, is in the heart, deeper than all our thoughts. Any uncertainty about God's will makes a joyful obedience impossible. Believe most confidently that the Father is willing to make known what He wants you to do. Count upon Him for this. Expect it certainly.

3. In view of the darkness and deceitfulness of the flesh and fleshly mind, ask God very earnestly for the searching and convincing light of the Holy Spirit.

There may be many things which you have been accustomed to think lawful or allowable, which your Father wants different. To consider it settled that they are the will of God because others and you think so, may effectually shut you out from knowing God's will in other things. Bring everything, without reserve, to the judgment of the Word, explained and applied by the Holy Spirit. Wait on God to lead you to know that everything you are and do is pleasing in His sight.

III. On Obedience unto Death.

There is one of the deeper and more spiritual aspects of this truth to which I have not alluded. It is something that as a rule does not come up in the early stages of the Christian life, and yet it is needful that every believer know what the privileges are that await him. There is an experience into which whole-hearted obedience will bring the believer, in which he will know that, as surely as with his Lord, obedience leads to death.

Let us see what this means. During our Lord's life, His resistance to sin and the world was perfect and complete. And yet His final deliverance from their temptations and His victory over their power, His obedience, was not complete until He had died to the earthly life and to sin. In that death He gave up His life in perfect helplessness into the Father's hands, waiting for Him to raise Him up. It was through death that He received the fullness of His life and glory. Through death alone, the giving up of the life He had, could obedience lead Him into the glory of God.

The believer shares with Christ in this death to sin. In regeneration he is baptized by the Holy Spirit into it. Owing to ignorance and unbelief he may know little experimentally of this entire death to sin. When the Holy Spirit reveals to him what he possesses in Christ, and he appropriates it in faith, the Spirit works in him the very same disposition which animated Christ in His death. With Christ it was an entire ceasing from His own life, a helpless committal of His spirit into the Father's hands. This was the complete fulfillment of the Father's command: Lay down Thy life in My hands. Out of the perfect self-oblivion of the grave He entered the glory of the Father.

It is into the fellowship of this a believer is brought. He finds that in the most unreserved obedience for which God's Spirit fits him, there is still a secret element of self and self-will. He longs to be delivered from it. He is taught in God's Word that this can only be by death. The Spirit helps him to claim more fully that he is indeed dead to sin in Christ, and that the power of that death can work mightily in him. He is made willing to be obedient unto death, this entire death to self, which makes him truly nothing. In this he finds a full entrance into the life of Christ.

To see the need of this entire death to self, to be made willing for it, to be led into the entire self-emptying and humility of our Lord Jesus,—this is the highest lesson that our obedience has to learn —this is, indeed, the Christlike obedience unto death.

There is no room here to enlarge on this. I thought it well to say this much on a lesson which God Himself will, in due time, teach those who are entirely faithful.

IV. Of the Voice of Conscience.

In regard to the knowledge of God's will, we must see and give conscience its place, and submit to its authority.

There are a thousand little things in which the law of nature or education teaches us what is right and good, and in regard to which even earnest Christians do not hold themselves bound to obey. Now, remember, if you are unfaithful in that which is least, who will entrust you with the greater? Not God. If the voice of conscience tells you of some course of action that is the nobler or the better, and you choose another because it is easier or pleasing to self, you unfit yourself for the teaching of the Spirit, by disobeying the voice of God in nature. A strong will always to do the right, to do the very best, as conscience points it out, is a will to do God's will. Paul writes, 'I lie not, my conscience bearing me witness in the Holy Ghost.' The Holy Ghost speaks through conscience: if you disobey and hurt conscience, you make it impossible for God to speak to you.

Obedience to God's will shows itself in tender regard for the voice of conscience. This holds good with regard to eating and drinking, sleeping and resting, spending money and seeking pleasure,—let everything be brought into subjection to the will of God.

This leads to another thing of great importance in this connection. If you would live the life of true obedience, see that you maintain a good conscience before God, and never knowingly indulge in anything which is contrary to His mind. George Muller attributed all his happiness during seventy years to this, along with his love of God's Word. He had maintained a good conscience in all things, not going on in a course he knew to be contrary to the will of God. Conscience is the guardian or monitor God has given you, to give warning when anything goes wrong. Up to the light you have, give heed to conscience.

Ask God, by the teaching of His will, to give it more light. Seek the witness of conscience that you are acting up to that light. Conscience will become your encouragement and your helper, and give you the confidence, both that your obedience is accepted, and that your prayer for ever-increasing, knowledge of the will is heard.

V. Of Legal and Evangelical Obedience.

Even when the vow of unreserved obedience has been taken, there may still be two sorts of obedience—that of the law, and that of the gospel. Just as there are two Testaments, an Old and a New, so there are two styles of religion, two ways of serving God. This is what Paul speaks of in Romans, when he says, 'Sin shall not have dominion over you, for ye are not under law but under grace' (6:14), and further speaks of our being 'freed from the law,' so 'that we serve in newness of the spirit and not in the oldness of the letter' (7:6); and then again reminds us, 'Ye received not again the spirit of bondage unto fear, but ye received the Spirit of adoption' (8:15).

The threefold contrast points very evidently to a danger existing among those Christians of still acting as if they were under the law, serving in the boldness of the letter and in the spirit of bondage. One great cause of the feebleness of so much Christian living is because it is more under law than under grace. Let us see what the difference is.

What the law demands from us, grace promises and performs for us.

The law deals with what we ought to do, whether we can or not, and by the appeal to motives of fear and love stirs us to do our utmost. But it gives no real strength, and so only leads to failure and condemnation. Grace points to what we cannot do, and offers to do it for us and in us.

The law comes with commands on stone or in a book. Grace comes in a living, gracious Person, who gives His presence and His power.

The law promises life, if we obey. Grace gives life, even the Holy Spirit with the assurance that we can obey.

Human nature is ever prone to slip back out of grace into the law, and secretly to trust to trying and doing its utmost. The promises of grace are so divine, the gift of the Holy Spirit to do all in us is so wonderful, that few believe it. This is the reason they never dare take the vow of obedience, or, having taken it, turn back again. I beseech you, study well what gospel obedience is. The gospel is good tidings. Its obedience is part of that good tidings—that grace, by the Holy Spirit, will do all in you. Believe that, and let every undertaking to obey be in the joyous hopefulness that comes from faith in the exceeding abundance of grace, in the mighty indwelling of the Holy

Spirit, in the blessed love of Jesus whose abiding presence makes obedience possible and certain.

VI. Of the Obedience of Love.

This is one of the special and most beautiful aspects of gospel obedience. The grace which promises to work all through the Holy Spirit is the gift of eternal love. The Lord Jesus (who takes charge of our obedience, teaches it, and by His presence secures it to us) is He who loved us unto the death, who loves us with a love that passeth knowledge. Nothing can receive or know love but a loving heart. And it is this loving heart that enables us to obey. Obedience is the loving response to the divine love resting on us, and the only access to a fuller enjoyment of that love.

How our Lord insisted upon that in His farewell discourse! Thrice He repeats it in John 14—'If ye love Me, ye will keep My commandments.' 'He that keepeth My commandments, he it is that loveth Me.' 'If a man love Me, he will keep My word.' Is it not clear that love alone can give the obedience Jesus asks, and receive the blessing Jesus gives to obedience? The gift of the Spirit, the Father's love and His own, with the manifestation of Himself; the Father's love and His own making their abode with us: into these, loving obedience gives the assured access.

In the next chapter He puts it from the other side, and shows how obedience leads to the enjoyment of God's love—He kept His Father's commandments, and abides in His love. If we keep His commandments, we shall abide in His love. He proved His love by giving His life for us; we are His friends, we shall enjoy His love, if we do what He commands us. Between His first love and our love in response to it, between our love and His fuller love in response to ours, obedience is the one indispensable link. True and full obedience is impossible, except as we live and love. 'This is the love of God, that we keep His commandments.'

Do beware of a legal obedience, striving after a life of true obedience under a sense of duty. Ask God to show you the 'newness of life' which is needed for a new and full obedience. Claim the promise, 'I will circumcise thine heart, to love the Lord thy God with all thy heart; and thou shalt obey the Lord thy God.' Believe in the love of God and the grace of our Lord Jesus. Believe in the Spirit given in you, enabling you to love, and so causing you to walk in God's statutes. In the strength of this faith, in the assurance of sufficient grace, made perfect in weakness, enter into God's love, and the life of living obedience it works. For it is nothing but the continual presence of Jesus in His love can fit you for continual obedience.

VII. Is Obedience Possible?

I close with once again, and most urgently, pressing home this question. It lies at the very root of our life. The secret, half-unconscious thought that to live always well-pleasing to God is beyond our reach, eats away the very root of our strength. I beseech you to give a definite answer to the question.

If in the light of God's provision for obedience, of His promise of working all His good pleasure in you, of His giving you a new heart, with the indwelling of His Son and Spirit, you still fear obedience is not possible, do ask God to open your eyes truly to know His will. If your judgment be convinced, and you assent to the truth theoretically, and yet fear to give up yourself to such a life, I say to you too, Do ask God to open your eyes and bring you to know His will for yourself. Do beware lest the secret fear of having to give up too much, of having to become too peculiar and entirely devoted to God, keep you back. Beware of seeking just religion enough to give ease to the conscience, and then not desiring to do and be and give God all He is worthy of. And beware, above all, of 'limiting' God, of making Him a liar, by refusing to believe what He has said He can and will do.

If our study in the school of obedience is to be of any profit, rest not till you have written it down—Daily obedience to all that God wills of me is possible, is possible to me. In His strength I yield myself to Him for it.

But, remember, only on one condition. Not in the strength of your resolve or effort, but that the unceasing presence of Christ, and the unceasing teaching of the Spirit of all grace and power be your portion. Christ, the obedient One, living in you, will secure your obedience. Obedience will be to you a life of love and joy in His fellowship.

Obedience to the Last Command

'Go ye therefore and make disciples of all the nations.' —Matt. 28:19.

'Go ye into all the world and preach the gospel to every creature.'—Mark 16:15. *#8216;As Thou didst send Me into the world, even so send I them into the world'* — John 17:18; 20:21.

'Ye shall receive power, when the Holy Spirit is come upon you: and ye shall be My witnesses unto the uttermost parts of the earth.'—Acts 1:8.

All these words breathe nothing less than the spirit of world conquest. 'All the nations,' 'all the world,' 'every creature,' 'the uttermost parts of the earth,'—each expression indicates that the heart of Christ was set on claiming His rightful dominion over the world He had redeemed and won for Himself. He counts on His disciples to undertake and carry out the work. As He stands at the foot of the throne, ready to ascend and reign, He tells them, 'All authority hath been given unto Me in heaven and on earth,' and points them at once to 'all the world,' to 'the uttermost parts of the earth,' as the object of His and their desire and efforts. As the King on the throne, He Himself will be their helper: 'I am with you always.' They are to be the advance guard of His conquering hosts even to the end of the world. He Himself will carry on the war. He seeks to inspire them with His own assurance of victory, with His own purpose to make this the only thing to be thought of as worth living or dying for—the winning back of the world to its God.

Christ does not teach or argue, ask or plead: He simply commands. He has trained His disciples to obedience. He has attached them to Himself in a love that can obey. He has already breathed His own resurrection Spirit into them. He can count upon them. He dare say to them: 'Go ye into all the world.' Formerly, during His life on earth, they had more than once expressed their doubt about the possibility of fulfilling His commands. But here, as quietly and simply as He speaks these divine words, they accept them. And no sooner has He ascended than they go to the appointed place, to wait for the equipment of a heavenly power from their Lord in heaven, for the heavenly work of making all the nations His disciples. They accepted the command and passed it on to those who through them believed on His name. And within a generation, simple men, whose names we do not even know, had preached the gospel in Antioch and Rome and the regions beyond. The command was passed on, and taken up into the heart and life, as meant for all ages, as *meant for every disciple.*

The command is for us, too, for each one of us. There is in the Church of Christ no privileged clan to which alone belongs the honor, nor any servile clan on which alone rests the duty, of carrying the gospel to every creature. The life Christ imparts is His own life, the spirit He breathes is His very own Spirit, the one disposition He works is His own self-sacrificing love. It lies in the very nature of His salvation that every member of His body, in full and healthy access with Him feels himself urged to impart what he has received. The command is no arbitrary law from without. It is simply the revelation, for our intelligent and voluntary consent, of the wonderful truth that we are His body, that we now occupy His place on earth, and that His will and love now carry out through us the work He began, and that now in His stead we live to seek the Father's glory, in *winning a lost world back to Him.*

How terribly the Church has failed in obeying the command! How many Christians there are who never knew that there is such a command! How many who hear of it, but do not in earnest set themselves to obey it! And how many who seek to obey it in such way and measure as seems to them fitting and convenient.

We have been studying what obedience is. We have professed to give ourselves up to a whole-hearted obedience. Surely we are prepared gladly to listen to anything that can help us to understand and carry out this our Lord's last and great command: the gospel to every creature.

Let me give you what I have to say under the three simple headings: Accept His command. Place yourself entirely at His disposal. Begin at once to live for His kingdom.

I. Accept His Command.

There are various things that weaken the force of this command. There is the impression that a command given to all and general in its nature is not as binding as one that is entirely personal and specific; that if others do not their part, our share of the blame is comparatively small; that where the difficulties are very great, obedience cannot be an absolute demand; that if we are willing to do our best, this is all that can be asked of us.

Brethren! this is not obedience. This is not the spirit in which the first disciples accepted it. This is not the spirit in which we wish to live with our beloved Lord. We want to say, each one of us—If there be no one else, I, by His grace, will give myself and my life to live for His kingdom. Let me for a moment separate myself from all others, and think of my personal relation to Jesus.

I am a member of Christ's body. He expects every member to be at His disposal, to be animated by His Spirit, to live for what He is and does. It is so with my body. I carry every healthy member with me day by day, in the assurance that I can count upon it to do its part. Our Lord has taken me so truly up into His body that He can ask and expect nothing else from me. And I have so truly yielded myself to Him that there can be no idea of my wanting anything but just to know and do His will.

Or let me take the illustration of 'the Vine and the branches.' The branch has just as much only one object for its being as the vine—bearing fruit. If I really am a branch, I am just as much as He was in the world—only and wholly to bring forth fruit, to live and labor for the salvation of men.

Take still another illustration. Christ has bought me with His blood. No slave conquered by force or purchased by money was ever so entirely the property of his master, as my soul, redeemed and won by Christ's blood, given up and bound to Him by love, is His property, for Him alone to do with it what He pleases. He claims by divine right, working through the Holy Spirit in an infinite power, and I have given a full assent, that I live wholly for His kingdom and service. This is my joy and my glory.

There was a time when it was different. There are two ways in which a man can bestow his money or service on another. In olden time there was once a slave, who by his trade earned much money. All the money came to the master. The master was kind and treated the slave well. At length the slave, from earnings his master had allowed him, was able to purchase his liberty. In course of time the master became impoverished, and had to come to his former slave for help. He was not only able, but most willing to give it, and gave liberally, in gratitude for former kindness.

You see at once the difference between the bringing of his money and service when be was a slave, and his gifts when he was free. In the former case he gave all, because it and he belonged to the master. In the latter he only gave what he chose.

In which way ought we to give to Christ Jesus? I fear many, many give as if they were free to give what they chose, what they think they can afford. The believer to whom the right which the purchase price of the blood has acquired, has been revealed by the Holy Spirit, delights to know that he is the bond slave of redeeming love, and to lay everything he has at his Master's feet, because he belongs to Him.

Have you ever wondered that the disciples accepted the great command so easily and so heartily? They came fresh from Calvary, where they had seen the blood. They had met the risen One, and He had breathed His Spirit into them. During the forty days, 'through the Holy Ghost He had given His commandments unto them.' Jesus was to them Savior, Master, Friend, and Lord. His word was with divine power; they could not but obey. Oh, let us bow at His feet, and yield to the Holy Spirit to reveal and assert His mighty claim, and let us unhesitatingly and with the whole heart accept the command as our one life-purpose: the gospel to every creature.

II. Place Yourself at His Disposal.

The last great command has been so prominently urged in connection with Foreign Missions that many are inclined exclusively to confine it to them. This is a great mistake. Our Lord's words, 'Make disciples of all nations; teaching them to observe all things whatsoever I have commanded you,' tell us what our aim is to be—nothing less than to make every man a true disciple, living in holy obedience to all Christ's will.

What a work there is to be done in our Christian churches and our so-called Christian communities ere it can be said that the command has been carried out! And what a need that the whole Church, with every believer in it, realize that to do this work is the sole object of its existence! The gospel brought fully, perseveringly, savingly to every creature: this is the mission, this ought to be the passion, of every redeemed soul. For this alone is the Spirit and likeness and life of Christ formed in you.

If there is one thing that the Church needs to preach, in the power of the Holy Ghost, it is the absolute and immediate duty of every child of God, not only to take some part in this work, as he may think fit or possible, but to give himself to Christ the Master, to be guided and used as He would have. And therefore I say to every reader who has taken the vow of full obedience—and dare we count ourselves true Christians if we have not done so?—place yourself at once and wholly at Christ's disposal. As binding, as is the first great command on all God's people, 'Thou shalt love the Lord thy God, with all thy heart,' is this the last great command too— 'The gospel to every creature.' Ere you know what your work may be, ere you feel any special desire or call or fitness for any work,—if you are willing to accept the command, place yourself at His disposal. It is His as Master to train and fit and guide and use you. Fear not; come at once and forever out of the selfish religion which puts your own will and comfort first, and gives Christ what you see fit. Let the Master know that He can have you wholly. Enroll yourself at once with Him as *a volunteer for His service.*

God has in these few past years filled our hearts with joy and thanksgiving at what He has done through the Student Volunteer Movement. The blessing it is bringing the Christian Church is as great as that coming to the heathen world. I sometimes feel as if there were only one thing still needed to perfect its work. Is there not a need of an enrollment of Volunteers for Home Service, helping its members to feel that as intense and undivided as is the consecration to which the Volunteer for foreign work is stirred and helped is the devotion Christ asks of every one, whom He has bought with His blood, for His service in saving the world? What blessings have not these simple words, 'It is my purpose, if God permit, to become a foreign missionary,' brought into thousands of lives! It helped them into the surrender of obedience to the great command, and became an era in their history. What blessings might not come to many who can never go abroad, or who think so, because they have not asked their Master's will, if they could take the simple resolve By the grace of God I devote my life wholly to the service of Christ's kingdom! The external forsaking of home and going abroad is often a great help to the foreign volunteer, through the struggle it costs him, and the breaking away from all that could hinder him. The home volunteer may have to abide in his calling, and not have the need of such an external separation—he needs all the more the help which a pledge, given in secret, or in union with others, can bring. The blessed Spirit can make it a crisis and a consecration that leads to a life utterly devoted to God.

Students in the school of obedience study the last and great commandment well. Accept it with your whole heart. Place yourselves entirely at His disposal.

III. And Begin at Once to Act on Your Obedience.

In whatever circumstances you are, it is your privilege to have within reach souls that can be won for God. All around you there are numberless forms of Christian activity which invite your help and offer you theirs. Look upon yourself as redeemed by Christ for His service, as blessed with His Spirit to give you the very dispositions that were in Himself, and take up, humbly but boldly, your life calling, to take part in the great work of winning back the world to God. Whether you are led of God to join some of the many agencies already at work, or to walk in a more solitary path, remember not to regard the work as that of your church, or society, or as your own but as the Lord's. Cherish carefully the consciousness of 'doing it unto the Lord,' of being a servant who is under orders, and simply carrying them out; your work will then not, as so often, come between you and the fellowship with Christ, but link you inseparably to Him, His strength, and His approval.

It is so easy to get so engrossed in the human interest there is in our work, that its spiritual character, the supernatural power needed for it, the direct working of God in us and through us, all that can fill us with true heavenly joy and hope is lost out of sight. Keep your eye on your Master, on your King, on His throne. Ere He gave the command, and pointed His servants to the great field of the world. He first drew their eyes to Himself on the throne: 'All power is given Me in heaven and on earth.' It is the vision, the faith, of Christ on the throne that reminds of the need, that assures us of the sufficiency of His divine power. Obey, not a command, but the living Almighty Lord of Glory; faith in Him will give you heavenly strength.

These words preceded the command, and then there followed, 'Lo, I am with you alway.' It is not only Christ on the throne—glorious vision!—that we need, but Christ with us here below, in His abiding presence, Himself working for us and through us. Christ's power in heaven, Christ's presence on earth—between these two pillar promises lies the gate through which the Church enters to the conquest of the world. Let each of us follow our Leader, receive from Himself our orders as to our share in the work, and never falter in the vow of obedience that has given itself to live wholly for His will and His work alone.

Such a beginning will be a training time, preparing us fully to know and follow His leading. If His call for the millions of dying heathen come to us, we shall be ready to go. If His providence does not permit our going, our devotion at home will be as complete and intense as if we had gone. Whether it be at home or abroad, if only the ranks of the obedient, the servants of obedience, the obedient unto earth, are filled up, Christ shall have His heart's desire, and His glorious thought—the gospel to every creature—find its accomplishment!

Blessed Son of God! Here I am. By Thy grace, I give my life to the carrying out of Thy last great command. Let my heart be as Thy heart. Let my weakness be as Thy strength. In Thy name I take the vow of entire and everlasting obedience. Amen.

Note on the Morning Watch.

'By, the observance of the morning watch is commonly meant the spending of at least the first half-hour of every day alone with God, in personal devotional Bible study and prayer.

'There are Christians who say that they do not have time to devote a full half-hour to such a spiritual exercise. It is a striking fact that the busiest Christians constitute the class who plead this excuse the least, and most generally observe the morning watch. Any Christian who will honestly and persistently follow this plan for a month or two will become convinced that it is the best possible use of his time, that it does not interfere with his regular work, and that it promotes the wisest economy of time....

'In India, in China, in Japan, hundreds of students have agreed to keep the morning watch....

'The practical question for each of us is, Why should not I keep the morning watch? Next to receiving Christ as Savior, and claiming the baptism of the Holy Ghost, we know of no act attended with larger good to ourselves and to others than the formation of an undiscourageable resolution to keep the morning watch.'

These quotations are from an address by John R. Mott. At first sight the closing statement appears too strong. But think a moment, what such a revelation implies.

It means the deep conviction that the only way to maintain and carry out the surrender to Christ and the Holy Spirit, is by meeting God very definitely at the commencement of each day, and receiving from Himself the grace needed for a walk in holy obedience.

It means an insight into the folly of attempting to live a heavenly life without rising up into close communion with God in heaven, and receiving from Himself the fresh bestowal of spiritual blessings.

It means the confession that it is alone in personal fellowship with God, and in delight in His nearness, that proof can be given that our love responds to His, and that we count His nearness our chief joy.

It means the faith that if time enough be given for God to lay His hands on us, and renew the inflowings of His Spirit, our soul may be so closely united to Him that no trials or duties can separate us from Him.

It means a purpose to live wholly and only for God, and by the sacrifice of time and ease to prove that we are willing to pay any price to secure the first of all blessings the presence of God for all the day.

Let us now look again at that sentence—, 'Next to receiving Christ as our Savior, and claiming the baptism of the Holy Spirit, we know of no act attended with larger good to ourselves or to others than the formation of an undiscourageable resolution to keep the morning watch.' If our acceptance of Christ as Lord and Master was whole-hearted, if our prayer for and claiming of the Holy Spirit to guide and control was sincere, surely there can be no thought of not giving God each day sufficient time, our very best time, for receiving and increasing in us what is indispensable to a life for Christ's glory and in His service.

You tell me there are many Christians who are content with ten minutes or a quarter of an hour. There are, but you will certainly not as a rule find them strong Christians. And the Students' Movement is pleading with God, above everything, that He would meet to train a race of devoted, whole-hearted young men and women. Christ asked great sacrifices of His disciples; He has perhaps asked little of you as yet. But now He allows, He invites, He longs for you to make some. Sacrifices make strong men. Sacrifices help wonderfully to wrench us away from earth and self-pleasing, and lift us heavenward. Do not try to pare down the time limit of the morning watch to less than the half-hour. There can be no question about the possibility of finding the time. Ten minutes from sleep, ten from company or amusement ,ten from lessons. How easy where the heart is right, hungering to know God and His will perfectly!

If you feel that you do not feel the need of so much time, and know not how to wait, we are content you should speak of your quiet time, or your hour of prayer. God may graciously, later on, draw you out to the morning watch. But do not undertake it unless you feel your heart stirred with the determination to make a sacrifice, and have full time for intimate intercourse with God. But if you are ready to do this, we urge you to join. The very fact of setting apart such a period helps to awaken the feeling: I have a great work to do, and I need time for it. It strengthens in your heart the conviction: If I am to be kept all this day without sin I must have time to get near to God. It will give your Bible study new point, as you find time, between the reading, to be still and bow in humility for the Holy Spirit's hidden working, and wait till you get some real apprehension of God's will for you, through the Word. And, by the grace of God, it may help you to begin that habit of specific and definite intercession of which the Church so surely stands In need.

Students! you know not whether in your future life your time may be more limited, your circumstances more unfavorable, your Christian earnestness feebler. Now is the accepted time. Today, as the Holy Ghost saith. Listen to the invitation of your brethren in all lands, and fear not to form an undiscourageable resolution to spend at least half an hour each morning with God alone.

www.ingramcontent.com/pod-product-compliance
Lightning Source LLC
LaVergne TN
LVHW091341110826
845155LV00043B/3

* 9 7 9 8 8 8 0 9 2 4 8 7 5 *